Anonymous

The rights of the clergy vindicated

A plea for canon law in the United States

Anonymous

The rights of the clergy vindicated
A plea for canon law in the United States

ISBN/EAN: 9783337233341

Printed in Europe, USA, Canada, Australia, Japan

Cover: Foto ©Suzi / pixelio.de

More available books at **www.hansebooks.com**

JURA SACERDOTUM VINDICATA.

THE RIGHTS

OF

THE CLERGY VINDICATED;

OR,

A PLEA

FOR

CANON LAW IN THE UNITED STATES,

BY

A ROMAN CATHOLIC PRIEST.

"Canonum statuta custodiantur ab omnibus : et nemo, in actionibus, vel judiciis ecclesiasticis suo sensu, sed eorum auctoritate ducatur."—*Ex Con. Meldensi in Gallia, A. D.* 845.

NEW YORK:
JAMES SHEEHY, PUBLISHER,
33 MURRAY STREET.
1883.

Entered according to Act of Congress, in the year 1883,
BY JAMES SHEEHY,
In the Office of the Librarian of Congress, at Washington.

O MARY IMMACULATE!

THE

AUGUST PATRONESS

OF

THE CHURCH IN THE UNITED STATES,

BLESS THIS LITTLE BOOK,

ITS READERS, ITS PUBLISHERS,

AND

ITS HUMBLE AUTHOR.

****

TO

THE MOST REV. ARCHBISHOPS

AND

RT. REV. BISHOPS OF THE UNITED STATES.

VENERABLE AND BELOVED PRELATES:
With the heart of a dutiful child towards my Holy Mother, the Catholic Church, with sentiments of unbounded veneration for your dignity, of ready and humble obedience to your authority, and of undying loyalty to your true interests and welfare, I address you, dearly beloved Archbishops and Bishops, to whom has been entrusted the care of Christ's flock in this portion of His Fold.

I most earnestly, and at the same time, most respectfully beg of you, in the name of hundreds, if not of thousands of the clergy of the United States, to remedy the evil which I indicate in the following pages, viz.: that of priests being uncanonically dismissed from their dioceses and thrown helplessly on the world, to the infinite degradation of the sacerdotal character, to the dishonor of our Holy Religion, and to the great scandal of the faithful. You have, it is true, in Plenary Council, already legislated against this crying abuse. Yet it continues to exist. I need only bring this fact to your attention, and your zeal for God's glory, the Church's welfare, and the honor of the Priesthood will cause you to enforce the laws from the non-observance of which this monstrous evil has arisen.

By the very nature of my subject, I have sometimes been obliged to state the truth plainly, at which you will not, I hope, be offended. Your venerable body cannot be held responsible for uncanonical proceedings on the part of a few, or even of many individual members thereof.

Before God and my own conscience, I assure you, in conclusion, dearly beloved Archbishops and Bishops, that the end I had in view in writing and publishing the following sheets, is the welfare, not only of my brethren of the clergy, but your own likewise, as well as that of the Catholic Church in these United States.

Your humble and devoted servant in Christ,

A. R. C. P.

PREFACE.

I had begun to write the following pages, when the "Instructio" *Quamvis*, of July 20, 1878, from the Sacred Congregation of the Propaganda, appeared, defining the manner in which, for the present at least, all criminal and disciplinary causes of clergymen in the United States should be settled.

The prescriptions of this Document, which was issued with the explicit approbation of our Most Holy Father Leo XIII., now gloriously reigning, if rigidly and conscientiously carried out, would remedy, not only the evils for which it was primarily and directly intended, but the evil also I had in view in writing, viz.: that of dismissing clergymen from their dioceses, and abandoning them to themselves and to the charity of the public, whence so many other grave evils flow.

What reasons then, it may be asked, had I for offering my humble suggestions to the consideration of the venerable hierarchy of the United States?

After seriously reflecting over the matter, and taking counsel of holy and learned men, I came to the conclusion that my humble work already begun, would, if finished, be of service to the Church, for the following reasons: First, from facts that have come to my certain knowledge, since the publication of the above-mentioned

"Instructio" of the Sacred Congregation, the evil of which I treat seems at present as far as ever from being abolished. I cannot prudently and with propriety even outline these facts to prove my assertion. The reason is obvious. I am most solicitous that no word escape my pen which could be construed, or even distorted, into an unseemly or odious personality, or at which any one, even the most sensitive, could take offence. Let it then suffice for me to say, that incontrovertible facts have come to my knowledge, since the promulgation of the "Instructio" of July 20, 1878, which facts proved conclusively to my mind, that I would be serving the Catholic Church in the United States by continuing and publishing the work I had commenced.

For any irregularity in the ecclesiastical government of this country, or non-observance of the laws of discipline enacted for it, certainly no blame can attach to Rome. Time and again Rome has made wise and salutary provisions for the protection of the clergy of the United States in their just rights, one of which most undoubtedly is, that every clergyman, even though he should have erred, so long as he is not contumacious, must be protected and cared for by his own proper bishop. This right has been proclaimed anew in the late "Instructio" of July 20, 1878, issued by the Sacred Congregation of the Propaganda, when it prescribes the manner of inflicting punishment on clergymen derelict to duty, though it leaves the punishment itself to the equity of the bishop, who is supposed to be conversant with the canons and decisions of the Church in such matters.

Neither can the blame of this evil, of uncanonically dismissing priests from their dioceses, attach to the Venerable Episcopate of the United States as a body, who, in Plenary Council, have already legislated against it by positively forbidding any bishop in these States to abandon his subject before he has secured another superior. "Statuunt Patres nullum harum provinciarum sacerdotem, ad aliam diœcesim transire volentem, a proprio Episcopo dimittendum, nisi certo constet eum ab alio Episcopo recipiendum. Si qui autem in posterum aliter dimissi fuerint, non recipiantur." II. Plenary Council of Baltimore, 122.

It is not, therefore, for want of salutary laws and wise prescriptions on the part of Rome, or of the ecclesiastical legislative assemblies of the Church in the United States, that results the evil of which I complain, but from the ignoring altogether of these laws and prescriptions on the part of many charged with their execution. Most assuredly I would never have had any occasion to speak of the evil of dismissing priests helplessly from their dioceses, if in all cases of delinquent clergymen, canonical punishments had been canonically inflicted. Any work, therefore, however humble, intended to call the attention of the hierarchy to the importance and necessity of a vigorous observance of the laws of ecclesiastical discipline enacted for the United States, I consider at this very moment to be not only not inopportune, but calculated to do much good.

Another reason that induced me to finish and publish my work was, that it is calculated to show, in general, the spirit of mercy and clemency, actuating the Church in her conduct towards the clergy, and in particular, her uncompromising love of justice, as illustrated by her judicial legislation, and by the Decisions of her Sacred Congregations.

Finally, the rules for inaugurating and conducting canonical trials, as well as other canonical documents and authentic Decisions of Rome found in my humble work, will be a safe guide in interpreting the true sense of the "Instructio" of July 20, 1878, sent to the hierarchy of the United States by the Sacred Congregation of the Propaganda, or a key that will unlock its meaning, and lay open to our view its hidden treasures, and the inestimable blessings it confers on the bishops and clergy, as well as on the faithful of the United States.

For these reasons I determined to finish what I had begun, and present my views, supported by authority, with regard to an evil that has existed in the Church in the United States for a long time: an evil which it was earnestly hoped and expected from year to year, would be remedied effectually by our venerable prelates; but which, on the contrary, seems to be gaining ground as time advances and the clergy become more numerous. That evil, as I have already said, is the dismissing of priests from their dioceses, to roam over the land, "Quasi oves perditæ aut errantes." This, all will acknowledge, is a grave evil and a serious abuse. Every true bishop, in all things faithful and loyal to Holy Church, as well as every priest and enlightened Catholic in the land, deplores it. It is not only a great disorder in itself, but the fruitful source of other disorders. The existence of this evil none will deny. That it is uncanonical, and utterly condemned and reprobated by the highest authorities in the Church of God, I prove conclusively in the following pages.

A desire to benefit my brethren of the clergy, and thus serve my Holy Mother, the Catholic Church, as well as the love and reverence I have for the sacerdotal character and dignity, urge me to raise my feeble voice against this evil, in the hope that our zealous and beloved prelates may heed it, and unite to root out this vile weed, which disfigures the fair garden of the Church in these United States. To see it growing unchecked and spreading daily, saddens the hearts of the good, and of all those who cherish the honor and glory and fair fame of the Catholic Church. Besides, it has been, and is still injuring religion, by bringing the priestly character into contempt, and casting odium on our holy religion.

It is, moreover, in consequence of this very abuse, and of the insecurity in general of the clergy as to their rights, that a spirit of estrangement has arisen of late years among many of them and their bishops, and is apparently gaining strength. For many years past, much has been said publicly, and much more privately, on abuse of episcopal authority. Such abuse is often imaginary, or exaggerated, but sometimes, alas, it is but too well founded, as when a clergyman is ruthlessly and uncanonically driven from his diocese, and consigned to the cold charities of the world.

Should this unpretending little volume help even remotely to the practical establishment in the United States of the Canon Law of the Church, which regulates the mutual relations of the bishop with his clergy, and settles in a just and canonical manner any difference that may arise between them; or should it even conduce to the enforcement of the canons of discipline enacted by the II. Plenary Council of Baltimore for that purpose; or help in any degree to bring about a strict and rigorous observance of the legislation promulgated by the Sacred Congregation of the Propaganda, July 20, 1878, it will have accomplished a great good. The conscientious observance of the wise and salutary laws of the Church, made for the mutual welfare of the hierarchy of the first and second order, would give the death-blow to that spirit of estrangement and want of confidence between them, which, it is no stretch of imagination to say, exists in some, if not in many dioceses, whilst it would surely promote and strengthen in every diocese, the spirit of charity and unity between the episcopate and the clergy, so essential to their mutual happiness, and to the well-being and prosperity of religion.

I ask my brethren kindly to overlook the many defects of my humble production. A plain, simple, earnest instruction or exhortation sometimes has a more powerful effect, and is often more productive of lasting good, than a discourse sparkling with brilliant thoughts, clothed in the most beautiful imagery, and expressed in faultless language. I have not written a line in these pages that has not come from thorough conviction. I have adduced nothing but what is based on incontrovertible facts, or supported by irrefragable authorities. I certainly never had the ambition to write book or pamphlet, nor would I have undertaken this little work; but feeling not only a desire, but a strong impulse to do something for my unfortunate brethren, and encouraged by a holy, learned and experienced priest, I took up my pen to ask mercy and justice for the erring of the Lord's anointed, hoping that some .one else possessed of a larger experience, a better knowledge of Canon Law, and an abler pen, may be prompted to take up the subject, and convince all our venerable prelates, effectively and successfully, if I fail in the task, of the importance and urgent necessity of canonical punishments, canonically inflicted for canonical faults; and of being guided by the laws made for their observance, and in general by the Canon Law of the Church in all their official relations with their clergy. "Canonum statuta custodiantur ab omnibus: et nemo in actionibus vel judiciis ecclesiasticis, suo sensu, sed eorum auctoritate ducatur," is as safe a principle and as binding on ecclesiastical superiors in the nineteenth century as it was in the ninth, in the United States as in other parts of the Church.

Before committing to print what I have written, I reflected, prayed and took counsel. But the more I considered in all its bearings and under all its aspects, the evil of dismissing priests uncanonically from their dioceses, the more convinced did I become that I would be serving our beloved bishops themselves as well as the clergy by placing before them this evil in its true light, and showing them how unequivocally it is condemned by the spirit and letter of the laws of our Holy Mother the Catholic Church.

In the accomplishment of this praiseworthy task not one disrespectful word of the Venerable Prelates of the United States has escaped my pen. Thank God, I am incapable of such treachery. To them and to the holy Church over which they preside I am loyal to the core of my heart. Were I to speak of the Episcopate of the United States as a body, my sentiments could find expression only in a high and just tribute of praise for their piety, zeal and learning. Most of them have been men of heart, just and merciful to the clergy over whom they were placed. From the patriarch Carroll of Baltimore, the bishops in this country in general have been merciful, just and good men, who have deserved well of the Church and of the Holy See. As a rule, they have governed their clergy prudently, mercifully, justly, wisely and well.

But there have been exceptions to this wise and prudent use of episcopal authority, and of late years these exceptions are apparently becoming more numerous. No one who has given any attention to the matter will deny this. All know it, not only the inferior clergy but our venerable prelates themselves.

In calling the attention, therefore, of all interested in the welfare of the Church, to her wise laws regulating the relations of ecclesiastical Superiors and their subjects, I say naught; nor could I say aught against the venerable Episcopate of the United States as a body, whose character and dignity I most profoundly and religiously reverence, and to whose authority, exercised in unison and in accord with that of Rome, I most humbly and cheerfully bow.

But I echo only the voice of Rome, and of all bishops and priests who possess her spirit, when I offer an humble and respectful remonstrance against those ecclesiastical Superiors who, in the government of their clergy, act in direct opposition to the Canon Law of the Catholic Church, ignore entirely the instructions of the Sacred Congregation of the Propaganda, and openly violate the statutes made for the good of religion by the venerable Fathers of the Church in this land, assembled in Plenary Council at Baltimore.

Not only will none of my brother priests blame me for this, but in the words of a learned and zealous clergyman who, a few years ago, whilst editing a Catholic journal, raised his voice successfully against an outrage analogous to the one I am combating, I have " no just reason to fear the frown of episcopal authority for calling attention to, and protesting energetically against an abuse that covers the priesthood with shame as with a mantle."

I am, moreover, certain that I have said nothing whatever in the following pages at which any right-minded person can take umbrage. Having carefully reviewed what I have written, and having weighed it all in the " Scales of the Sanctuary," I find that I have given utterance to my honest convictions only, which, from the authorities I have cited in their support, seem to be in harmony with the teaching and discipline of the Church for ages. I have tried to write in a kind and respectful spirit, and I certainly have not written as strongly as the abuse treated, inflicting such terrible and lasting injury on individuals, and dishonor on religion and the priesthood, would seem to justify.

Nevertheless, I ask pardon beforehand for any word that may have escaped my pen, and that would seemingly give pain. Far be it from my mind and heart to wound unnecessarily! But every one who has had much experience of men and things in general, knows that sometimes the truth cannot be told without inflicting more or less pain. And yet, of any unpalatable truth I may be obliged to utter in connection with my subject, I believe I can say of it with the poet Dante:

> "Though when tasted first, the voice shall prove
> Unwelcome ; on digestion, it will turn
> To vital nourishment."

When pain accompanies the telling of the truth, done for the benefit of our fellow-man, or for the welfare of religion, or through any other praiseworthy or justifiable motive, whilst it is a sacred duty to make it known, the blame, if there be any, must rest on the circumstances that called it forth, not on the individual who utters it. To withhold the truth when it should be spoken, is often the extreme of cruelty. He who, standing by the bedside of his friend unprepared to meet his God, and whose sands of life are fast running out, would not open his lips to warn him of his danger, through fear of wounding his feelings, or of incurring his anger or displeasure, would be but a dumb devil leagued with hell to compass his eternal ruin. The surgeon, who in mistaken mercy, would anoint an ulcer, and then bandage it up, leaving it to gather and foster corruption, until it brought death to the patient, most assuredly would not be his friend. On the contrary, he only would be a true friend of the sufferer, who would not spare him, but using the knife with an apparently merciless hand, would probe and cut to the very bone if necessary, to let out the foul matter that threatens life or limb. Though such treatment gave temporary pain, it would in the end prove highly beneficial to the sick man.

If, therefore, dear reader, any thing in the following pages is met with, apparently sharp or plainly stated, it is simply because it could not otherwise have been said well or truthfully. Yet more, it is said because religion and charity and justice demanded it. It is said to serve and to save, not with the most remote intention of giving pain. My apology, if any is needed, as well as my justification, will be found in these words of Divine Inspiration, "Better are the wounds of a friend, than the deceitful kisses of an enemy." (Prov. xxvii. 6.)

I send forth my little book on a mission of mercy. Like its humble author, it may be somewhat rough and unpolished, but it is truthful, honest and sincere in its utterances. If it has any weight, as I sincerely hope it will, in urging every ecclesiastical superior throughout the country to follow the Canon Law of the Church as far as practicable in his relations with his clergy, or at least to carry out the regulations laid down in the II. Plenary Council of Baltimore, as well as those of the last "Instructio" from Rome of July 20, 1878, it will redound to the honor and glory of the mitre. If it puts but one of our revered and honored prelates on his guard, and causes him to reflect most seriously before pronouncing sentence,—or rather, to be only the executive of the sentence pronounced by his ecclesiastical court, or Quasi Judicial Counsel, it will not have been written in vain. If it induces but one bishop to look upon an erring clergyman not contumacious, with a little of the compassion and mercy which the Great Pastor of souls had for sinners, my time will have been well employed. If, above all, in consequence of this humble little volume seeing the light of day, but one single priest in the United States is spared the humiliation and all the other evils accompanying the being helplessly cast forth from his diocese, to wander over the country like a sheep without a shepherd, then will I have been more than rewarded for the hours snatched from other duties to accomplish this work.

I have the well-founded hope, in view of the eminent, venerable and weighty authorities by which I prove all that I advance, that our revered prelates themselves, and the devoted clergy, will approve of my humble effort in behalf of ecclesiastical discipline and in the interests thereof. My object is to promote their mutual happiness, as well as to offer my humble tribute for the protection of the good name and honor of the Priesthood. My hopes may not be realized, or but in part, and the end I have in view in writing and publishing this little book, viz.: the entire abolition of what I consider a monstrous evil, may not be attained, but I humbly trust that God will bless my purpose, and that my brethren in the Holy Ministry, while kindly giving me the credit of a pure and upright intention at least, will deal gently with the shortcomings and imperfections of my work. Yet, with all its imperfections, I flatter myself that no canonist, at least, will condemn the matter, whatever may be said of the manner, or of the method of its presentation.

It may be objected to the success, and even to the propriety of publishing my humble work, that it has no *Imprimatur*. To this I answer, that I have the sanction of my own conscience, and the approbation of an enlightened and experienced churchman, a sound theologian and an able canonist. He heartily approved of the motives that prompted my book, and of the work itself, which he read over, and assured me that it was calculated to benefit the Church and the clergy. Yet all this would not be sufficient to justify me in publishing my book without the *Imprimatur*, if there was a positive law of the Church requiring it, for I hold firmly to the doctrine that "Obedience is better than sacrifice." But there is no such law now in force. I need no *Imprimatur*. A few lines will make this clear.

The *Imprimatur* is required for Bibles only and explanations and annotations on Holy Writ, in which category of books my humble volume, as is evident, cannot be classed.

The *Imprimatur* is required for Bibles only and explanations and annotations on Holy Writ, if the Council of

Trent, which framed and promulgated this law of *Imprimatur*, restricted it to Bibles only and annotations and explanations of Holy Writ. Such in fact is the case.

The council of Trent requires the *Imprimatur* for Bibles only and explanations and annotations on Holy Writ. This will appear evident to any one who will carefully read the decree itself of the Council of Trent, "Decretum de editione et usu Sacrorum Librorum," Sess. iv., enacting the law of *Imprimatur*. I may also refer the reader to Konings, Theol. Mor. *Trac. de Cens.* N. 1741.

If we inquire into the motive or reason of this law, we are still more confirmed in what is already clear from the wording of the decree, that the law of *Imprimatur* was intended by the Venerable Fathers of Trent to guard the purity, integrity and sanctity of the Holy Scriptures, and had them alone for its object. They wished to stem the wild torrent of fanaticism, impiety and crime that was let loose on the Christian world, when Luther gave to the poor, uneducated laborer, or to the soldier in his barracks, the same liberty of expounding the divine Word, as to the reverent scholar whose life was spent in its study, and who interpreted it with the light of the Church's teaching for fifteen hundred years illuminating its pages, and aided by the learned commentaries of sainted Doctors and Fathers.

To remedy, therefore, the abuses of Bible reading, and of Bible interpreting, and to obviate the inconveniences and evils, the crimes and abominations of all kinds that were desolating society in consequence of every one's being allowed to follow his private judgment as to the sense and meaning of the inspired Word, as well as to guard the faithful against mutilated editions and false, or incorrect interpretations of the same, the holy and Œcumenical Council of Trent promulgated the law of *Imprimatur*. The faithful were thus secured in the possession of a correct version of God's Holy Word, as likewise of a proper and authentic interpretation of the same. Her wisdom shines forth conspicuously in the light of the past and of the present. The murders and adulteries and butcheries, the crimes without number, and the untold abominations that have been perpetrated in the name of the Bible, from the days of M. Luther to our own times, silently but eloquently, sadly but convincingly, prove the wisdom of the Catholic Church in protecting and guarding with her *Imprimatur*, the sacred deposit of divine revelation entrusted to her keeping, from the profanation of the impious, the abuse of the ignorant, and the contempt of the irreligious.

This view of the matter which I have taken is confirmed by Konings, whose theology most of the bishops of the United States have formally approved. He says *Trac. de Cens.* N. 1741 : " Excommunicationes.......... contra imprimentes, aut imprimi facientes sine ordinarii approbatione, libros de rebus sacris tractantes, i. e., libros sacræ scripturæ et eorundem librorum adnotationes et expositiones; DE HIS ENIM, AC DE HIS SOLIS agitur in allegato Decreto."

I would have put my name to my humble work, but for the following reasons, which I think will amply justify me for not so doing. 1. My name would add no weight to the work, for I am but an humble, obscure priest, known only to the few amongst whom the providence of God has placed me. 2. I do not desire the notoriety, or inconvenience of being known as the author of even so small and unpretending a volume. 3. I believe I echo only the sentiments of the clergy of the United States, or of the majority of them at least, on the subject treated, and it is this that will command attention, without regard to the individual who gives expression to it. 4. My authorities, which can be easily verified, speak for themselves. And, finally, it is my intention to ask my publishers to get up copies suitable for presentation to our Most Holy Father and to the Cardinal Prefect of the Propaganda, which I will send to them with my humble autograph.

One word as to the plan. A considerable part of the work is occupied in showing the spirit of the Church towards the clergy. After proving conclusively, by the most unexceptional authorities, that they cannot be uncanonically dismissed from their dioceses, and abandoned to ruin, I lay down the manner in which the Church wishes them to be treated when charged with any canonical fault, which is to be tried canonically; and if found guilty to be canonically punished. I speak, therefore, briefly of the different kinds of canonical trials, and give the most important decisions and principles governing them. As the Quasi Judicial Counsel, or Commission of Investigation, commanded by Rome, takes the place in the United States, for the present at least, of the canonical trial, I give entire the " Instructio " of July 20, 1878, promulgated by the Sacred Congregation of the Propaganda, and devote a chapter to its explanation, made by the aid of the Canonical Principles and Decisions previously given.

From the open and well-known fact that the provisions of the above-mentioned "Instructio" are not observed as they should be, and are even in danger of being ignored entirely, the only means, in my humble judgment, to have them enforced, as well as all the other laws of discipline enacted for this country, is the appointing by Rome of an Apostolic Delegate to the United States. I therefore devote a chapter to the importance and necessity of having an Apostolic Delegate in our midst for a few years at least, until our ecclesiastical government is established on the permanent basis of Law and Order.

I then conclude with what is a natural corollary of the whole book, viz.: the absolute, most just and undeniable obligation which devolves on every bishop or administrator of a diocese to protect and provide for every priest, not contumacious, who is his subject.

I may, possibly, if there is much demand for my humble work, issue another edition of it; and will do so, if urged thereto by those whose judgment and piety convince me that my work is serviceable to Holy Church, and if the proceeds of the present edition enable me to do so. As my brethren of the clergy, or some members of the episcopate may have valuable suggestions to make which will enhance the value of the work, all communications addressed to my publisher will reach me, and will be regarded by me as sacred and confidential, as far as the name of the writer is concerned.

I am indebted to a venerable and worthy clergyman for many pertinent hints, and for documents and authorities which I had not at hand, as well as for material aid in helping me to have my book published. I hereby publicly thank him for his uniform courtesy, his kind and sustaining encouragement, and for the pecuniary and other assistance he gave me in getting out this work; and from my heart I pray that God may spare him yet many years for the good of the Church and the salvation of souls. He has no ambition whatever for the "Mitre," although his gentleness, learning and piety would grace it well.

I will say, in conclusion, that whilst on the one hand, I cannot be indifferent to an appreciation of my humble efforts to succor my brethren, by showing forth the charity and compassion of the Church for them, and by bringing to the attention of all her laws of mercy and justice that protect them as long as they are obedient to her authority, yet, on the other hand, conscious of the rectitude of my motives in writing, and of the conformity of what I have written with the teaching and practice of Rome, unkind, or even harsh and unjust criticisms will not disturb me. As I am now minded, I will not heed them. My defence is in my cause, which in the depths of my soul I believe to be an eminently just one. Should any further defence of it, however, be required, I entrust it to our learned Doctors, who, in accepting the honorable title of D. D., have, *eo ipso*, accepted the mission it imposes of defending bravely and fearlessly every tittle of the Church's doctrine, authority and discipline.

In all that I have written I most cheerfully and unreservedly submit my poor judgment to that of the Holy Roman Apostolic See and its Sacred Congregation of the Propaganda, which has charge of the interests of the Church in these United States.

Feast of our Blessed Lady, " Help of Christians," May 24th, 1832.

CHAPTER I.

ORIGIN OF CANON LAW.

The Catholic Church is the most perfect organization on earth. This is not surprising, for she is the creation of the Incarnate Wisdom of God. She is His beautiful and Immaculate Bride, "A glorious Church, not having spot or wrinkle, or any such thing, but holy and without blemish." (Eph. v. 27.)

The Catholic Church being therefore the creation of God, possesses eminently all the characteristics of God's works. She is permanent and immutable, incapable of being improved by man, and perfectly adapted to the end for which Jesus Christ instituted her, viz.: to apply to man the merits of the Redemption, and to guide him in the way of all truth. Hence she is infallible, that she may teach the truth unerringly, and holy, to make man a good citizen of earth, and to fit him for his eternal destiny in heaven.

The Catholic Church is holy. In this nineteenth century she is as holy as when her divine Founder himself was bodily present in the midst of his apostles, "Speaking to them of the kingdom of God," or as when the Holy Ghost descended upon them on Whit-Sunday. The same Holy Spirit still abides with the Church. Nor is Jesus absent from her. He not only watches over, protects and cherishes his Church, but he has deigned even to remain bodily present with her, dwelling within the lowly and humble tabernacle of the Catholic altar, as truly and as really as he once did in the stable at Bethlehem, or in the poor cottage of Mary at Nazareth.

In the long ages that have elapsed since the birth of the Catholic Church on Pentecost Sunday, not for one single moment has the smallest sin even, stained her spotless robe of sanctity; nor in the years to come will that sanctity ever be tarnished, for she is "the Church of the living God," the "Fold," of which Christ is the "Shepherd," the "Bride" of which he is the "Bridegroom," the "Body" of which he is the "Head." Such close and intimate relations with Jesus Christ necessarily imply on her part absolute and essential holiness.

The Catholic Church is also the Teacher and Guardian of truth, commissioned by the Almighty himself, to fulfil this office towards the human race until the end of time, "Go teach all nations.... and behold I am with you all days even to the consummation of the world." (Matt. xxviii. 19-20.) "Thou art Peter (a rock), and upon this rock I will build my Church, and the gates of hell shall not prevail against it." (Ib. xvi. 18.) The Catholic Church, therefore, is likewise infallible,—"the pillar and ground of the truth." (1 Tim. iii. 15.)

The members of the Church, however, even her ministers and officials, are not always holy, though the children of an immaculate Mother. This is no fault of hers, but of their own perverse nature and abuse of the graces that flow to them through her. Again, though she is infallible, they can err, and often do err, except in those things in which they follow her unerring teaching.

The Church being governed, therefore, by imperfect and fallible men, who may sin, and who can err, she has not left them, even in matters of discipline and ecclesiastical government, to their own judgment and wisdom in ruling the different portions of the kingdom of Christ committed to their care. According to times and circumstances, she has devised and promulgated wise and salutary laws for their guidance.

This is the origin of the disciplinary Canon Law of the Church, which is a body of Canons, or Rules, for the maintenance of good order and discipline amongst all the members of the household of the Faith. These Canons, or Rules, are calculated to promote piety and virtue, to correct disorders, and to protect the children of God in their just rights, liberties, and privileges, which they possess as members of the Church, or which were bestowed upon them by her. They are derived from various sources, as the Holy Scriptures, Tradition, the writings of the Fathers, the Constitutions of the Apostles, Decrees of Popes, Decisions of Sacred Congregations, Councils, etc., approved and promulgated by the Sovereign Pontiff, the Supreme Legislator in the Church.

CHAPTER II.

IN THE CATHOLIC CHURCH, NO ONE POSSESSES ABSOLUTE, MUCH LESS ARBITRARY POWER.

In consequence of the wise and salutary Canon Law of the Church, derived principally from the above-mentioned sources,—sources of such weight, wisdom and authority,—it follows that Law and Order are the normal condition of the Catholic Church. The flock and the shepherd, the faithful and their bishops and priests, are all subject to law, and amenable to it. To no one, among the hierarchy of either the first or second order, has she ever entrusted absolute, much less arbitrary power.

Even the Supreme and visible Head of the Catholic Church, the Bishop of Rome, the Successor of St. Peter, the Vicegerent of Christ on earth, does not possess absolute power, in the sense that his power is unconditional, unrestricted or unlimited. Far less is his power arbitrary, capricious, or despotic. As the Supreme Ruler and Legislator in the Church, and the Father of all the faithful, his authority must be absolutely obeyed; but that authority is never exercised without consulting his Sacred Congregations of Cardinals, or in opposition to the laws and constitution of the Church.

Even when the Holy Father exercises his unique prerogative of Infallible Teacher of the Universal Church, though we firmly believe, and know well that he cannot err, because protected by Unerring Truth, and his teaching is therefore absolute and irreformable, yet he is guided in the exercise of this power by the voice of revelation, both written and unwritten, by the counsel of the Church teaching throughout the world, and by the rules of consummate wisdom and prudence. In the exercise, therefore, of this sublime power, attached only to the Chair of St. Peter, there is nothing partaking of the nature of absolute, much less of arbitrary power.

It is, indeed, very true, that when the Supreme Pontiff of the Church speaks *ex cathedra*, all the children of God, from the humble peasant to the mitred prelate, or crimson-robed cardinal, must bow in lowly reverence, to accept the words of the successor of the Fisherman of Galilee, as they would had they fallen from the lips of Peter, or been uttered by the Son of God Himself. But this acceptance of the teaching of Jesus Christ, through His Vicar on earth, is eminently conformable to reason itself. For right reason dictates submission of our will and intellect to God, Who can neither deceive us, nor be Himself deceived.

Now God teaches us, either directly by word of mouth, as Jesus Christ taught when on earth, or by the ministry of another, who by His appointment is gifted with infallibility. The Prophets of the Old Law and the Apostles of the New were endowed with such infallibility. The visible Head of the Church, teaching *ex cathedra* in matters pertaining to faith or morals, possesses this privilege of infallibility. The late Œcumenical Vatican

Council has solemnly defined it,—therefore, has the Holy Ghost spoken it.

In defining the Pope's infallibility, as teacher of the Universal Church, the Council of the Vatican only affirmed with her infallible authority that this doctrine is contained in the "Deposit of Revelation." How clear, in fact, are not the words of Divine Inspiration that bear on this article of our Holy Faith: "Thou art Peter (a rock), and upon this rock I will build my Church, and the gates of hell shall not prevail against it." (Matt. xvi. 18.) "I have prayed for thee that thy faith fail not, and thou being once converted, confirm thy brethren." (Luke xxii. 32.) "Feed my lambs.... Feed my sheep." (John xxi. 15–17.)

We see, therefore, that even the Supreme Ruler in the Catholic Church, the Sovereign Pontiff, does not possess absolute, far less arbitrary power. In the exercise of a power which no other individual on earth possesses, that of teaching the Universal Church, in Faith and Morals, with the infallible certainty that he cannot err, he is dependent on Law and Order. He is, moreover, guided by the Hand of God, whose wisdom has hedged him round with infallibility. Hence, I may add, this prerogative of infallibility in teaching, possessed by the Father of Christendom, is a blessing to mankind. and an inestimable boon to the human race.

As Supreme Legislator in the Church, the Holy Father can abrogate any ecclesiastical law, or dispense therefrom. This, however, he cannot do arbitrarily, but only for weighty reasons, after mature deliberation, and with due regard to the established canons, discipline and constitution of the Church.

If, then, the august Head of the Universal Church, the Supreme Pastor, from whom all jurisdiction flows to the subordinate pastors, does not possess absolute, much less arbitrary power, with much more reason can we affirm, that none of these subordinate pastors possess such power. For them, as well as for the Visible Head of the Church, and the humblest of the clergy and of the faithful, LAW rules supreme. No matter how high the position they may hold in her service, or exalted the station they may occupy in society, all the children of the Catholic Church must submit to the laws which her wisdom has laid down for their guidance and government, from the mighty monarch of a vast empire, to the lowliest member of her household, from the humblest cleric to the Supreme Pontiff " Urbis et orbis."

Not only this, but as citizens of the state, she inculcates in her children and requires of them a conscientious obedience to all the just laws of the government under which they live, of whatsoever form it may be.

This love of Law and Order, which in practice she carries out so perfectly, and preaches so uncompromisingly, this duty of obedience to lawful authority, so admirably illustrated within her, and so conspicuously manifested in the loyal bearing of the true and faithful Catholic to his king, or ruler, wherever his lot may be cast, the Catholic Church has ever proclaimed, and still proclaims to the nations of the earth. In this as in every age, she echoes the teaching of the great Apostle of the

Gentiles: "Let every soul be subject to higher powers; for there is no power but from God; and those that are, are ordained of God. Therefore, he that resisteth the power, resisteth the ordinance of God. And they that resist, purchase to themselves damnation. Wherefore be subject of necessity, not only for wrath, but also for conscience' sake." (Rom. xiii. 1-2, 5.)

The governments and people of these latter days, however, have not heeded the teaching of the Catholic Church, as to the necessity and importance of obedience and submission to lawful authority. In consequence, instead of peace, and prosperity, and happiness, the appendage and offspring of Law and Order, they are now reaping the sad fruits of their infidelity, in beholding on every side discontent and anarchy, bankruptcy and ruin, and miseries of all kinds daily multiplied. Whether empires, or kingdoms, or republics, if they are so often threatened, or convulsed with social and political revolutions,—now thrown into consternation by the bold and impious assassination of the head of the nation; now petrified with horror and aghast at seeing the cherished monuments of antiquity—commemorative of the worthy deeds of their fathers, or recording the glories of the State—wrapped in flames kindled by the radical torch of the communist or socialist; or again, appalled with fear and dread, at seeing the flood-gates of anarchy let loose, and a people considered conservative and law-abiding forgetting in a moment all the principles of right and justice, becoming intoxicated with demoniacal desires of blood and destruction against those who they believe, or imagine wronged them, and rushing madly on with wild and frenzied gesticulations and angry shouts, with fury in their eyes, madness in their brains, hatred in their hearts and strength in their sinewy arms, threatening, like a wild and turbulent torrent, ruin and desolation to all they meet in their path —if, I repeat, the governments of our day behold not unfrequently these evidences of lawlessness, they have none to blame but themselves. They have practically set God aside, persecuted more or less His Church and her august Head, trampled on her divine authority, and they are now reaping bountiful crops of disorder and confusion, insecurity and revolt, having lavishly sown the seeds of these fruits of evil, when they set their faces against God's Holy Church and His Vicar on earth. They have rejected or set at naught Divine authority, the only and stable foundation of all human authority; and their own subjects, walking in their footprints, and imitating their example, despise their authority, and endeavor to free themselves therefrom.

Law and Order rule supreme in the Catholic Church, both in her teaching and in her practice. In opposing all absolute and arbitrary power, not only in her own officials and rulers, who possess power and exercise authority within her, but even in those who govern the people, and in ever inculcating obedience to law in both rulers and subjects, the Catholic Church has ever proved herself to be the guardian and strength of just governments of every form, whilst she is hostile in principle to every government that has not in view the public and common good. Because of her advocacy of Law and Order, she is to-day the only grand, conservative power on earth, and the firm pillar of every State. For all who heed her voice must walk in the path of obedience to authority, which is the path of peace and prosperity. And when, for the preservation of Law and Order and the attainment of peace, the State is obliged to engage in war, there are no braver or more loyal soldiers than her children, of whatsoever clime or color, race or tongue, as, in times of peace, there are no better citizens than those who obey her laws and hearken to her voice.

We see, therefore, that the Catholic Church is eminently distinguished for her love of Law and Order. She is the uncompromising enemy of absolute and arbitrary power either in Church or in State, whilst she is the staunch friend and incorruptible advocate, as well as the fearless teacher of submission to lawful authority and to all just laws. None of her officials possess absolute, much less arbitrary power. They must be guided and governed by *law*. The Canon Law of the Church is the Rule by which they are expected to square their conduct.

Canon Law is the result of the wisdom and experience of ages.

It was composed or put together by some of the wisest and holiest of men.

It is at the foundation even of all the celebrated civil codes of the Christian era.

It was the principles of right and justice taught by

the Canon Law of the Church, that wrested from a tyrant the *Magna Charta* of human liberties.

The Canon Law of the Church is drawn from teachings the most venerable, from documents the most worthy of our admiration, and from sources that command our respect and obedience, viz.: From the teachings of the Word of God; from the writings of the renowned Fathers and Doctors of the Church; from the Decrees of Sovereign Pontiffs, the Vicegerents of Christ in the government of the Church Militant, and of their Sacred Congregations of Cardinals, composed of men venerable for their age, distinguished for their learning and experience, and remarkable for their piety and incorruptible justice; from the laws and regulations of the venerable and saintly bishops of the Church, who, in council assembled, enlightened by experience and guided by piety, justice and charity, enacted, from age to age, wise and salutary statutes for the good government of the Church.

Canon Law is founded on the eternal and immutable principles of justice.

It is animated by the breath of Divine Charity.

It has, in fine, been promulgated by the highest authority on earth.

In all cases, where its principles and rules are applicable, it is the only sure and safe guide of action for all possessed of ecclesiastical authority.

"The principles," says Smith, in his Preface to *Notes*, *etc.*, "underlying ecclesiastical jurisprudence, are, like those of moral theology, unchangeable, and the same in every country: their application, however, is different, accidentally at least, in the various parts of the Christian world.

"The principles themselves of Canon Law flow from the essential constitution of the Church; hence they are as fixed as is the essence of the Church. I am not one of those who think that the combined wisdom of nineteen centuries, as concentrated in ecclesiastical jurisprudence, is wholly inapplicable to this country, or altogether out of date,—that we need a system of ecclesiastical legislation entirely distinct from that which was laid down by the Fathers of the Church, and the immortal Pontiffs of old.

"While it may be said that Canon Law is, to a certain limited extent, the outgrowth of circumstances of time and place, yet it must not be forgotten, that everywhere exists the same Church, the same hierarchy, and in consequence, substantially the same relation between bishops, priests and laity."

CHAPTER III.

OUR ANOMALOUS CONDITION OF ECCLESIASTICAL GOVERNMENT.

The Catholic Church, as we have just seen, entrusts absolute, much less arbitrary power to the keeping of no one man, either in the ranks of the inferior clergy, or of the episcopate. A learned Catholic prelate, Rt. Rev. Silas Chatard, fresh from the "Eternal City," of whose fountains of piety and learning he had drunk for many years, openly proclaimed this truth but a few years ago, when he said "The Catholic Church does not favor—has never favored—arbitrary power."

Civil governments, even, have made the discovery that absolute or arbitrary power in the hands of one man is hostile to the interests of the state and of its citizens. Neither the President of the United States nor England's monarch possesses such power. Both are amenable to Law for their official acts. Both are bound by wise, constitutional restrictions, to hinder them from abusing their power.

If we desire to see the evil fruits of the tree of Absolutism, and the baneful effects of arbitrary power in the civil order, we have only to turn our eyes to the governments, at the head of which reigns the Czar of Russia, or the Sultan of Turkey, or the Chancellor of Prussia, the last of whom has at least been the power behind the throne. The constitutions of these governments do not, indeed, confer upon their rulers absolute, much less arbitrary power. The evils under which these nations have been groaning in past years, and which even now press heavily upon them, result from the attempt to override law, and rule with a despotic sceptre.

Men are men after all, whether they rule in Church or in State; whether they exercise authority in the free republic of America, in the kingdoms and monarchies of Europe, or in the more remote empires of the East. They can, therefore, abuse their authority, whether it be spiritual or temporal, regal or sacerdotal, unless the occasion of abusing it be taken from them by constitutional restrictions and safeguards. To say they could not or would not sometimes misuse, or abuse their power, would be to contradict the experience of all time, and to proclaim that the sacerdotal or regal unction takes from spiritual and temporal rulers their human nature and human infirmity. Hence is it, that the Catholic Church, wise beyond all human governments, directed and guided as she is by the Holy Ghost, has never entrusted absolute, much less arbitrary power to any of her officials or ministers.

The exceptional, or rather the anomalous and uncanonical form of ecclesiastical government, as it has been, alas, but too often administered in the United States, especially as regards the relations of the bishop with his clergy, beyond a doubt has approached the absolute: nay, has often been none other than the arbitrary and sometimes capricious will of one man. Louis XIV. of France, in the consciousness and pride of power, put an end to all discussion and remonstrance, by the simple but significant words, " L'état, c'est moi." In like manner, some of our prelates have closed the mouths of those appealing to the laws of the Church for redress against grievances, by declaring their *ipse dixit* the *law*. " Ego sum jus canonicum," are words that fell from the lips of a bishop of the United States, yet living, to show the extent of his power, and the folly of resisting his will. In fact, " I am the bishop," is the only and *ultima ratio* that some prelates in the United States have sometimes given for their acts, how incomprehensible soever they were in themselves, or opposed to the spirit and letter of the Canon Law of the Church.

The neglect, on the one hand, of proper and merited punishment, and on the other, the excessive and uncanonical punishment inflicted sometimes on clergymen, show how far we have strayed from the normal ecclesiastical discipline of the Church.

It is not often, thank God, considering the great number of priests and the many dangers to which they are exposed, that we hear of any of them straying far from the narrow path of virtue and ecclesiastical discipline. And when a priest does err, his fault, as a rule, is such, that in another it would not excite comment, or scarcely be noticed. Great, indeed, is the dignity of the Christian Priesthood, and eminent the sanctity it demands. This the people themselves know. What in a layman might be only a light transgression, may, in a clergyman, be a grave fault.

But priests are not impeccable. They are men, and are liable to err, and now and again do err. It is in such cases that our anomalous condition of ecclesiastical government is conspicuously made manifest. Some have sinned grievously, and either no note of censure whatever has been passed upon them, or they were punished lightly: others have sinned lightly and have been punished most rigorously. In most cases, there has been an immense disproportion between the fault and the punishment.

In fact, when I consider on the one side, a priest's fault of frailty or surprise, certainly not of malice, and the punishment I have known, without admonition, warning, citation or trial, to have been inflicted for it, that of being dismissed from his diocese and made a helpless outcast on the world, I am forced to confess, that the Episcopal code of ecclesiastical penalties, followed too often in practice in these United States for the punishment of clerical delinquents, bears a strong resemblance to the ancient code of the celebrated Draco. This latter has been summed up in one word: "Death for larceny; and for parricide or treason there remains—only death."

In like manner, suspension and exile, a fate sometimes worse than death, "Nonnunquam morte durior," has been often decreed for ordinary faults into which any one is liable to fall, and there remains no other punishment to be inflicted on the public apostate, or the contumacious rebel to authority. In the absence of canonical procedure and canonical punishments, this Draconian code embraces the sum and substance of the ecclesiastical criminal code of the United States as it has been reduced to practice by some at least, if not by many of our prelates. Banishment, exile and social death, is the punishment that has been meted out alike to the shameless reviler of Holy Mother Church, and to the poor victim of surprise and frailty.

Nay, more, in this unique code of unauthorized ecclesiastical discipline, the greater the crime the easier seems the pardon. Should a clergyman make a great deal of noise in the world, and raise his impious hand against the mother that bore him in Christ, à *la Hyacinthe* or *Döllinger*, his ecclesiastical superior would most eagerly make some provision for him in a monastery, or some other place of retirement, should he show the least desire of returning to the Church which he insulted and outraged. I do not find fault with this. It is right. It is according to the spirit of the Church's mercy and charity. Like her Divine Founder, the Catholic Church "wishes all men to be saved." But why, on the other hand, should that same ecclesiastical superior absolutely refuse to do any thing for, and close his doors against the poor priest, whose fault, compared with that of the former, was as a mole-hill compared to a mountain, and who, in poverty and evil repute, in hunger and nakedness, is true and loyal to the Faith of his fathers, and whose desire is to walk in its precepts? No matter how sincerely determined he is to return to the path of ecclesiastical discipline, and to redeem his error, he oftentimes receives only harsh and unkind treatment. He is thrown helplessly on the world. Every door of return into the ark seems closed against him. Even those to whom he has a right to look up to for encouragement, guidance, protection, mercy and justice, seem by their uncanonical treatment, determined to drive him to desolation, ruin, and despair.

Such has been our anomalous condition of ecclesiastical government in the past! But it is said that henceforth a different state of things will exist in the United States in consequence of the recent "Instructio" from Rome of July 20, 1878, taking action in the matter, and insisting upon Quasi Judicial Investigations and canonical punishments for canonical faults. We all hope that such will be the case, but I am sorry to say that there is many a Thomas among the clergy, who will not believe that this is going to bring much relief, until he sees the good results with his own eyes. Four years have elapsed since its promulgation, and so far at least these results are not very apparent. Sixteen years ago we had a like promise given by our venerable prelates themselves in the Second Plenary Council of Baltimore, and since that time, I doubt very much if throughout the length and breadth of the United States, there has been one canonical trial and one canonical punishment of an erring clergyman. The present dispensation, promulgated under more favorable auspices, and coming directly from our most Holy Father himself, has not, so far at least, been attended with much better success. From present appearances it looks as if the "Instructio," like the Council of Baltimore, would be "put on the shelf."

As absolute or arbitrary power in the hands of any one man, as we have seen, can be, and often is abused, so our abnormal condition of ecclesiastical government, which up to the present has, practically at least, approached nearer the absolute or rather arbitrary, than any other form, can give rise to many inconveniences and evils, —has actually been attended with many grave inconveniences and evils,—and from its very nature is always liable to be abused.

If law is the promoter, guardian and safeguard of peace, stability and good will, its antithesis, the absolute and still more the arbitrary will of one man, must, sooner or later, occasion discord, dissatisfaction and confusion. It is folly to object, that he who exercises power absolutely or arbitrarily is a holy man, such as are our venerable prelates. As long as he is a frail mortal, liable to err in his judgments, grave inconveniences and evils and abuses may frequently flow from his administration. This is sufficient to condemn it. Moreover, the Church herself, as we have already seen, is opposed to all government of her subjects that is not according to *law*. From her knowledge of the heart of man, and her experience of men, she knows how easy it is, for even the best and holiest of men to be mistaken when he has no other guide of conduct but his own absolute will.

Our anomalous condition of ecclesiastical government comes directly from the non-observance of the laws enacted for the good government of the Church in this country. In the II. Plenary Council of Baltimore, laws were made to be observed by all the bishops of the United States in their treatment of their clergy. These laws, though few in number, and of easy observance, have been almost entirely ignored. They are, in most dioceses, simply a myth, as far as their practical observance goes. Of them can be said very truthfully, what a loyal and conscientious Catholic journalist said of another Decree, N. 370 of the same Council, which declares, "public and frequent invitations to foundations of perpetual masses, inserted for several months in public newspapers, among secular matters," to be "an intolerable abuse and a profanation of sacred things." Having inserted such an advertisement in his paper, he defended himself for so doing in the following words, which speak the plain truth, not only of the Decree in question, but of those likewise made for the protection of the clergy, and in general of all the Decrees of discipline put together by the Fathers of the Council of Baltimore at the sacrifice of so much time, labor and trouble.

"The published Acts and Decrees of the Plenary Council of Baltimore, A. D. 1866, form a handsome volume. Not only that,—we keep it as a book of reference, and marvel very much at seeing how utterly it is disregarded.... When we first received it, we supposed that it was to be law for the Catholics of the United States.

"We accordingly wrote to a venerable religious monastery, saying that we must discontinue its advertisements.... We received in due time a letter certifying that the bishop of the diocese where the monastery was, sanctioned its publication in our columns. Right on the hand of this, the bishop of another diocese sent us, under his own head, personally known to us, an advertisement of the same identical character. When we found some of our bishops disregarding the prescriptions, and when we saw right and left that the handsome Acts and Decrees of the Second Plenary Council were put on the shelf,—after the best advice we could reach being taken,—we resumed the publication," etc. N. Y. Freeman's Journal, Sept. 13, 1873.

With much greater reason, as being more universally violated, the same just criticism could be made with regard to the Decrees of the same Council, marked 77 and 122, the one granting a canonical trial to ecclesiastics charged with any delinquency, the other forbidding bishops to dismiss any priest from his diocese until he has secured another bishop. These Decrees are certainly more openly and frequently set at naught, than the one to which the distinguished journalist mentioned above alludes. Priests are frequently dismissed from their dioceses, not only before they have secured another bishop, but often with the utmost probability that they will find no bishop who will receive them, or, if he observes the law strictly, who *can* receive them. "Si qui autem in posterum aliter dimissi fuerint *non recipiantur*." II. Plenary Council of Baltimore, N. 122.

Again, rarely has there been any judicial or canonical proceedings had towards a clergyman charged with any infraction of the law. In these cases, some, if not many bishops, without any previous admonition or exhortation whatever, without the shadow of a trial or even serious investigation, without apparently thinking of the counsels of the Gospel, or of the instructions of the Church and the admonitions of her Sacred Canons, have proceeded at once to pronounce a peremptory and absolute sentence, sometimes even arbitrarily casting forth the delinquent from his diocese, a sad fact which is generally made known to him in a few curt words, as: "I have nothing more, sir, to do with you. Go and look for another bishop."

But, my dear bishop, who may speak thus, permit an humble priest, who loves your eternal welfare, to say to you kindly and in the sincerest friendship, that these words so easily spoken—the terrible consequences of which to yourself in eternity, and to the priest for time and eternity, no one can tell—do not relieve you of your responsibility to your erring child. You are his spiritual father, who should love him, as the Council of Trent has it, " tanquam filium et fratrem." Until you hand over your Crozier to another, canonically appointed to fill your place, or until it falls from your hands palsied in death, *you are that poor priest's bishop, with all the dread responsibilities of a bishop towards him.* Instead of looking after your strayed sheep, instead of trying to lead it back into the fold, in pursuance of the teaching and example of your divine Model and Master, you may abandon it by telling it to seek another shepherd and other pastures, but neither the Gospel, nor the Church, nor her Sacred Canons justify such action.

Pardon the digression. As I was saying, seldom has a priest in this country, charged with a fault, the advantage of canonical proceedings. Not only have some bishops not endeavored to arrive at the truth by means of the process indicated in N. 77 of the II. Plenary Council of Baltimore, nor inflicted punishment according to the spirit and letter of the Holy Canons, but frequently they do not consult even their own Council in the matter. Their own will is the only law by which they have been governed. Right or wrong, just or unjust, their sentence, pronounced without any form of trial, and based sometimes on uncertain data, has been conclusive.

If this sentence should happen to be unjust, which, to say the least, is a possible contingency, the only hope of redress heretofore, has been a journey to Rome, for an appeal to the Metropolitan or Senior Bishop was not in order, as a bishop's sentence in the United States has generally been *ex informata conscientia*, which allows recourse only to the Holy See.

It was in view of this additional hardship imposed on priests in the United States, resulting from this method of procedure, that Kenrick, as far back as 1861, said: "Attamen, ut ingenue loquar, cum nulla forma judicii servatur, datur ansa Presulibus detrahendi, veluti omnia pro arbitrio agentibus: et appellationis ad Metropolitam remedio denegato, nulla reis spes relicta videtur, nisi itinere Romam suscepto." Theol. Mor. Trac. XXII, *de Cens* N. 85.

Few have the means to undertake a journey to Rome to have an unjust sentence righted. Many, had they even the means, have not the courage. Rather than expose themselves to the danger of incurring the bishop's ill-will, and all its possible consequences, they prefer to suffer injustice in silence, rather than journey to Rome, or appeal by letter to the Holy See.

I think I have said sufficient to show how anomalous has been the condition of our ecclesiastical government in these United States. There is no excuse or palliation for it. If even the few laws of discipline already enacted were only observed there would be an immense change for the better. There would then be no need to speak of the evil of dismissing from their dioceses priests not contumacious before they had secured another bishop. This evil arises undoubtedly from the non-observance of the ecclesiastical discipline already enacted for the protection of the clergy in this country by Roman Pontiffs, Sacred Congregations, and the II. Plenary Council of Baltimore. The laws already made, bishops as well as priests should scrupulously observe. In their relations with each other, especially if any misunderstanding arises between them, or some offence is charged against a clergyman, these laws, and not the bishop's sole will, should be his rule and guide of action. "Canonum statuta custodiantur ab omnibus: et nemo in actionibus vel judiciis ecclesiasticis, suo sensu, sed eorum auctoritate ducatur." Nothing whatever of importance should be left to the arbitrary ruling of any one man, who, no matter how just or holy he may be, is liable to err, and to be influenced in his judgment by biassed motives.

CHAPTER IV.

NECESSITY OF A COMPREHENSIVE AND WELL DEFINED CODE OF ECCLESIASTICAL DISCIPLINE FOR THE UNITED STATES.

The United States still ranks in the category of missionary countries. Its ecclesiastical affairs are exclusively under the supervision of the Sacred Congregation of the Propagation of the Faith, established by Gregory XV. for the government of the Church in all those countries where dioceses are not organized canonically, with chapters, ecclesiastical courts, etc.

Up to a comparatively recent period, this rank of a purely missionary country was befitting this land. In the early days of our republic especially, and for many years after, even a bishop's lot was that of a hard-working missionary, who was necessitated to take his share of the labor of the confessional, and often even to attend the sick call. Nay, many a time and oft, he had no other means of conveyance in visiting his diocese but that of the pilgrims of old,—and on foot, wearied and almost exhausted, he arrived in the dusk of the evening, at the little log chapel where he was to give confirmation on the following morning.

But a wonderful change has taken place since those days. On every side of us, from the Atlantic ocean to the Pacific, we see incontrovertible evidences of the stability of the Catholic Church in the United States. We have the honor of having even a Cardinal in our hierarchy, which is a favor Rome rarely grants to purely missionary countries, and a strong proof that she no longer looks upon the United States altogether in that light.

In fact, besides our Cardinal, we have several archbishops and many bishops, large and flourishing dioceses, crowded and well defined quasi parishes, magnificent cathedrals and churches, academies and colleges and schools, asylums and hospitals, and religious houses of almost every Order in the Church.

A bishop, in most parts of the United States, has now every facility of communication with his priests and people. He has his comfortable mansion, as well as his stately cathedral. He has generally a sufficient number of clergy, to surround himself with priests who can attend to all the wants of his cathedral church, and leave him free to devote himself exclusively to the affairs of his diocese, as well as to enable him to carry out to the letter, the grand, imposing ceremonies of the *Pontificale*. Nor, in fine, is he stinted in means to minister to his material wants, for there are few, if any bishops in the United States but have an abundance for all their necessities and conveniences.

Moreover, the Catholic Church has a firm footing in this country. She is not trammelled in her actions by *Concordats*, or by the interference of the State. In fact, the Church is more free in the United States to preach the Gospel, and to exercise her Divine Mission among men, than she is in the old Catholic nations of France and Italy. There seems to be no obstacle whatever in the way of introducing any ecclesiastical laws that the changed circumstances of our condition may require. In fact, all the laws of ecclesiastical discipline which have now as just an application as when they were enacted, and are as much needed now as then, could be easily introduced, not to speak of the facility there is of observing all the laws already made.

As soon as the Faith becomes established in a country, the Church wishes that all her laws of ecclesiastical discipline observed throughout the Church, should be gradually introduced. Her entire code for the guidance, protection and general good of her rulers and those governed, cannot be promulgated at once with the planting of the Faith, because of the obstacles to its observance that may exist. As these obstacles, however, disappear, she wishes that all her canons for the general government and well-being of her subjects should gradually obtain.

Amongst these canons are reckoned those of ecclesiastical discipline, regulating the relation of the bishop and his clergy, under which falls the subject of uncanonically dismissing priests from their dioceses, which will be discussed in these pages.

I may here remark, once for all, that when I speak of Canon Law in connection with my subject, I refer, of course, to what relates to ecclesiastical discipline, more particularly to that which regulates and determines all the relations between the bishop and his clergy. I am not ignorant of the fact, that many of the Sacred Canons have become obsolete on account of circumstances, whilst others could not be introduced because of their impracticability, though the spirit of piety, charity, justice and mercy that dictated them, is, and ever will remain unchangeable.

Rome has intimated more than once her desire that Canon Law, as far as possible and practicable, should be introduced and observed in the United States, especially as regards the bishop's relation with his clergy. Her wish is unmistakably seen from several Decisions of her Sacred Congregations in matters pertaining to this country, and from the Instructions given from time to time to the bishops of the United States. The desire of Rome that the Church in this country should gradually conform to the general discipline in vogue elsewhere, is also evident from her refusal to sanction indefinitely, or even *ad viginti annos*, the privilege of ordaining in this country to the extraordinary Title of the Mission, to which regular canonical titles must succeed as soon as possible. The wish of Rome that our hitherto anomalous condition of ecclesiastical government should cease altogether, and something definite and satisfactory take its place, is also apparent from the latest promulgation of our Holy Father to the American bishops, insisting upon the creation in every diocese of Ecclesiastical Commissions of Investigation, or Quasi Judicial Councils, for the ascertaining of the truth in all ecclesiastical causes. It is the beginning of the end.

Moreover, our late lamented and sainted Father, Pius the Great, who loved the Church so well, guarded her

so faithfully, and defended her so bravely; who so
nobly and unflinchingly and perseveringly fought the
good fight of Faith against the enemies of God and man,
and who, when he breathed his pure soul into the hands
of his Creator, was no doubt welcomed into Heaven,
amidst the joyful acclamations of the Church triumphant,
with our beloved Mother Mary, whom he proclaimed
Immaculate, at their head—Pius IX., one of the greatest
and most glorious of the Popes who have reigned since the
days of Peter, expressed the desire a short time before
his death, that the United States should take her place
under the general laws of discipline observed in Catholic
countries. His illustrious successor, Leo XIII., seems to
be of the same mind. He has already taken the first
steps towards its accomplishment, in rigorously requiring
that the late "Instructio" of July 20, 1878, be observed
by all the archbishops, bishops and vicars apostolic of
the United States. Many of the latter, I believe, coincide with the views of Rome, of the immortal Pius IX.,
and of his most worthy successor Leo XIII. This we
can, at least, infer from the II. Plenary Council of Baltimore. Smith, in his preface to *Notes* on the same, says:
"The desire of gradually introducing into this country, as
far as practicable, the ecclesiastical discipline prevalent
throughout almost the entire Church, was strongly and
repeatedly expressed by the Fathers of the late National
Council of Baltimore. Its decrees tend both avowedly and
implicitly to promote the accomplishment of this object."

Notwithstanding, however, the wonderful progress
of the Catholic Church in the United States, and the

readiness with which all the laws of discipline already enacted could be carried out, and others even added, we are yet in the position of a purely missionary country. Up to the present time there has been scarcely a shadow of change in ecclesiastical discipline as practised in the government of the clergy in this country, and that followed by the illustrious and venerable Carroll, when he was Prefect Apostolic of the whole United States. Things now are ripe for a change for the better, or for the substitution of Law and Order for our hitherto anomalous condition of ecclesiastical government. That the time is opportune nothing is more certain. The recent action of heaven-inspired Rome is a conclusive proof of this.

The multitude of Catholic Churches, the interests of the faithful, of religion in general, and of the clergy especially, both bishops and priests, require a more definite ecclesiastical discipline, than when the country was one vast diocese. This is necessary, to keep every thing in order, and for the comfort and edification of the faithful and of the body ecclesiastic. It is of the utmost importance, because of the great number of bishops and priests, that their mutual relations should be clearly determined, and especially that all difficulties and misunderstandings which may arise between them, should be justly settled, without derogating from the rights of either. This can be effected only by a comprehensive and well defined code of ecclesiastical discipline, binding upon all, and whose special laws must be observed faithfully and conscientiously by our venerable prelates themselves, as well as by the clergy.

It was the longing and ambition of the inhabitants of every province conquered by the Roman Eagles to become citizens of Rome. In like manner, do we, the clergy of the United States, long for the day, which does not seem to be remote, when we will have over us the ægis of the benign, just, and merciful discipline of the Church of Rome, and we hope that our venerable prelates will help to bring about this consummation so anxiously looked for.

CHAPTER V.

THE EVIL OF DISMISSING UNCANONICALLY ANY CLERGYMAN FROM HIS DIOCESE.

Before I proceed briefly to portray the evil to which these humble pages are intended to call the attention of the venerable authorities of the Church in the United States, a few preliminary words are necessary, that I may not be misunderstood.

It is, indeed, sometimes a sad necessity, and now and again, an unfortunate priest may leave no other alternative to his bishop but to abandon him to his folly, until he returns to better dispositions. But such a sad necessity takes place in one case only. It is when an erring priest is likewise contumacious. Contumacy, and contumacy alone, cuts him off from the Church's mercy, and from the protection and clemency which, in all other cases, he has a right to expect from his bishop, the Church's representative towards him.

M. Luther, who tried to rend apart the seamless garment of Christ, His Church, would have been pardoned his impious revolt against Divine Authority, had he followed up any of his many protestations of obedience and submission to the Holy See, which he made whilst the fear of God and his grace seemed yet to influence him for good; but putting aside the former and trampling the latter under foot, it was only when he had yielded completely to the terrible passions of disappointed ambition, pride and lust, and imitating the example of Lucifer, the first "reformer," exclaimed, as he did, " Non serviam," or, in other words, became contumacious, that he was abandoned by the Catholic Church.

Luther was a child of the Church and a priest. Had he at any time, even at the last moment of his unfortunate career, returned to the mother whose very life he had attempted, she would have welcomed him with open arms, received him to repentance, pardoned him, and thrown about him her mantle of mercy and protection. But he cut himself loose from her by contumacy.

It was contumacy that shipwrecked Simon Magus, Ebion, Cerinthus, Arius, Nestorius, Macedonius, Photius, and all through the long line of Heresiarchs to Luther, Calvin, Zwinglius, Henry VIII. and Co. Aaron, a High Priest of the Old Law, and Peter, a High Priest of the New, both sinned grievously, the former by openly sanctioning the worship of the Golden Calf, the latter by thrice denying his Divine Master, but they were not contumacious. They wept and did penance for their sin. God pardoned them. Nay, more, *He reinstated them in their office, and permitted them afterwards to minister before Him, and even among the very people whom they had scandalized by their fall from grace.*

Contumacy is the only obstacle then, which prevents a clergyman from experiencing the Church's clemency and protection, and ought to be the only obstacle that would exclude him from the mercy and protection of his bishop.

It will be well, therefore, to define here, before I proceed further, the precise meaning of contumacy, as the word will frequently occur in the following chapters. Moreover, a priest who is contumacious is excepted from the benefit of the law, forfeits all his rights, and can expect no mercy from his bishop, or from the Church, of which the bishop is the representative, until he humbles himself and submits to Authority.

Contumacy is defined: "Inobedientia a legitime vocato erga judicem, in iis quæ ad judicem pertinent, commissa, ita quoad sensum omnes." Schmalzgruber, *in tit.* 14, *lib.* 2, *Decretal N.* 38.

It is clear from this definition, that contumacy in the canonical sense of the word, has rarely, if ever, been found associated with delinquency in this country. For contumacy necessarily supposes the existence of ecclesiastical courts. True, ecclesiastical tribunals of justice have been legislated for by the II. Plenary Council of Baltimore, but unfortunately without any practical result. They ended with that legislation. The statute which ordains ecclesiastical trials (N. 77) has been a dead letter from the day it was promulgated to this day. The realization of its salutary ends never took place. It never got further than being printed, sent to Rome as an evidence of the zeal of our venerable prelates in the cause of justice. Having been returned, revised by Rome, it fell into disrepute. It was openly and generally disregarded as if it were of no account whatever. One or another bishop may have observed its provisions for aught I know, but the majority utterly disregarded it. This I do know. Ecclesiastical courts existing therefore only on paper, not in reality, there could not by any possibility have been disobedience to them, or to any order issued from them, and consequently, there could not, heretofore, have been any contumacy in the proper sense of the word, on the part of delinquent clergymen.

Such, however, will not be the case in the future. As canonical courts, or at least quasi judicial Counsels must be established in every diocese, each clergyman will be amenable to the Counsel of his diocese, and if wilfully disobedient to it, in the legitimate exercise of its jurisdiction and functions, he will, as a matter of course, and according to the definition given above, incur the brand of contumacy.

Gladly, heretofore, would the most part of ecclesiastics in the United States have submitted to the most rigorous sentence of a properly constituted ecclesiastical court, rather than suffer the penalty that has sometimes been decreed against them of being driven ignominiously from their dioceses, and abandoned helplessly to want and misery ; and in consequence either forced to work at some secular employment to gain their bread, or to beg it from the charity of the faithful.

The dismissal from his diocese, with or without a judicial investigation, of a priest charged with, or guilty of any offence, is an evil that has resulted immediately from our anomalous condition of ecclesiastical government. It is an evil that loudly calls for redress, and one that imperatively demands of our Most Rev. and Rt. Rev. Prelates a speedy and efficacious remedy.

Rome has long endeavored to remedy this evil, but

she has never taken more effectual steps in the matter than her recent action of imperatively requiring ecclesiastical tribunals in every diocese of the United States. This is intended to remedy the evil effectually, for the simple reason, that even a quasi judicial investigation requires, if the accused be found guilty, a canonical punishment; and it is most assuredly no canonical punishment to dismiss a priest from his diocese, and abandon him to ruin and desolation. There is not, nor ever will be, a canon to this effect.

It would seem, then, that I have no further need to speak of an evil, for which the remedy has been prescribed. But, alas! this salutary "Instructio" of July 20, 1878, seems already a dead letter. A prescription alone will not cure disease. It must be compounded and administered to the patient. In like manner, the prescriptions of the "Instructio" will avail nothing, unless they are carried out in practice. As I remarked in my preface, the quasi judicial investigations commanded by the "Instructio" must be made according to the spirit and letter of the same, otherwise the evil against which I speak would continue to exist, and become, perhaps, greater than before. There is, even now, therefore, more reason for protesting against the uncanonical penalty that so many priests have suffered in the past, of being helplessly dismissed from their dioceses, and of speaking of the canonical investigation that will remedy it, now that every priest can demand and insist on such investigation, lest the same fate of being made castaways may yet be decreed against them, notwithstanding the panoply and imposing array—on paper—of judge and jury.

I will, therefore, proceed to expose the evil of helplessly dismissing a priest from his diocese. A clergyman contracts many and grave obligations: obligations that cease only with his life; obligations which require for their faithful discharge much self-denial and constant vigilance, even when surrounded with all the helps which religion and the seclusion of his state afford. Without these helps and this seclusion, it is morally impossible for him to be faithful. Above all is this the case, when thrown into the very jaws of danger and temptation, which always occurs when his bishop dismisses him uncanonically from his diocese. Such action on the part of his bishop is a sure and almost infallible means of speeding a priest to utter ruin. For, abandoned by him, his father and only protector on earth, he is often made a wreck for time, and sometimes even for eternity, though such a sad result is not directly and explicitly intended.

To prove this, we have only to look at the unhappy results of such abandonment. We have only to follow the priest thus forsaken by his bishop and dismissed from his diocese, from the first step he takes in his helpless obedience to the uncanonical, and therefore irregular and unjust sentence of exile pronounced against him, to his last steps on earth, towards the doors of some public hospital, thence to be carried, perhaps, to an obscure and untimely grave.

The fate of a priest in this country, whom his bishop

abandons, is a hard and sad one indeed, and suggestive of more miseries and sorrows than my humble pen could depict. Had I even the ability, I have not, for obvious reasons, either the desire or the inclination to portray the helplessness, the bodily privations, the anguish of mind and grief of heart, the desolation of soul from shattered hopes and bitter disappointments, the feeling akin to despair, of being made an exile from home and relatives and friends, and even altar, and an outcast amongst men; much less could I adequately describe the dishonor to religion, the disgrace to the priesthood, and the injury to Holy Church, which follow in the wake of almost every priest forsaken by his bishop and thrown upon his own resources. It would be a sad and sombre picture, indeed, scarcely relieved by a single ray of light. I will simply glance at its outlines. Details are unnecessary. It needs no coloring. It is too painful already, in its naked reality.

A priest cast off by his bishop, who ought to be his best friend on earth, abandoned by him whom the Church gave him as his protector and guardian, is the most forlorn, pitiable, helpless object on the face of God's beautiful earth. Every religious house, and every Catholic Institution in the land is closed against him. They are not bound to provide for him for whom a bishop of the Catholic Church is bound in justice and charity to provide. There is a door open to the drunkard to reform him, to the orphan to feed and clothe him, to the insane to protect and care for him. To every class, and to every creed and nationality, will the passport of poverty, affliction, bodily suffering or mental infirmity, open the doors of our charitable Catholic institutions. There is but one for whom there seems to be a refuge nowhere: the unfortunate priest abandoned by his bishop. Were he contumacious the fountains of pity would be justly dried up with regard to him, for then he would have absolutely no one to blame for his miseries but himself and his abominable pride and obstinacy that holds him back from humbly bowing his neck to the sweet yoke of obedience and authority. But, though having erred, he is generally humble and penitent. He loathes his error, and sighs for forgiveness and reconciliation. He would enter any monastery. He would do any amount of penance for his sin. But, in the wide world there is no refuge for him where he can gain admission. It seems that there is no room for him anywhere.

Is it not strange—and I put the question to our venerable prelates, the faithful clergy and the devoted laity—is it not passing strange, that amidst the multitude of religious establishments and priests and churches and cathedrals, there is not in this land, a door of welcome open to the poor, erring priest, against whom the bishop has closed his? It is, indeed, strange, and, alas, but too true!

When a priest has been forsaken by his bishop, even a *confrère*, willing, or even anxious to keep him, can do little or nothing for him. By giving him hospitality, he often exposes himself to incur the displeasure, and sometimes even the ill-will of his bishop. Though willing to brave this, yet he and his *protégé* would be placed in an awkward position; for is it not disedifying at least to a congregation, to have a priest for one's guest, who is not allowed to say mass? In consequence, he cannot remain any length of time with his dearest and most devoted friend amongst the clergy. Nay, he is precluded from finding a home even under his own paternal roof, for, not to be allowed to offer up the holy sacrifice, implies some serious crime, or grave unworthiness, and the crushing disgrace and humiliation attached to it he is unwilling to bring to the home of friend, much less of father or mother, brother or sister.

He has, therefore, no alternative left, but to make application to some other bishop. He does so, but unsuccessfully. He then applies to another, and to another, and to still another, but to no purpose. There is no room for him. In vain does he approach bishop after bishop. Some will not even see him. Some will treat him kindly, and pass him gently to the next, whilst one or another advise him to return to his own bishop, who, by the Canon Law of the Church, by the Title of his ordination, and by the titles of mercy, charity and justice, is bound to care for him as long as he is not contumacious. But his own bishop refused, perhaps, even to see him, before he started on what proved for him only a wild goose chase. He knows that it is useless for him to return. What then will he do? What *can* he do? Were he a mechanic, or a farmer, or even a laborer, he might find employment. But—HE IS A PRIEST.

It has been said, and even advocated, that a priest in this country, who has been forsaken by his bishop, ought to turn his hand or brains to some use to earn a living for himself. I know of two bishops even, in the United

States, who recommended unfortunate priests, whom they had uncanonically dismissed from their dioceses, to seek some secular employment to earn their bread. In my humble judgment, such advice was equivalent to telling them to positively peril the salvation of their immortal souls. For, if it is difficult even, for one to save his soul in his vocation, with all the helps, natural and supernatural, which it affords, it is beyond comparison far more difficult for him to secure his salvation outside of his calling. Such, at least, is the teaching of all ascetic writers.

It is false, and a pernicious error, and contrary to the spirit and teaching of the Church, as I shall prove in the proper place, to say that a priest who may have erred, even grievously and repeatedly, is allowed to abandon his cassock, and take up the spade, or become a lawyer, doctor, farmer, or tradesman to gain the means of subsistence.

A priest is never permitted to abandon his state and enter secular life. Nay, if he have a particle of the spirit of the Priesthood within his heart, he cannot force himself to follow any other avocation than the one to which God called him. The mysterious mark of the priesthood of Jesus Christ imprinted on his soul by the Sacrament of Order, holds him back. The Church asserts positively that it is unbecoming and degrading to the sacerdotal dignity to engage in secular pursuits, " Cum indecorum omnino sit atque a clericorum qui Sacris Ordinibus constituuntur, dignitate prorsus alienum, ut ipsi aut mendicatis subsidiis, aut ex sordido quæstu, ea quæ ad victum necessaria sunt, sibi comparare cogantur." Instr. S. C. de P. F. *de Tit. Ord.* How unworthy soever he may be, he feels the truth of these words in the very inmost recesses of his being. How far soever he may have strayed in forbidden paths, he cannot bring his mind to lay aside his cassock forever, and assume the garb and occupation of a layman. Even for him such occupation is "sordidum." Sheer necessity and absolute want may, indeed, force him to it, but as long as he lives, the priesthood, which, in his proper and legitimate sphere, would be the joy and comfort of his life, becomes for him an overwhelming weight of bitterness and sorrow. His heart will ever be torn with anguish and bowed down with grief, though possessed of every earthly pleasure and comfort, until he again enters "in domum Domini," and takes his place therein, even though it be that of a penitent, unless he has lost all faith and every hope of happiness here and hereafter. This phenomenon can be explained only by the power and grace of the Sacrament of Order working in him, preserving him often from what might prove the shipwreck of his salvation, and urging him on to seek, sometimes even almost against hope, a path of life in accordance with his sacred character.

The clergyman dismissed from his diocese and abandoned by his bishop, not being allowed to work, and ashamed to beg, and unsuccessful in every application to this or another bishop, who certainly cannot be blamed for not receiving him, as he has no claim whatsoever on them, knows not what to do, or whither to turn his face for a refuge.

In this perplexing and troubled state of mind, he is informed of a certain monastery, where he will probably be welcomed. Hope revives in his heart. He has read of the monasteries of old, synonymous with charity and hospitality. If the monks received with kindness, and treated with thoughtful and Christian charity, the poorest of God's poor; if, through respect for him, Who, when on earth, " Had not whereon to lay His Head," they bathed their feet, and set out the bountiful repast, and provided the comfortable couch; they will doubtless be moved to compassion towards him, who, moreover, bears impressed on his soul the priestly character. Besides, being in all probability of the number of the poor, he has this additional motive to hope for a kind reception.

Thus soliloquizing, he starts for the monastery of which he has heard, hoping there at least he will find a shelter and an asylum, where he can live as becomes the priestly character. He wends his way thither, only to find on his arrival all his bright anticipations blasted, for he learns that the regulations of the monastery do not allow him to stay longer than a few days at most, unless he has a letter from his bishop authorizing them to receive him. No blame can attach to them for refusing him an asylum in his helplessness, for it is very true, as they may inform him, that his bishop is the proper person to provide him with a home. But, alas! it was his bishop, and he knows it to his sorrow, that made him homeless and a wanderer on the face of the earth.

A brother clergyman perhaps whom he approaches in his distress, tells him of some college where he may find employment as a teacher. So anxious is he to be in some place where he can live according to the spirit of his calling, that he is willing to teach, even, for his board. Sore at heart for his many disappointments, he makes application at the college for any position, however humble, in which he can be of service. He receives for answer, that every position therein has been filled. Again they may give him the information he has heard repeated so often, that it is his bishop, who, in charity and justice, is bound to do something for him. He feels, however, that if he returns, he will only do as he did before,—close his doors against him! Besides, he is now probably without means, and far away from home and friends.

I have, dear reader, given but a very imperfect outline of the position in which many a good priest even, in the United States, has been placed, by being dismissed from his diocese. I say advisedly, of many a good priest, for his transient fall, of no very serious nature, did not vitiate him, or make of him a bad priest.

If, now, we withdraw our eyes from the unfortunate priest himself, and view this act of helplessly dismissing him from his diocese, in all its baneful consequence of sin and shame and scandal, of dishonor to the Church, injury to religion, to the priestly character and dignity, and to immortal souls, we have, indeed, abundant cause of tears and sadness. I need not dwell on this manifold phase of the evil. Every bishop, priest and almost every layman in the United States is conversant with it. Few there are who have not seen with their own eyes, this evil in its sad consequences, or have not heard of it with their own ears. Often has it been made the subject of even the newspaper paragraph.

All the calamities and miseries that overwhelm an unfortunate priest who has been dismissed from his diocese and thrown helplessly on the world, are insignificant—are nothing at all—compared to the injury inflicted thereby on the Catholic Church, on the honor of the priesthood of Jesus Christ, and on immortal souls. I will not sadden the hearts of my readers, by enumerating all the other evils and scandals that flow, as a consequence, from this one evil, of helplessly and uncanonically dismissing a clergyman from his diocese. They have been summed up in one word by the immortal Pontiff, St. Pius V., over three centuries ago, when legislating against this very evil of which I complain, whence so many others follow, viz.: that of priests being left helpless and without an ecclesiastical superior: "Cum .... per sæculum vagantes vel, mendicare, vel sordidum questum exercere, non sine ipsorum dedecore, et ordinis vilipendio, et quam plurimorum fidelium scandalo." Bulla *Romanus Pontifex*.

It is against this evil of uncanonically dismissing priests from their dioceses, so prolific in unholy fruits of ruin to the individual, as well as of disorder in the Church, scandal to the faithful and loss of souls, that I enter my solemn protest in these pages, in the name of hundreds of my fellow-clergymen, and of tens of thousands of the devoted laity.

The establishment in every diocese, on a true and

solid foundation, *i. e.*, according to the spirit and letter of the late "Instructio" *Quamvis*, of July 20, 1878, and according to the Canon Law of the Church, of ecclesiastical tribunals of justice, ought, as I have more than once remarked, to give the death-blow to this evil and all its baneful consequences. For canonical tribunals, whether courts, or quasi judicial investigations, unless they be made a sham and a mockery, will and must inflict canonical punishments, of which helplessly dismissing a priest from his diocese and abandoning him to ruin, is not one. And yet, so universal and of such long standing has been this evil, that many even now fear that it will not be abolished, and, therefore, a voice of remonstrance is not out of place, and may be most opportune, and productive of beneficial results, especially when backed by the voice and authority of Rome.

This evil of which I speak, is certainly not an imaginary one, as regards the past, at least. It has been a tangible, palpable, sad reality, witnessed every day of the three hundred and sixty-five days of the year, in its sad consequences of roaming priests and sacerdotal scandals. It brings dishonor on religion, contempt on the sacerdotal character, odium on the bishops and clergy in general, is weakening the faith of the good, and destroying that of the lukewarm. Why this evil has been allowed to go unchecked so long is to me a mystery and a wonder. Mercy, justice, charity, the welfare of Catholicity, even our common humanity cry out against it. It has been the "Abomination of Desolation" in the Church in the United States.

CHAPTER VI.

THE SECOND PLENARY COUNCIL OF BALTIMORE, AND THE SPIRIT AND LETTER OF THE COUNCIL OF TRENT, PROHIBIT THE UNCANONICAL DISMISSAL OF ANY CLERGYMAN FROM HIS DIOCESE.

It was to remedy this evil, of which I spoke in the preceding chapter,—that of dismissing from his diocese any priest not contumacious, and thus consigning him to almost certain ruin,—that the Fathers of the II. Plenary Council of Baltimore made the following statute: "Statuunt Patres, nullum harum Provinciarum Sacerdotem, ad aliam diœcesim transire volentem, *a proprio episcopo dimittendum, nisi certo constet eum ab alio episcopo recipiendum.* Si qui autem in posterum aliter dimissi fuerint, non recipiantur." N. 122.

That the animating spirit of the above Decree was to remedy the evil of dismissing priests uncanonically from their dioceses, is evident from the words of Cardinal Barnabo to the Fathers of the Council, suggesting the statute itself, " Imo Patres 7mæ Synodi Baltimorensis, *ut omnem vagandi viam clericis præcluderent,* jam Can. V. statuerant," "Nullum harum Provinciarum sacerdotem," etc.

Some of our venerable prelates have not observed the above salutary decree. When a priest erred, their only solicitude seemed to have been, not how they would correct and save him, but how they could get rid of him. Many bishops have given letters dimissory to clergymen, though they knew well that they had secured no other bishop, and knew very well, too, that no other bishop could receive them. "Si qui autem in posterum *aliter* dimissi fuerint *non* recipiantur." Is this complying with the injunction of the Council of Baltimore, "Nullum sacerdotem a proprio episcopo dimittendum, nisi certo constet eum ab alio episcopo recipiendum"?

That I state only the plain, simple truth in this matter, the great number of priests shifting every day from the east to the west, and from the north to the south, abundantly proves. There is scarcely a month, and in many places not a week passes but witnesses one or more priests seeking in vain for some refuge, where, sheltered from the gaze of the world, they can lead a life in conformity with the nature of their calling. Can any adequate reason be given for this sad state of things, other than the positive disregard of the above quoted statute of the II. Plenary Council of Baltimore, as well as that other Decree of the same Council granting to every ecclesiastic charged with any offence, a fair and impartial trial, which necessarily implies a definite sentence? It is self-evident that this crying evil of homeless and wandering priests would not exist, if the above statute of the Council of Baltimore were observed by all our venerable prelates.

And back of this violation of the Decree of Baltimore, is the direct and positive disregard of a higher and more venerable authority, the Council of Trent, or the very voice of the Church itself. This Holy and Œcumenical Council admonishes bishops of the duties of love and protection they owe their clergy. It reminds them of the anxious solicitude they should have for their welfare, and the obligation they are under of caring for them as a father for his children, a brother for his brethren, or a pastor for the members of his flock. But, for the edification of my readers, I will give the very words of the venerable Fathers, found in Sess. xiii., cap. 1, *de Refor.*

"Eadem sacrosancta Tridentina Synodus, in Spiritu Sancto legitime congregata.... intendens nonnulla statuere, quæ ad jurisdictionem pertinent episcoporum.... illud primum eos admonendos censet, ut se *Pastores* non *percussores* esse meminerint, atque ita præesse sibi subditis oportere, *ut non eis dominentur, sed illos, tanquam filios et fratres diligant: elaborentque ut hortando, et monendo, ab illicitis deterreant, ne, ubi deliquerint, debitis eos pœnis coercere cogantur.* Quos tamen, *si quid per humanam fragilitatem peccare contigerit,* illa Apostoli est ab eis servanda præceptio, ut *illos arguant, obsecrent, increpent in omni bonitate et patientia : cum sæpe plus erga corrigendos agat benevolentia quam austeritas ; plus exhortatio, quam comminatio; plus charitas, quam potestas. Sin autem ob delicti gravitatem virga opus fuerit ; tunc* cum *mansuetudine* rigor, cum *misericordia* judicium ; cum *lenitate* severitas adhibenda est, ut *sine asperitate,* disciplina populis salutaris, ac necessaria conservetur ; *et qui correcti fuerint* EMENDENTUR ; aut si resipiscere noluerint, ceteri, salubri in eos animadversionis exemplo, a vitiis deterreantur ; *cum sit diligentis, et pii simul pastoris officium, morbis ovium levia primum adhibere fomenta; post, ubi morbi gravitas ita postulet, ad acriora, et graviora remedia descendere:* sin autem nec ea quidem proficiant illis submovendis, ceteras saltem oves a contagionis periculo liberare."

Here we have the very inspired voice of the infallible Church, instructing and admonishing her bishops how to act towards their clergy, either to prevent them from going astray, or to save them, should it happen that they sin. In hearkening to this voice there need be no fear of being mistaken. In following, to the letter, these admonitions and instructions of the Council of Trent, there is no danger of being led astray, or of being "too lenient."

This evil of homeless priests, wandering from diocese to diocese, or again, of priests homeless at home, begging their daily bread from the charity of the clergy and of the laity, would most certainly not exist, if every bishop in the United States heeded and followed in practice the above wise and salutary instructions and admonitions with regard to their clergy, besides observing towards them the method of acting laid down by the Fathers of the II. Plenary Council of Baltimore. To any one reading the Councils of Trent and of Baltimore this is evident. It needs no further proof. It is as clear as the noonday sun.

It is now over three centuries since the venerable Fathers of Trent gave the above instructions and admonitions to the bishops of the Catholic Church, and to-day they read as if they had in view the uncanonical manner in which some bishops in the United States have treated their clergy.

How grandly harmonious do not the words of the venerable Fathers of Trent, full of wisdom and breathing the spirit of Divine Charity, now strike on our ears, after the lapse of more than three hundred years! " Sacro sancta Synodus in Spiritu Sancto legitime congregata, illud primum eos (episcopos) admonendus censet, ut se pastores, non percussores esse meminerint; atque ita præesse sibi subditis oportere, ut non eis dominentur, sed illos, tanquam filios et fratres diligant." How their words breathe the spirit of paternal solicitude with which the Church wishes the hearts of all her bishops to be filled towards their clergy! "Elaborentque, ut hortando, et monendo, ab illicitis deterreant; ne, ubi deliquerint, DEBITIS eos PŒNIS coercere cogantur." How they inculcate still the love of a Father for his erring child, and a Father's efforts to bring him back to the path of duty! "Quos tamen, si quid per humanam fragilitatem peccare contigerit, illa Apostoli est ab eis servanda præceptio, ut illos arguant, obsecrent, increpent in omni bonitate et patientia; cum sæpe, plus erga corrigendos agat benevolentia quam austeritas; plus exhortatio quam comminatio; plus charitas quam potestas." And, finally, when punishment becomes necessary, and the rod of correction must be used, how they insist that the bishop make use of it with the feelings of a *Father!* "Sin autem, ob delicti gravitatem, virga opus fuerit; tunc cum mansuetudine rigor, cum misericordia judicium, cum lenitate severitas adh.benda est, ut sine asperitate, disciplina populis salutaris ac necessaria conservetur: et qui correcti fuerint *emendentur.*"

Oh! grand, beautiful, merciful, and admirable spirit of the Holy Catholic Church! It is full of sweet gentleness, and withal replete with justice. It possesses the firmness of a Father and at the same time the tenderness of a Mother. It is none other than the benign, just and merciful spirit of Jesus Christ himself. Would that all ecclesiastical superiors were possessed of this spirit! Acting towards their clergy in the spirit of charity, compassion, benignity, mercy and justice, so beautifully and so forcibly described by the holy and Œcumenical Council of Trent, the utmost harmony and affection would subsist between them and their subjects. Great indeed is the love, surpassing that of flesh and blood, between the simple laic and the true Pastor, but greater far is the love and affection and confidence that exist between a true bishop and his clergy.

It is the fault in a great measure of some of our bishops themselves,—and I say it in all kindness and friendship and Christian charity, and most respectfully,—if in some dioceses a spirit of coldness and want of confidence has arisen between them and their clergy. It is chiefly their fault, if the spirit of love, reverence and filial affection is disappearing, and that of indifference or stolid obedience is taking its place. It is chiefly their fault if priests are found roaming from diocese to diocese, friendless, homeless and penniless. It is chiefly their fault if Rome, of late years, has been deluged with complaints from the clergy. These and many other evils result from the admonitions and instructions of the Council of Trent being disregarded, and the laws enacted at Baltimore by the Fathers of the II. Plenary Council being set at naught.

How, I ask, can the conduct of that ecclesiastical superior be reconciled with the Decree of the Council of Trent which I have quoted, or with the later ones of the Council of Baltimore, who will not even condescend to grant an interview to an erring but penitent priest; who pitilessly closes his door against him, and makes him a helpless outcast upon the world? Do the II. Plenary Council of Baltimore, the Holy and Œcumenical Council of Trent, the sacred canons of the Church, or the canons of charity, justice and mercy proclaimed by the Gospel, justify such action?

I am indeed pained to be forced, in connection with my subject, to speak so plainly, but, alas! every priest in the United States, who has been any number of years on the mission, knows that I utter only the plain, unvarnished truth; and if his own bishop is mild, and gentle, and merciful, and just, and a bishop according to God's own heart, he is not ignorant that the same cannot be said of some others.

How, again I ask, reconcile with the above-quoted decree of the Council of Trent, breathing in every word the spirit of charity and paternal affection, the conduct of that ecclesiastical superior, who, when that poor man whom he has uncanonically dismissed from his diocese finds a home or a refuge, makes use of his authority to oblige his kind benefactors to drive him forth from beneath their roof, and thus force him to become again a wanderer on the face of the earth? More than one instance of this kind could be cited, were it either proper or prudent. Many a priest throughout the land can vouch for the truth of what I assert.

It is far from being a pleasure to expose these sad facts,—it grieves me much to do so,—but justice to the dead and mercy to the living demand the revelation. The images of men who were good and true, and who were driven to desolation and ruin, or suffered the extreme of mental anguish or bodily privations, in consequence of uncanonical action on the part of their bishops, seem to rise up before me and to plead in behalf of the clergy in the United States of this and future generations, entreating me to remind those of our venerable prelates who may need it, of the wise and salutary admonitions and instructions of the Council of Trent, and to humbly and earnestly entreat them to follow to the letter these admonitions and instructions in their official dealings with their clergy. Their voice—and it is the voice of a multitude—as well as the glory of the Priesthood and the honor of the Catholic Church, have more weight with me than the paltry fear of offending those bishops, who base the government of their clergy on other principles than those laid down by the II. Plenary Council of Baltimore, by the "Instructions" from Rome, or by the Holy and Œcumenical Council of Trent.

How, again I ask, reconcile with the above decree of Trent, full of the spirit of paternal charity, of mercy and of rightly understood justice, the conduct of that ecclesiastical superior, who never drops one word of reproof, warning or exhortation to him who is in danger; for whom the admonition of the Apostle, "Arguent, obsecrent, increpent, in omni bonitate et patientia," is a dead letter; who, when he punishes, never blends mildness with vigor, or mercy with justice, or lenity with severity; who, in a word, follows but one canon of discipline towards delinquent priests, and that of his own making, or one method of acting towards them, and that is, to discard them altogether, and abandon them to utter ruin and desolation? Every bishop and every priest in the United States knows that in this I speak only the simple truth, a truth attested every day by the number of shipwrecked priests that are met with, who, having in the beginning but slightly erred, were made complete wrecks by being dismissed from their dioceses by their ecclesiastical superiors, who, in so doing, not only set at naught the admonitions and instructions of the Council of Trent, and the Decrees of the Council of Baltimore, and utterly disregarded their duty as laid down by these venerable authorities, but ignored even the dictates of charity and justice, and the very instincts of our common humanity. It has, indeed, given me much pain, and cost me an effort to speak these plain truths, but my subject imperatively demands it, the evil that I combat requires it, so that, from these scant intimations, our venerable prelates may see for themselves what mighty reasons I had for raising my feeble voice in behalf of the Rights of the Clergy of the United States.

Besides the Council of Trent and the II. Plenary Council of Baltimore, I may here introduce another authority, condemnatory of this evil of uncanonically dismissing priests from their dioceses. Rome, of late years, has put an almost insurmountable obstacle to it. Now no priest can be transferred from his own diocese and affiliated to another without a special concession of the Holy See. This I gather from the following reply to a question asked of the Sacred Congregation by the holy, learned and devoted Coadjutor Archbishop of Cincinnati, Most Rev. Wm. Henry Elder, D. D.

" Quæritur si sacerdos ex una diœcesi ad alteram transire velit, approbante ordinario suo, estne necesse emittat novum juramentum? Et ad tale jusjurandum num requiratur nova Concessio S. Sedis?"

To this the answer was: "Affirmative ad utrumque."

Yet, notwithstanding the merciful instructions and admonitions of the Council of Trent, notwithstanding the Instructions from Rome, and the special enactments made by Rome for the protection of priests in the United States, notwithstanding the legislation of the II. Plenary Council of Baltimore to the same end, we are saddened and grieved to the heart almost every day by the sight of priests, " quasi oves perditæ aut errantes," made such by their ecclesiastical superiors.

The Church certainly does not desire such a state of things. Rome has several times signified her abhorrence of it, and her wish that an end be put to it. Every true and good bishop throughout the land, as well as every priest who loves his Church and reverences the priestly dignity, deplores it, whilst the intelligent laity are amazed at it.

We need not search far for the remedy for this evil. The Doctors and Fathers of the Church have prescribed for its cure. The instructions and admonitions of the venerable Fathers of the Council of Trent are intended to guard against it. The Canon Law of the Church, the Decrees of Pontiffs and Decisions of Sacred Congregations, as we shall see further on, condemn it. But we need not search even so far,—the remedy is at hand. The venerable Fathers of the II. Plenary Council of Baltimore prescribed the cure for it. They framed a statute which aims directly at this evil of abandoning a priest before he is under another superior. I have already quoted it. It is as follows:

" Statuunt Patres, nullum harum Provinciarum sacerdotem, ad aliam diœcesim transire volentem, a proprio episcopo dimittendum, NISI CERTO CONSTET EUM AB ALIO EPISCOPO recipiendum. Si qui autem in posterum aliter dimissi fuerint non recipiantur."

Let even the above wise and salutary Decree be scrupulously observed by each of the venerable prelates of the United States, and the evil of homeless, wandering and mendicant priests will disappear forever.

Again, the late " Instructio " of July 20, 1878, directed to the archbishops, bishops and Vicars Apostolic of the United States, which requires that every priest charged with any canonical offence, be granted a quasi judicial investigation of his case, and if found guilty, be canonically and definitely punished, will remedy the evil, if the provisions of that

Instruction are only carried out. And I here humbly and most earnestly entreat our venerable and beloved prelates, in the name of the clergy of the United States, to observe *in toto*, in all its details, the *modus agendi* there laid down for them by Rome. I would inform them in the spirit of sincere friendship, that already there is much dissatisfaction at the little notice this Instruction has received at the hands of the episcopate of the United States. Many have even ventured to affirm that it would soon be entirely ignored. God forbid that any one of our venerable prelates, much less any considerable number of them, should openly disobey the Vicar of Christ!

But to return to my subject. For the wise and good government of the Church in these United States, we must substitute the laws of the Council of Trent, and of the Council of Baltimore and of the Instructions from Rome, for the sole arbitrary will of one man, no matter how just, learned, holy or wise he may be. This is the salutary salve that will heal all the wounds of the body ecclesiastic in these United States, and particularly the one indicated in these humble pages,—that of dismissing uncanonically any clergyman from his diocese, an evil which I will now proceed to discuss more fully, and to show by other authorities how opposed it is to the spirit and teaching of the Church, and how frequently and unequivocally it is condemned by her in one form or another.

CHAPTER VII.

CHARITY AND JUSTICE FORBID THE UNCANONICAL
DISMISSAL OF A CLERGYMAN FROM HIS DIOCESE.

No one who has read the preceding chapters but will admit, that the dismissing from his diocese of any clergyman, and casting him forth helplessly on the world, is an evil much to be deplored in itself, and prolific of many sad consequences.

But perhaps this evil is one of the many that exist in "this valley of tears," and for which there is no remedy. Perhaps it is one of those unavoidable, necessary evils to be ranked amongst those to which the old adage applies, "what can't be cured must be endured." Is such the case? No! This evil can be cured. It results from the non-observance of the laws of the Church, and for its remedy, it needs only that these laws be enforced.

A bishop or other ecclesiastical superior cannot lawfully dismiss a priest from his diocese, and abandon him to ruin, for even serious and repeated misconduct, as long as he is not contumacious. We have already seen that this is forbidden by Decree N. 122 of the II. Plenary Council of Baltimore, as well as by the spirit and letter of the Council of Trent. It is, moreover, condemned by the laws of Charity and Justice, by Decrees of Roman Pontiffs, the Decisions of Sacred Congregations, by the teachings of Theologians and Canonists, as well as by the very nature and dignity of the priestly character, all of which will clearly appear as I proceed.

In this chapter I will show, that both Charity and Justice forbid a bishop to dismiss helplessly from his diocese any clergyman not contumacious.

I. Charity forbids it. True and well regulated charity for priest and people, may require a bishop, or other in authority, to remove or suspend a priest *positis poncndis*, to punish him even severely for his delinquencies, but always and ever according to canonical rules. But suspending him, or punishing him, is a far different thing from driving him forth from his diocese and abandoning him altogether, thus placing him in imminent peril of his very salvation. This the law of charity, the first of all laws, the greatest of the commandments, absolutely forbids.

In Tractatu de Charitate *Art*. 2, N. 278, Konings says, "Necessitas (dicitur) gravis, ut cum quis, nisi adjuvetur ab alio, difficillime effugere valet periculum animæ vel vitæ corporis, alteriusve gravis mali."

N. 279: " Si proximus sit in gravi necessitate, sive spirituali, sive temporali nemo ei *per se tenetur* succurrere cum gravi incommodo."

" Dixi 1° *per se;* nam teneretur, etiam cum periculo vitæ QUI AD ID OBLIGARETUR vel RATIONE OFFICII, ut ANIMARUM PASTORES."

Suarez says: " Quod PASTOR scil. EPISCOPUS et PAROCHUS TENETUR, ETIAM CUM MAGNO SUO DAMNO TEMPORALI, PROCURARE MAGNAM UTILITATEM SPIRITUALEM

SUBDITI." St. Liguori, l. ii., N. 27, and Kenrick, Trac. xiii., N. 84, teach the same doctrine.

The application of the above principles to the case of dismissing from his diocese a priest who is not contumacious, is apparent. These eminent theologians teach that a bishop is obliged by the law of charity to help his subject, "in gravi necessitate," even at the risk of his life, "cum periculo vitæ." According to this teaching, he ought to be willing to lay down his life for the humblest member of his diocese placed in grave spiritual or temporal necessity. *A fortiori*, he ought to be willing, and is bound to make every temporal sacrifice, even to the giving of his life, to succor "in gravi necessitate sive spirituali, sive temporali," any of his clergy, who, because of their character and dignity, are the first fruits and most excellent of his flock.

Now, when a bishop dismisses a priest from his diocese, and abandons him altogether, not only does he, his Pastor, not succor him in grave necessity, but as a rule he actually places him therein. For, of such a priest generally, nothing is more true, than "nisi adjuvetur ab alio, difficillime effugere valet periculum animæ vel vitæ corporis, alteriusve gravis mali." This I have already abundantly proved in a preceding chapter, when I dwelt on the evil of uncanonically dismissing any priest from his diocese. Moreover, that a clergyman forsaken by his bishop, is *ipso facto* as a rule, placed in grave spiritual and temporal necessity, is a truth so evident, that none will be found to deny it.

Therefore, according to the above-mentioned theologians, whose teaching on this point is in accordance with that of all others, a bishop is forbidden by the law of charity to dismiss his subject helplessly from his diocese, because such an act is diametrically opposed to charity. For it places him *ipso facto* in a position which, as a rule, will bring with it grave spiritual and temporal necessities, as well as other momentous evils. From this it follows as a necessary corollary, that any bishop, who, by the act of uncanonically dismissing a clergyman from his diocese, has thus placed him in grave spiritual or temporal necessity, is bound *sub gravi* to redeem his error, and relieve the same as soon as possible from such an unhappy situation, even at the sacrifice of his life, were that necessary.

It may have been this thought preying upon the mind of a bishop of whom I was told, who, having in the beginning of his administration, uncanonically dismissed two priests from their diocese, made the most strenuous efforts afterwards to find them, to repair the wrong he had done them and his own soul, and his efforts proving unsuccessful, he sorrowed over it to the hour of his death.

Charity forbids the dismissing uncanonically from his diocese of any clergyman, not only on account of the many evils it inflicts on him, whom, as a rule, it places in grave spiritual and temporal necessity, but likewise on account of *the consequences* of such an act.

I have already spoken of the evils that attend a priest, who is made an orphan without bishop or diocese, or rather whom the bishop or the diocese abandons. Such a clergyman is far more helpless than the veriest orphan that has lost his natural protectors. Forsaken by his lawful superior and guardian, not only can he with the utmost difficulty avoid dangers to soul and body, but oftentimes, scandal to religion, dishonor to the Church and to the Holy Priesthood, follow almost as closely on his peregrinations as the shadow does the body. These disorders arising from the uncanonical dismissal of priests from their dioceses, and the scandals given by clergymen thus abandoned, result as a rule from their exposed and helpless condition. They follow directly, and as our poor human nature is constituted, almost necessarily from it. Had those clergymen who have given scandal in village, town or city, during their wanderings, been cared for and protected; had the admonitions and instructions of the Council of Trent, or even Decree 122 in the Acts of the II. Plenary Council of Baltimore been observed in their regard, these disorders and scandals would never, or rarely have occurred. But, driven from their dioceses uncanonically, and abandoned by their bishops, is it any wonder that, discouraged, desolate and despairing, such as these should have recourse to the lethean bowl, to drown momentarily, at least, the thoughts of their miseries and sorrows! The consequences generally are, much scandal and injury to religion.

It seems to me, that the scandals and disorders that follow in the wake of a priest uncanonically dismissed from his diocese, are more imputable to his bishop thus dismissing him than to the priest himself.

My assertion holds good, and is irrefragable, if this act of the bishop dismissing his subject uncanonically from his diocese—which act, as a rule, is the immediate cause of the scandal and dishonor he brings on religion— has all the conditions required by theologians to make the evil consequences of his act imputable to him. Three conditions are required to make the evil consequences of an act imputable to the agent, viz.: 1. He must have foreseen *saltem in confuso*, the evil consequences of his act. 2. He must not have been necessitated to place the act whence evil flowed. 3. He must have been under an obligation not to put the act or cause of evil.

Now, to apply these principles laid down by all theologians to the act of a bishop uncanonically dismissing his subject from his diocese, I affirm that in ninety-nine cases out of every hundred, if not the even hundred, which is far more probable, more or less scandal and disorder result from this act, and follow it almost as certainly as effect follows cause. *The scandals of clergymen in most cases result directly from their being cast by their bishops on the open and dangerous sea of the world, unprovided with anchor or sail, oar or compass.* They are placed by those who ought to protect them, and whose duty it is to try to rescue them from danger, in a position that requires a miracle of grace, and the extraordinary protection of Heaven to save them.

Not only, therefore, is it condemned by charity and most unjustifiable in an ecclesiastical superior to abandon his subject, and thus place the immediate cause of scandals and disorders, but—*he is even responsible before God and man for such scandals and disorders.* They are imputable to him, if the act whence they flowed possesses the three conditions, which make the consequences of any act imputable to the agent.

1. Does the bishop foresee *saltem in confuso*, the scandals and disorders which follow the abandoning of a clergyman to the charity of the public, without a home or a refuge of any kind? He cannot but foresee them. The sad consequences of disedification, scandal, and disorder, which generally result from a clergyman's being placed in a position in which it is morally impossible for him to comply with the duties of his state, which is always the case when he is abandoned by his bishop, are so evident and well known, that they need not be detailed. It does not require a very profound knowledge of human nature, or much experience of men and things in general, to foresee the evil results of this act. *Ex contingentibus*, all bishops and priests know what most probably will be the consequence of a priest being altogether forsaken by his superior. From the bishop's knowledge, then, of what, as a rule, does occur, can he conscientiously say, that he did not foresee the disorders and scandals that followed from his act of uncanonically dismissing his subject, not only *in confuso*, but with a *moral certainty?*

2. The second condition to make the evil consequences of an act imputable to the agent, is, that he was under no necessity to place the act, whence evil consequences followed.

Now what necessity under heaven can a bishop, or other constituted in authority, allege for uncanonically dismissing a priest from his diocese, and abandoning him to public charity, which is the immediate and almost certain cause of scandal and disorder? If he is under the necessity of punishing him, or of even suspending him, this does not imply that he should expose him to ruin, and drive him to desolation. His bishop could easily have found an asylum for him in some religious house or monastery, thus reconciling duty with conscience, the priest's spiritual and temporal safety, and the good of religion. Such restraint and retirement is, and is looked upon by the Church, as a more or less grievous punishment, according to its duration; so much of a punishment, in fact, that it cannot be inflicted—enclosure in a monastery at least, or place of penance—without having been preceded by a canonical investigation. Should even religious house or monastery fail the bishop, he could easily shelter him under his own roof, for there is no bishop in the United States so indigent, that he could not give a poor priest a share at his table, and a cot in some corner of his palace. Under no circumstances, therefore, can I see that a bishop can plead necessity for uncanonically dismissing any clergyman from his diocese, thus placing him in grave spiritual and temporal necessity, and putting the immediate occasion of disorders and scandals.

3. The third condition required by theologians to make the evil consequences of an act imputable, is that the agent be under an obligation not to put the cause of the act whence evil flows.

Now the act of dismissing uncanonically from his

diocese any clergyman, is *not* lawful, because it is *uncanonical.* It is therefore unjust, which brings me to the law of justice which forbids this evil.

II. Justice condemns the uncanonical dismissal of any clergyman from his diocese. A bishop is under a strict obligation of justice *not* to put this act whence, as a rule, scandals and disorders flow. A few words will make this clear.

The Title of ordination gives to all clergymen not contumacious, as I shall clearly prove further on, a strict and just right to an honest subsistence, or "congrua sustentatio." Now, a bishop who abandons his subject to the charity of the public, positively violates *ipso facto* this right given by the Church and acknowledged by all canonists. He sins, therefore, against justice, by uncanonically dismissing any priest from his diocese. He is under an obligation to provide and care for him by granting to him "congrua sustentatio," the right to which the Title of his ordination gives him, and this right he clearly violates when he casts him forth on the world, to work, beg or starve.

There is, moreover, a just law of the II. Plenary Council of Baltimore forbidding a bishop to dismiss a priest from his diocese before he has secured another bishop. The spirit and letter of the Council of Trent forbid it, as we have seen, and many Decisions of the Church, as we shall see.

I conclude, therefore, from the above reasoning, founded on the teaching of theologians, that not only is a bishop, or other possessed of authority, forbidden to abandon any priest not contumacious, but that, moreover, he is responsible before God and man for all the evils and scandals and disorders that may result from such abandonment. They are imputable to him. *Qui est causa causæ, est causa causati,* under the circumstances and conditions mentioned above. Terrible thought! calculated to fill the hearts of those in authority with a salutary fear, and to induce them in all their dealings with their clergy, to act according to Law and Order, which alone will relieve them of their dread responsibility and accountability to God for the consequences of their acts. " Canonum statuta custodiantur ab omnibus: et nemo in actionibus, vel judiciis ecclesiasticis, suo sensu, sed eorum auctoritate ducatur."

The charity a bishop should show towards a delinquent clergyman, is beautifully and strikingly exemplified in the conduct of Jesus Christ, the Great Model and Exemplar of all bishops, in his treatment of the erring Peter after his fall. Peter had sinned most grievously! He had sinned frequently—not less than three times did he openly and shamelessly deny his Divine Master!

Had Jesus Christ, the meek and merciful Saviour, the great and only Bishop of the Church, all others being but His Vicars or representatives—had He, Who in condemnation of the fault-finding of the Pharisees with His spirit of mercy and forgiveness towards sinners, previously uttered these memorable words of reproof, " Go, then, and learn what this meaneth, I will have mercy and not sacrifice, for I have come to call not the just but sinners to repentance"—had our beloved Redeemer, I repeat, the

Supreme Head of the Church, turned away from sinful Peter, though only in sorrow and indignation at his base treachery—had He treated him harshly, and driven him forth from His presence, Peter, like Judas, might have yielded to despair, and died miserably. His fall, like that of the latter, would have been recorded; his repentance —perhaps never. Peter, when he fell, was even a bishop destined to be Christ's vicegerent on earth. Yet, notwithstanding his repeated infidelity, Jesus had compassion and mercy on him. He seeks the opportunity of making him feel the ingratitude and unworthiness of his conduct, and as soon as that opportunity presents itself He profits by it, and with a look that speaks volumes to his heart, He pardons, comforts and strengthens His poor, weak, and erring Apostle. That mild, tender look of compassion, full of sweet reproach and sorrow, penetrates the generous soul of Peter, and in its very depths excites remorse and stirs it to heartfelt contrition. By it his great love for his Divine Master was rekindled. He went forth from his presence a changed man, " Et egressus foras, flevit amare." Peter was saved through the mildness and charity of Jesus Christ, and afterwards became the glory, the pillar, and the solid rock upon which He built His Church.

It is, in fact, when the heart of man is bowed down in sorrow and oppressed with grief; it is when it is wounded and bleeding from the shafts of sin; it is when one is overwhelmed with shame and confusion and humiliation at the contemplation of his errors and his folly, that the Christian wand of pity, compassion, charity and mercy, will excite in his soul fervent gratitude, and move it to generous resolves and sincere efforts at reformation. A kind word spoken then, a mild look even, a just rebuke gently but firmly given, words of fatherly admonition sink gratefully into the bruised and wounded soul, and in general are productive of penance and reform. This we see exemplified in our dear Redeemer's delinquent Apostle Peter, whose grief for having denied his Master, called forth by His look of mercy, was so overwhelming, poignant, intense and lasting, that tradition tells us, his cheeks became furrowed from his constant weeping.

There was one other of the Apostolic college who fell, but, alas, never to rise! It was Judas, the traitor, the son of perdition. But even him Jesus treated kindly and mercifully. This we gather from the Gospel itself. By His meek and gentle words and manner, Jesus endeavored to reclaim him from the frightful crime of treason he was meditating. The words, "Quod facis fac citius," addressed to him, the import of which the other Apostles did not understand at the time, were for Judas, a grace like the look He gave Peter. Again, the meek words so gently and so sorrowfully spoken, "Juda, osculo filium hominis tradis?" was a last condescension of mercy and love, to withdraw him from the frightful depths of the abyss of sin into which he had fallen. Even then gladly would the omnipotent hand of the world's Redeemer have reached down and drawn him forth. Even then He would have saved him. But all was of no avail. The terrible, blinding sin of avarice had taken complete possession of the soul of Judas. It hid from him the enormity of his crime, blinded him to his spiritual and eternal interests, and made him deaf to the warning he received from the lips of even his God and Saviour. This terrible example of the perdition of an Apostle shows us the danger of allowing any passion to get control of our hearts. Judas was lost through the vice of avarice, which led him to betray and sell the Son of Man for thirty pieces of silver. But it was not his divine Master that drove him to ruin. It was his own perverse and wicked heart. To every bishop and to all other ecclesiastical superiors, I can say, without the fear of giving offence: "Inspice et fac secundum exemplar." They cannot err in copying this Divine Model.

There was a venerable, saintly Archbishop in the West, John Martin Henni, who died but recently, whose ministry of many years was crowned with "honor and glory" and abundant success, who was loved by priests and people as perhaps no other bishop in the United States was ever loved, and most deservedly, for he was ever a *Father* to his flock. This holy, learned and venerable man was once reproached, I am told, with being "too merciful to priests." His reply was worthy of his illustrious namesake, St. John the Evangelist, or of a St. Charles Borromeo, or of a St. Francis of Sales, or of a St. Thomas of Villanova, for these holy Bishops were extremely merciful to their clergy. "It may be," it is said that he modestly replied, "that I am too merciful to priests, but when I appear in the presence of Jesus Christ, and He has only this to reproach me with, I will answer him, 'Dear Master, I tried only to imitate at a distance the example You gave me. You ever pardoned and received to Your friendship the penitent Prodigal. Could I have acted otherwise than do what You Yourself taught me to do by word and example?'" The fruits of his merciful government are apparent. The clergy he left behind him compare favorably for piety and learning with any diocese in the land, and there is scarcely six miles of the archdiocese he founded where there is not a cross-crowned church, or chapel, convent or school to attest the glory and success of his administration.

From the principles of Charity and Justice which I have enunciated, confirmed by the example of Jesus Christ Himself, and illustrated in the lives of those Bishops around whose brows the Church has placed the aureola of sanctity, I think I am not mistaken, but can fearlessly assert without danger of contradiction, that in no case and for no fault how grave soever, is a bishop justified in abandoning an erring priest, if he is penitent, and has the least desire to comply with the duties of his calling, or to live as becomes his sacred character. Charity and Justice both demand of him that he put no obstacle to his return into the way of salvation, and he certainly places an almost insurmountable obstacle to this, when he dismisses him uncanonically from his diocese.

God's mercy and charity are not straitened towards sinners, neither should be the mercy and charity of a bishop. So long as a clergyman is not lost to all sense of religion, as long as he shows any disposition or desire to reform, —in a word, as long as he is not contumacious, his bishop, both in charity and justice, is obliged by his very office

as bishop to give him all the assistance in his power to
enable him to redeem his error, or at least he should give
him the opportunity of saving his soul. His office of
bishop enjoins on him the obligation of doing all that in
him lies to bring back the wanderer into the path of rectitude. If he cannot employ him in the ministry, he must
in conscience, in charity and in justice give him a decent
subsistence in some college, seminary, religious home,
monastery or ecclesiastical asylum. He cannot, without
sinning grievously, consign him to the streets to beg or
starve.

Priests, after all, are men and not angels. The Sacrament of Order does not confirm them in grace, or change
their human nature, or give them, instead, one more perfect. It only strengthens them, and gives them the assurance that they will receive all the graces they need
to fulfil well and faithfully the duties of their sublime
calling, if they place no obstacle in the way. Alas! we
know well from our own weakness, from the temptations
that assail us, and the prayer and vigilance that is ever required to combat them successfully, and from the teaching
of the Church, how frail we are by nature, and how liable
we are to err! What enemies has not a priest, above all
others, to contend against! If Solomon, endowed by the
Almighty with a special gift of wisdom and understanding, fell; if David, a man "according to God's own
heart," fell; if Peter, taught in the very college of the
Apostles, and by Jesus Christ Himself, fell; and 'another
Apostle fell, and never after rose, need we, after all, be
surprised, if now and again, a poor, frail, weak vessel of

clay, is surprised into some fault, or led into it by his own evil inclinations, want of prayer and vigilance, or the assaults of hell? He ought to be allowed the opportunity of redeeming his error. At least he ought to be given an Asylum, or a Refuge of some kind, and not be made a helpless outcast on the world "in contemptum ecclesiæ." True charity imperatively and peremptorily imposes this obligation on his bishop. Moreover, it is not just that a priest be degraded for every fault, and it is degradation to all intents and purposes, aye, degradation of the deepest dye, to dismiss ignominiously from his diocese a delinquent not contumacious, and abandon him to public charity, to want and to destitution, to temporal, spiritual and eternal ruin.

Forgiveness of sin and reconciliation of the sinner, though he should even be a priest, is a fundamental tenet of Christianity. A priest alone, of all men, should not be excluded from the pale of salvation, and from the universal boon of pardon, which is almost done when he is abandoned by his bishop, because of the helpless, pitiable condition of soul and body in which such abandonment places him. On the contrary, a bishop, like his Divine Model, the Good Shepherd, should seek out and try to rescue the lost sheep, and not to drive him forth from his pastures and his companions, to fall an easy prey to wolves. The Pallium that surrounds the neck of an archbishop has this latter signification. He wears it only amid the sacred pomp and glitter of his most solemn and highest functions. Even then, the Church would remind him of the duty and privilege of his high office, the Pallium representing, as it does, the strayed sheep carried back to the fold on the shoulders of the Good Shepherd. The latter leaves "the ninety-nine in the desert, and seeks the one that is lost, and having found it, lays it upon his shoulders rejoicing, and coming home, calls together his friends and neighbors, saying to them : ' Rejoice with me, because I have found my sheep that was lost.' " (Luke xv., 4, 5, 6.)

In our present fallen state, there is no true justice without mercy. Of this we need no better proof than the teaching and example of the Great High-priest of the New Dispensation, and the profound and adorable mystery of Calvary that closed His suffering and penitential life. Mercy and forgiveness were essentially the characteristics of the Good Shepherd; mercy and forgiveness shine forth most conspicuously in the conduct of the Church in all ages towards her children ; and the heart of every priest, from the lowly curate to the Supreme Pontiff, should be full to overflowing with charity for the fallen, and forgiveness for the penitent and the prodigal.

In view, therefore, of this spirit of charity, mercy and forgiveness, preached and practised by our Beloved Redeemer during His life-time, from His Crib in Bethlehem to His Cross on Calvary, I cannot be wrong in asserting what I hope to prove further on, beyond the chance of cavil, that under no circumstances is a bishop justified in abandoning any priest not contumacious, or in driving him to despair and ruin by harsh treatment and uncanonical action. If a clergyman's crime is so enormous, and is so adjudged by the ecclesiastical court of his diocese, that no penance can sufficiently atone for it, so as to make him useful or acceptable in the ministry, let the bishop place him in some monastery, or religious house, where he can efface it by tears and penance, and secure for himself at least the possession of that heaven, towards which he rendered himself unworthy to guide others.

CHAPTER VIII.

TO DISMISS UNCANONICALLY A PRIEST FROM HIS DIOCESE, IS TO REDUCE HIM, AS A RULE, TO BEGGARY, OR OBLIGE HIM TO FOLLOW SECULAR PURSUITS TO GAIN A LIVELIHOOD, BOTH OF WHICH ARE POSITIVELY FORBIDDEN BY THE CHURCH.

The proposition enunciated in the heading of this chapter, contains two distinct points: first, that to dismiss a clergyman from his diocese, is, as a general rule, to reduce him to the condition of a mendicant, or necessitate him to engage in secular employments to gain a livelihood; and secondly, that for a priest, both of these means of gaining a living are positively forbidden by the Church.

That a priest dismissed from his diocese is obliged as a rule to beg, or to seek his living by engaging in secular pursuits, is so evident that it needs no proof. The greatest number by far of the secular priests of the United States are poor. They do not, indeed, take the vow of poverty, but their slender incomes oblige them to practise it to a considerable extent. Such, at least, has been my experience. I have never been able to put a dollar in any bank except, perhaps, where "the moth and the rust consumeth not, and where thieves do not dig through and steal." Priests in this country are obliged to live sparingly and frugally in their parishes to make both ends meet. The most part of them, I believe, practise from necessity, if not through a higher motive, the injunction of St. Paul: "Habentes alimenta et quibus tegamur his contenti sumus."

In most dioceses, the clergy are salaried, and receive from four or five hundred to eight hundred, or a thousand dollars a year. This amount may be variously increased by stipends and perquisites, to twelve, fifteen hundred, or two thousand dollars a year. But even when such is the case, as in large cities, there are innumerable calls on their charity, and these, with their own necessary wants, consume all that they receive, so that few priests have a penny at the end of the year to put aside as a provision in case of sickness, or other unforeseen accident.

If, therefore, a priest in the United States should be so unfortunate as to make a blunder, for which a bishop dismisses him from his diocese, he has no alternative left but to face the world and beg for his subsistence, or engage in some secular pursuit to gain it, both of which are positively forbidden by the Catholic Church.

In the first place, the Church does not wish her ministers in Sacred Orders to beg for the means of subsistence. It is disgraceful. It dishonors the Church and the Priesthood. It is indeed no disgrace to be poor. Poverty has been sanctified and ennobled by the example of the Incarnate Wisdom of God, Who willed to be born poor, to live poor, and to die poor. Millions in the ages that have passed since then, of every rank and station in life, from the humble servant girl to the heiress, from the peasant to the monarch, and from the simple clerk to the tiaraed

Pontiff, have voluntarily embraced poverty, taken her for their cherished spouse, and purchased at the cost of all they possessed on earth, this jewel of inestimable worth, of which the world will never know the value.

When, therefore, I speak of the disgrace attached to mendicity in a clergyman, I of course do not allude to that which is sanctified and dignified by a religious Profession. The humble Franciscan Friar in his coarse habit and sandaled feet, begging from door to door, is a far different spectacle from that of a secular priest reduced to a state of absolute poverty and want in consequence of being dismissed from his diocese, and who is forced through necessity to beg the means of subsistence. The one is edifying and calculated to excite admiration; the other is degrading, and of its very nature exposes the Priesthood to contempt, dishonor and infamy. For this reason is it most explicitly and peremptorily forbidden by the Church.

To prove this, I need only quote the following words of the Sacred Congregation of the Propaganda, "Cum indecorum omnino sit, atque a clericorum qui Sacris Ordinibus constituuntur, dignitate prorsus alienum, ut ipsi .... *mendicatis subsidiis* .... ea quæ ad victum necessaria sunt, sibi comparare cogantur." Instr. de Tit. Ord. This sentiment of the most eminent Cardinals is only a repetition of that proclaimed by the venerable Council of Trent long before, in Sess. XXI. c. ii., *de Refor.*—" Cum non deceat eos, qui Divino ministerio adscripti sunt, cum ordinis dedecore *mendicare.*"

In the second place, a priest is forbidden to engage in

secular business or pursuits to gain a subsistence. This is also clear from the Council of Trent and the "Instructio" above indicated. "Cum non deceat eos, qui Divino ministerio adscripti sunt, cum ordinis dedecore mendicare, aut *sordidum aliquem questum exercere ;"* and, " Cum indecorum omnino sit, atque a clericorum qui Sacris Ordinibus constituuntur, dignitate prorsus alienum, ut ipsi aut mendicatis subsidiis, aut *ex sordido questu*, ea quæ ad victum necessaria sunt, sibi comparare cogantur."

I will now produce other authorities to prove that the Church forbids her clergy, even under censure, to engage in secular pursuits, viz.: The Constitutions of the Apostles, Canons of Councils, Bulls, Decretals, and Encyclicals of Popes, and that of Abbot Siculus, a canonist, who, because of his great knowledge of Canon Law, received the title "Lucerna Juris."

The 7th Canon of the Apostles decrees deposition against any bishop, priest or deacon, who takes upon himself secular cares. It is couched in the following words: "Episcopus, aut presbyter, aut diaconus, nequaquam sæculares curas assumat, sin aliter dejiciatur."

The same penalty for the same fault is decreed in Canon 17 of the Council of Nice.

A Council of Carthage held A. D. 397, has the following : " Episcopi, presbyteri, et diaconi, vel clerici non sint conductores, neque procuratores, neque ullo turpi, vel inhonesto negotio victum quærant; quia respicere debent scriptum esse : Nemo militans Deo implicat se negotiis sæcularibus."

The Council of Chalcedon, Canon 3, speaks to the same purpose.

Likewise, the Council of Tarragone, held A. D. 516, in Canon 2.

These Canons can be found in the *Jus Antiquum* of Gratian.

The Council of Lateran, under Innocent III., A. D. 1215, speaks as follows: "Clerici, officia, vel commercia sæcularia non exerceant, maxime inhonesta."

Against clergymen who engaged in traffic foreign to their calling, the *Jus Antiquum* contained in Gratian decreed " depositio ab officio."

The Decretals of Gregory IX. and of Boniface VIII., authorized the use of canonical censures,—suspension, interdict, excommunication, anathema, against clergymen pursuing secular employments.

The *Jus Novum*, according to the Bulls of Pius IV., St. Pius V. and Benedict XIV., prescribes, moreover, confiscation of all profits made out of secular employments.

Alexander III., in a Decretal to the bishop of London, renews the prohibition of the above Pontiffs under anathema.

The Bull of Pius IV., 9 Nov., 1560, has reference not only to commercial gains, but, "aut alias contra sacros canones quomodolibet acquisita." This Bull is confirmed by that of St. Pius V., 30 Aug., 1567, *Romani Pontificis providentia circumspecta.*

Urban VIII., 22 Feb., 1633, and Clement IX., 17 June, 1669, forbade, *sub pœna excommunicationis*, all clergymen, whether missionary or otherwise, regular or secular, from engaging in any secular business, trade or traffic.

Under date of 4 Dec., 1872, EE. PP. Inquisitores Generales, decided that the censures and penalties decreed by the Constitution *Ex debito* of Urban VIII., 22 Feb., 1633, and by that of Clement IX., *Solicitudo*, 17 June, 1669, viz.: " excommunicatio latæ sententiæ," and for Regulars, " privatio officiorum, dignitatum et inhabilitas ad illa," and for both Regulars and Seculars, " necnon amissio mercium et lucrorum omnium," are as yet in full vigor, and the Sacred Congregation of the Propaganda has notified the missionaries of Asia and *America* of the same.

Benedict XIV., in his Constitution *Apostolicæ servitutis*, 25 Feb., 1741, extends and applies to clergymen who engage in secular business in the name of another, the penalties fulminated by former canons and constitutions, with confiscation of the profits of such business.

We read in the Panormitan, one of the most accredited canonists: " Puto ego negotiatorem clericum committere peccatum mortale, non ex eo solum, quod constitutiones canonicæ super negotionibus stant præceptivæ: sed quia stat prohibitum lege Divina, et quidquid est contra præceptum legis Divinæ, mortale peccatum est." The author of the Panormitan was Nicholas de Tudeschis, known better as the Abbas Siculus or Abbas Junior, and by canonists called Lucerna Juris.

Let those who might bring the silly objection that an erring priest does not fall under the Decrees and Constitutions above quoted, and that he at least can throw aside his cassock, and engage in secular pursuits, note the above words of this able and learned canonist. The law forbidding ecclesiastics to engage in secular pursuits is both ecclesiastical and Divine, binding all who have not been excepted or legitimately dispensed therefrom. Now as these Constitutions make no exception whatever but include all priests, "whether missionary or otherwise, secular or regular" (Urban VIII. and Clement IX.), and "all ecclesiastical persons, secular or regular, of any Order, Congregation, Society or Institute, notwithstanding any and all indults, privileges and exemptions whatever" (Clement XIII.), it is evident that delinquent clergymen are likewise included, and though having erred, this certainly is not a reason why they should be forced to violate these Constitutions, and thus incur additional guilt, and expose themselves to fall under the penalties of excommunication, etc., decreed by the Church against all clergymen who engage in commercial or business pursuits foreign to the clerical state.

Finally, Clement XIII., by an Encyclical, 17 Sept., 1759, approves, renews and confirms all canonical laws, and all the Constitutions of his predecessors, the Roman Pontiffs, against clergymen who engage in trade, or follow secular avocations, ... and decrees anew against them, all the penalties and censures contained in these Constitutions....
" We declare that these penalties concern all ecclesiastical persons, secular or regular, of any Order, Congregation, Society or Institute, notwithstanding any and all indults, privileges, and exemptions whatever.... We declare that

the business of Banking is also prohibited by the present, etc."

The expression used by Clement XIII., in the above quoted Encyclical, is substantially the same as that used by Pius IV., "aut alias contra sacros canones quomodolibet acquisita," *i. e.*, any trade, employment, craft, traffic, profession, or other secular pursuit; so that priests are forbidden to be civil judges, lawyers, bankers, soldiers, physicians, business managers, book-keepers, commercial travellers, etc. " Domestic employments" and "servile offices," are expressions that occur in the Encyclical of Clement XIII., though they are not forbidden under the same penalties. Yet he warns bishops to forbid clergymen under censure even, if necessary, from engaging in such occupations.

It may be objected, that the Constitution *Apostolicæ Sedis* of Pius IX., of hallowed memory, revoked all the above censures. I answer: 1. Even had it done so, which it did not, they nevertheless show the spirit of the Church from the very days of the Apostles, when it was written, " Nemo militans Deo, implicat se negotiis secularibus," and throughout all succeeding time. 2. The above Constitution of Pius IX., of cherished and happy memory, limited censures, *latæ sententiæ*, only. Those of *ferendæ sententiæ*, which comprise the most of those forbidding clergymen to engage in business, trade, etc., are still in full force. As an evidence of this we have the Title itself of the above-mentioned Constitution. " Constitutio qua ecclesiasticæ censuræ *latæ sententiæ* limitantur." It is also clear from the following sentence found therein:

"Decernimus, ut quibuscunque censuris, sive excommunicationis, sive suspensionis, sive interdicti, quæ per modum *latæ sententiæ*, ipsoque facto incurrendæ, hactenus impositæ, nonnisi illæ, quas in hac Constitutione inserimus eoque modo quo inserimus robur exinde habeant." 3. The Decision of 4 Dec., 1872, of the EE. PP. Inquisitores Generales, assures us that the censures of the Bull *Ex debito* of Urban VIII., 1633, and of Clement IX., *Solicitudo*, 1669, are still in full vigor.

From the perusal of the above authorities, forbidding clergymen most explicitly and under severe censures from engaging in secular pursuits, we are forced to conclude that no priest is allowed to exchange his state of life for worldly occupations. Those who advance, or advocate that a priest in this country, dismissed from his diocese and abandoned by his bishop, can lay aside his cassock, and seek the means of subsistence in secular avocations, can see from the authorities I have quoted, how unequivocally such doctrine is condemned. I would scarcely blame a priest so situated, to have recourse temporarily to some secular means of gaining his bread, provided he recited his office; but in the meantime, it would be his sacred and conscientious duty to appeal to Rome, which would not permit so grave a deordination and degradation of the priestly character and dignity. In any other case but dire and absolute necessity, a priest who engages in secular employments, not only violates the spirit and letter of the Church's teaching, innumerable Decrees of Roman Pontiffs, and canons of discipline, but also exposes himself at least to incur fearful and terrible censures, even that of excommunication and anathema.

From the fact which I have established by incontrovertible authorities, that a priest is forbidden to beg, or engage in secular employments, it follows as a necessary consequence, that it is unlawful for a bishop to dismiss uncanonically any priest from his diocese, because, as a rule, it immediately exposes him to the necessity of becoming a mendicant, or of having recourse to secular employments to gain the means of subsistence.

Not only does the Second Plenary Council of Baltimore forbid a bishop to dismiss any priest from his diocese before he has secured another superior; not only is it forbidden by the Council of Trent, which admonishes bishops to be true pastors over their priests, to labor by admonitions and exhortations to deter them from evil, and should they err to punish them, "ut emendentur," and not in a way that of itself is calculated to sink them in deeper misery, and drive them to desperation and ruin; not only is it forbidden by the law of charity, which in the heart of every bishop should first hold towards his clergy, whom, as the Holy and Œcumenical Council of Trent expresses it, he should love, "tanquam filios et fratres;" not only is it forbidden by the law of justice which imposes on a bishop an obligation of protection over every priest of his diocese not contumacious, and who is therefore bound in justice to give to every such clergyman the "congrua sustentatio" of which the Title of Ordination gives him the assurance, and to which it gives him the right; not only is it forbidden by the example of Jesus Christ, the Great Pastor of souls and the Exemplar of bishops, illustrated in His conduct towards His erring Apostle Peter ; not only is it opposed to the spirit of mercy, clemency and forgiveness, inherent in the Church, and which should be possessed in an eminent degree by her bishops,—but it is diametrically opposed to the spirit and teaching of the Catholic Church, as I have abundantly proved in this chapter.

I will now show, that whilst the Church forbids her clergy to beg, or engage in secular pursuits, she has enacted wise laws to preclude the necessity or the possibility of the one or the other.

The Catholic Church has legislated that each and every one of her ministers in Sacred Orders, so long as he submits to her discipline, receive a becoming support during his lifetime. This I will prove in the following chapter.

CHAPTER IX.

THE CHURCH HAS LEGISLATED THAT ALL HER MINISTERS IN SACRED ORDERS RECEIVE A BECOMING SUPPORT DURING THEIR LIFETIME.

The Church of God never does any thing by halves. She employs adequate means to carry out the ends of her legislation. If, on the one hand, as we have seen in the preceding chapter, she considers it disgraceful, and repugnant to the dignity of the clerical state for any member of it either to beg or have recourse to secular employments to gain a subsistence; on the other hand, she has legislated effectively to prevent his ever being reduced to want, by which he might be forced to submit to this, for him, humiliating necessity. The Church does not confine herself to the simple prohibition to demean the clerical dignity by mendicancy, or by engaging in secular pursuits. She goes further. To preclude the possibility of any clergyman being obliged, through dire necessity, to act contrary to the spirit and letter of her teaching in this matter, she has enacted wise laws, which, if observed, would secure to every clergyman during his lifetime a support becoming the dignity of his order. My object in this chapter is to prove this, and to show at the same time how the Church accomplishes it.

In fact, the providing of an honest subsistence for her clergy during their lifetime is but a logical consequence of her teaching, as laid down in the previous chapter, from the Council of Trent, the "Instructio" *de tit. ord.* of the Sacred Congregation of the Propaganda, as well as from Bulls, Decretals and Encyclicals of Roman Pontiffs. The Church, as I remarked, does nothing by halves. Her legislation is effective. She makes use of the proper means to attain the end thereof. When, therefore, in the Council of Trent, and in the above indicated "Instructio," we read the declaration that it is indecorous and entirely unbecoming in a clergyman to beg for his subsistence, or to seek it by secular pursuits, which latter are so strongly and frequently and persistently condemned in clergymen by Popes and Councils, we naturally look or seek to ascertain the manner in which priests or others in Sacred Orders are to obtain a living. Nor are we disappointed in our expectation. The manner in which clergymen are to obtain their subsistence is, in fact, proclaimed immediately after. It is minutely and thoroughly explained. In a word, *the Title of Ordination gives them a right to a becoming support as long as they live, and are not contumacious.* This we find clearly and fully explained, both in the Council of Trent, and in the "Instructio" *de tit. ord.* sent to the bishops of the United States. This explanation follows in both, immediately after the assertion that it is unbecoming the clerical dignity either to beg or exercise some secular calling to gain the means of subsistence.

Let us first take up the Council of Trent. The question of securing the material support necessary to a clergyman, is treated in Sess. XXI., Cap. 2. *de Refor.*

"Cum non deceat eos, qui Divino ministerio adscripit sunt, cum ordinis dedecore mendicare, aut sordidum aliquem questum exercere;.... statuit sancta synodus, ne quis deinceps clericus secularis, quamvis alias sit idoneus moribus, scientia, et ætate, ad Sacros Ordines promoveatur, nisi prius legitime constet, eum beneficium ecclesiasticum, quod SIBI AD VICTUM HONESTE SUFFICIAT, pacifice possidere. Id vero beneficium resignare non possit, nisi facta mentione, quod ad illius beneficii titulum sit promotus; neque ea resignatio admittatur, NISI CONSTITO, QUOD ALIUNDE VIVERE COMMODE POSSIT; et aliter facta resignatio NULLA SIT. Patrimonium vero, vel pensionem obtinentes, ordinari posthac non possint, nisi illi, quos episcopus indicaverit assumendos pro necessitate, vel commoditate ecclesiarum suarum; eo quoque prius perspecto, patrimonium illud, vel pensionem vere ab eis obtineri, TALIAQUE ESSE, QUÆ EIS AD VITAM SUSTENTANDAM SATIS SINT: atque illa deinceps sine licentia episcopi alienari, aut extingui, vel remitti nullatenus possint, donec BENEFICIUM ECCLESIASTICUM SUFFICIENS SINT ADEPTI; VEL ALIUNDE HABEANT UNDE VIVERE possint: antiquorum canonum pœnas super his innovando."

From the above Decree of the Council of Trent, we perceive at once the means the Church has selected to secure for her Sacred Ministers the means of subsistence for life. The sole and exclusive object of this legislation is to secure a certain and assured means of support for the clergy, so that they may never be exposed to the danger of bringing infamy on their sacred character and calling, by being necessitated to become mendicants, or to resort to secular employments to make a living, lest, as St. Pius V. expresses it, " Per sæculum vagantes, vel mendicare, vel sordidum questum exercere, non sine ipsorum dedecore, ac ordinis vilipendio, et quamplurimorum christifidelium scandalo cogantur." Bulla *Romanus Pontifex*.

In the above decree of the holy and Œcumenical Council of Trent, we cannot but see that its whole tenor and aim is to secure for those raised to Sacred Orders à becoming and suitable subsistence during their lifetime. Without the assurance of such support, it positively forbids any secular cleric to be ordained, how learned soever, or holy, or otherwise well disposed he may be, "Statuit sancta synodus, ne quis deinceps clericus secularis, QUAMVIS ALIAS SIT IDONEUS MORIBUS, SCIENTIA ET ÆTATE, ad Sacros Ordines promoveatur, nisi prius legitime constet, eum, beneficium ecclesiasticum, QUOD SIBI AD VICTUM HONESTE SUFFICIAT, pacifice possidere. Hence the Title of Ordination. If not possessed of such Title, giving him the assurance of, and the right to an honest subsistence during his life, he cannot lawfully be ordained by any bishop, how great soever the desire of the latter to ordain him, or how urgent soever his need of priests, or how distinguished soever for piety and learning the candidate himself may be. All this shows how supremely important in the eyes of the Church is the Title of Ordination.

If any thing is clearly and evidently and incontrovertibly proved from this decree of the Council of Trent, it is that every priest, deacon and subdeacon, is by the *Title* of his Ordination guaranteed *a lifelong and becoming support*. As long as he remains an obedient child of the Church, even though he should err, as I shall prove hereafter, no bishop on earth can lawfully dismiss him from his diocese and abandon him to poverty and want. His subsistence for life is secured, even before the august character of the Priesthood is imprinted on his soul. He must be ordained to a *Title*, which, as the word signifies, *entitles* him to a becoming and perpetual support, or gives him a *right* thereto, or, as the Sacred Congregation of the Propaganda expresses it: "De CONGRUA PERPET-UAQUE SUBSTENTATIONE provideatur." Instr. *de tit. ord.*

This right to an honest subsistence during his lifetime, which the Title of his Ordination gives a priest, is even stronger and more binding and lasting, than the right which one acquires to property by any title-deed on earth. For the possessor of the latter can, of his own free will, sell, or give away, or otherwise dispose of his property, whilst a clergyman is never allowed to resign his right to a becoming support, "Id vero beneficium resignare non possit..... neque ea resignatio admittatur, nisi constito, quod aliunde vivere commode possit, te aliter facta resignatio nulla sit," and again, "Alienari, aut extingui, vel remitti nullatenus possint—(scil. patrimonia, vel pensiones) donec beneficium ecclesiasticum sufficiens sint adepti; vel aliunde habeant unde vivere possint."

How solicitous the Church is, that the above decree of Trent should be observed, is evident from the fact that she forbids any bishop to ordain a clergyman without a Title, or what amounts identically and precisely to the same thing, without an assured means of support during his lifetime. Formerly, a bishop who ordained without a Title, incurred suspension from conferring orders, and from the exercise of his other episcopal functions, as can be seen from the Bull of Sixtus V., *Sanctum et salutare.* In the present discipline of the Church, a bishop would not only incur censure, but the obligation also of supporting at his own expense a priest whom he would ordain without a Title, until he secured a Title for him, or the means of subsistence. Coun. Lat. Inn. III. *c. cum sec. de Præb.*

In the Constitution *Apostolicæ Sedis* 12 Oct., 1869, of Pius IX., of blessed memory, the second of the suspensions "latæ sententiæ Summo Pontifici reservatæ," is the following, " Suspensionem per triennium a collatione ordinum, ipso jure incurrunt aliquem ordinantes absque titulo beneficii, vel patrimonii, cum pacto ut ordinatus non petat ab ipsis alimenta." Again, in the same Constitution we find the following: "Suspensionem per annum a collatione ordinum ipso jure incurrit, qui, excepto casu legitimi privilegii, ordinem sacrum contulerit, absque titulo beneficii vel patrimonii, clerico in aliqua congregatione viventi, in qua solemnis professio non emittitur, vel etiam religioso nondum professo." In this same Constitution all the censures decreed by the Council of Trent against those ordaining without a Title, are renewed.

That the Title of Ordination has solely and exclusively

for its object, the material well-being of the clergy, or is intended only to secure them a becoming support for life, and thus preclude the possibility of their ever being obliged to beg, or engage in secular employments, is also clearly seen from the Bull of St. Pius V., *Romanus Pontifex*, issued in 1568, a few years after the Council of Trent was brought to a close.

The Decree of the Council of Trent had reference to secular clerics only. St. Pius V. extended it to religious not yet professed. The Jesuits are made an exception, though even for them a special provision was made, lest leaving the order, or being expelled therefrom before their solemn profession, they might be obliged to beg, or engage in secular pursuits. The Jesuits are looked upon as professed, though having taken simple vows only, as can be seen from the Bull *Ascendente* of Gregory XIII., and that of Gregory XIV. *Ecclesiæ*. There was no difficulty about priests of religious orders who were professed, for their profession assured them an honest subsistence for life. But this was not the case with those who had not made such profession. They might leave the order, or be expelled therefrom. The holy Pontiff St. Pius V., in the Bull above indicated, requires that all religious not yet professed, who were to receive Sacred Orders, should possess a Title, like secular clerics, securing them the means of subsistence for life, upon which they could fall back, should they leave the Order, or be expelled therefrom. In other words, he decreed by this Bull, that the regulations of the Council of Trent should apply to religious not yet professed, as well as to secular clerics, lest having been ordained, and afterwards leaving the order, "they might wander about, and be compelled to beg or engage in secular employments, to their own dishonor, the disgrace of their sacred character, and to the scandal of the faithful,"—the very reasons, I may add, which should ever deter a bishop from abandoning any of his priests.

Such were the motives of charity, love for the honor of the Church and of the Priesthood, that moved St. Pius V. to extend to religious not yet professed the Decrees of the Council of Trent requiring a Benefice, Pension, or Patrimony for ordination. It shows that the same reason actuated the Venerable Fathers who framed the Decree of Trent, and proves that the sole and only object of the Title of Ordination, was to preclude the possibility of any one in Sacred Orders ever being obliged to beg or to have recourse to worldly pursuits to obtain a livelihood. This is effected by his Title of Ordination, which gives him the assurance of a lifelong subsistence, and a right to the same, without which the Priesthood might be dishonored and the faithful scandalized, "Cum........illud inconveniens eveniat, ut si promoti, a claustro exeuntes, et per sæculum vagantes, vel mendicare, vel sordidum questum exercere, non sine ipsorum dedecore, et ordinis vilipendio, et quam plurimorum Christifidelium scandalo, cogantur." Ex Bulla *Rom. Pontifex* Pii V., A. D. 1568.

It is evident, therefore, from the Council of Trent, that the Church has rendered effective her legislation forbidding the clergy to beg, or to follow secular avocations for a living, by securing to each and every one of them a life-long subsistence, which is effected by the Title of Ordination.

Let us now consider this question with regard to the United States, where the Council of Trent has not been formally promulgated; or rather, where priests are not, as a rule, ordained to the Titles therein mentioned. Secular priests in this country are ordained " Ad Titulum Missionis." Does this Title give the assurance of an honest subsistence, and confer the right thereto, the same as the Titles mentioned by the Council of Trent? It most certainly does, if it has the same meaning in the mind of the Church, as those of which the Council of Trent speaks. That the Title of the Mission has the same meaning essentially as any canonical Title in the Church, I prove by no less an authority than the "Instructio S. C. de P. F. de Tit. Ordinationis," addressed to all the bishops of the United States.

In this document the Sacred Congregation, in its introductory observations, speaks of the Title of the Mission, of which it treats *ex officio*, in precisely the same strain as the Council of Trent does of other canonical titles. It reads thus: "Cum indecorum omnino sit, atque a clericorum qui Sacris Ordinibus constituuntur, dignitate prorsus alienum, ut ipsi, aut mendicatis subsidiis, aut ex sordido quæstu, ea quæ ad victum necessaria sunt, sibi comparare cogantur, nemo ignorat, ab antiquissimis inde temporibus cautum fuisse, ut quicumque in ecclesia Dei ad Sacros Ordines essent promovendi, eisdem de congrua perpetuaque substentatione provideretur."

These words of the eminent Cardinals of the S. Congregation of the Propaganda, confirm in strong and unmistakable language, all that I have already said of the Title of Ordination, based on the Decree of the Council of Trent. For they inform us that from the earliest times precaution was ever taken, that all in the Church of God who were to be promoted to Holy Orders, should be provided with a becoming and life-long support, " DE CONGRUA PERPETUAQUE SUBSTENTATIONE PROVIDERETUR."

Whoever reads carefully throughout the above indicated " Instructio" of the Sacred Congregation of the Propaganda, cannot but see, that the same spirit pervades it which dictated the Decree of Trent concerning the Title of Ordination, and that it views the Title of the Mission in the same light as all ecclesiastical writers who have ever treated the subject, viz.: the clearly expressed solicitude and wish of the Church, that no priest, or cleric in Sacred Orders, should ever be without the assured means of subsistence.

Thus, N. 6 says: "Qui vero hujusmodi titulo (scil. missionis) ordinati sunt, ii ex Apostolico ministerio in missione, cui fuerunt addicti, *ad victum necessarium consequuntur.*"

This clause implies all that the Council of Trent or the Church ever required from the Title of Ordination, whose primary and essential end is to secure the necessaries of life, "ea quæ ad victum necessaria sunt." He who has been ordained to the Title of a Benefice, if incapacitated from duty, or if he has been suspended; nay, more, if he has been even deposed, but is not contumacious, must receive " congrua sustentatio" from the revenues of the benefice indicated by his Title: *a pari*, and this is implied in the above N. 6 of the "Instructio" *de Tit. Ord.*, as well as all through the same. Priests in the United States, ordained to the Title of the Mission, though relieved of duty for any cause whatever but that of contumacy, must receive a becoming support from the diocese or mission "cui fuerunt addicti."

It will scarcely be objected, that any diocese is too poor to give the necessaries of life to one or another clergyman, who may be thrown on its charity. No!' Not on its charity—there is question here of simple *justice.* Such objection would scarcely be heeded, I think, by any Christian, much less by any bishop or priest.

"Tenentur (sacerdotes ad Tit. Mis. ordinati,) prius juramentum emittere, quo spondeant missioni cui destinati sunt, vel destinabuntur, se fore perpetuam operam daturos, quod quidem ab iis qui hoc titulo frui volunt, S. Sedes ut missionum *quarum sumptium illi aluntur*, servitio consuleret, exigere constanter consuevit." Instr. *de Tit. Ord.*, N. 8.

Every priest, therefore, ordained to the Title of the Mission, is bound to take an oath to serve his diocese perpetually, from which oath none but the Holy See can absolve him: The reason of this oath is founded in justice, for it is just that a priest should obligate himself to serve the diocese or mission from which he receives his support, "quarum sumptibus alitur."

It may be here objected, that when a priest is not actually serving the mission, or his diocese, he has no right to a support therefrom, as when he is broken down in health, or suspended by his bishop, but N. 9 of the "Instructio" on the Title, says: "Necesse non est, ut qui ad SS. Ordines hoc titulo (scil. missionis) evehendus est, actualiter in missione versetur, sed sufficit, ut paratus sit ad missiones obeundas, quando et quomodo superiores eum mittendum censuerint ac ire jubeant." This, it is true, is principally intended for him who is to receive Sacred Orders, as is evident from the expression "evehendus est," but it is equally true of those who have received orders, or even of clergymen who have been suspended, as long as they are willing to obey the commands of their superiors, or are not contumacious, as I shall abundantly prove hereafter by many Decisions of Rome.

No. 11 evidently places the Title of the Mission on an equality with other Titles in the Church. In fact, there is not any difference between it and any other Title, in its essential end of securing "congrua sustentatio." It says: "Quemadmodum alii tituli, ita etiam hic (scil. missionis) de quo agitur, juxta canonicas sanctiones amitti potest, atque ab ordinariis auferri, de consensu tamen S. Congregationis, cujus est, sic ordinatos præstiti juramenti vinculo exsolvere. Quod si amisso titulo generatim, aut etiam titulo missionis, alter ei non substituatur, sacerdos haud propterea remanet suspensus, sed ordinarii tenentur compellere ordinatos ad alterius tituli subrogationem, prout sacris canonibus consultum est. Id Sacra hæc Congregatio in generalibus comitiis diei 1 Sep., 1856 declaravit."

The above is not a new law in force since 1871, but a declaration of what had been enacted as far back as 1856, and has reference to all ordained to the Title of the Mission. From it we also gather, that no secular priest in the United States can lose his Title, or in other words his right to "congrua sustentatio," unless with the consent of Rome, "de consensu tamen S. Congregationis." Should he even lose his Title, his bishop is bound (tenetur) to oblige (compellere) him, to seek another Title. And here I cannot help remarking, that if a bishop is bound in obedience to this "Instructio" from Rome, to compel a priest having lost his Title to seek another, with how much more reason is he obliged to put no obstacle in the way of his securing a Title? When he dismisses him helplessly from his diocese, he not only robs him as far as he can of his Title, but puts an almost insurmountable obstacle to the obtaining of another.

N. 12 of same "Instructio" says: " Pariter sacerdotes regulares, qui vota solemnia nuncuparunt, atque ex Apostolica indulgentia in sæculo vivere permittuntur, vel qui ediderunt vota simplicia et e suis Congregationibus, seu Institutis egressi sunt, ne cum proprii gradus dedecore, emendicare cogantur, ad sibi de canonico titulo providendum obligentur; in locis vero missionum ipsi probare saltem tenentur, sibi suppetere media quibus propriæ substentationi, ut par est, consulant."

I have just come across another authority, relating to the point I am discussing, viz.: that the Title of Ordination is only intended in the mind of the Church to secure to the clergy the means of subsistence. In a " Folium circa patrimonia ordinationis," of July 8, 1876, published in the ANALECTA JURIS PONTIFICII, 15 series,

Rome, A. D. 1876, I find in Col. 961 the following passage: "Jam vero mens et causa finalis, ob quam Concilium Tridentinum decrevit, ne dentur ordines sacri non habentibus beneficium, vel pensionem aut patrimonium, ea fuit, ne clerici mendicent in plateis, et civili operi mancipati, publicam a quolibet deposcant alimoniam. Quare, quoties provideatur mendicitati hujusmodi, satisfactum est menti et causæ finali legis, et consequenter dispositioni."

Now the Title of the Mission is, in this country, the means intended to fulfil the end of the "Instructio" of the Propaganda, and of the Council of Trent in their legislation concerning the Title of Ordination, and it must, therefore, effectually take away "causam mendicitatis," which it does by giving the right to "congrua perpetuaque substentatio."

Again, in Col. 948, I find the following: "The patrimony required for ordination is an alimentary pension. The Church insists upon it, to the end that her ministers may not be deprived of the necessaries of life. For this reason, the Council of Trent requires the patrimony to be sufficient to live upon, 'quæ ad vitam sustentandam satis sint.' The alimentary pension is a thing privileged in all legislation, and is exempted from seizure; for the stomach's demands are imperative and brook no delay."

From Col. 963 I take the following extract: " In 1850, at the request of the Rt. Rev. Bishop of Bruges, the S. Congregatio Concilii approved the quasi patrimonial Title, which gives the right to a pension out of the diocesan fund, to clergymen who cease to be occupied in the ministry. This fund is kept up by free offerings. It was suggested that every one to be ordained should be obliged to deposit a certain amount in the said fund, but the Sacred Congregation did not sanction such forced contributions."

Though the nature of "congrua sustentatio" attached to the Title can be readily understood from what has been said, yet, that I may not be misunderstood, and to forestall any objection that may arise for want of a clear perception of the question under discussion, I will here explain the true meaning of an "honest subsistence," or "congrua sustentatio," of which his Title gives a priest the assurance, and to which it gives him the right.

By an Honest Subsistence, "congrua sustentatio," or "sustentatio honesta," is meant that material support which includes, at least, all the necessaries of. life. A priest not on duty, whom the bishop or the diocese would support in a monastery, or. other religious house, would receive "congrua sustentatio," though such penalty could not legally be inflicted upon him without a canonical investigation. In other words, "congrua sustentatio" is what theologians call "pensio mixta," which is defined, "illa pensio quæ datur clerico, tantum propter honestam sustentationem," and must not be confounded with what is termed "pensio ecclesiastica," which is " illa pensio quæ datur clericis propter ministerium spirituale." Of this latter, a clergyman may be justly and properly deprived, of the former —NEVER— unless he is contumacious.

Innumerable instances indeed could be adduced where clergymen have been deprived of their benefices, and all the revenues and fruits thereof,—a thousand and more cases of suspension, deposition and degradation of delinquent clergymen, *but not one single instance can be authenticated where the Church deprived a priest, how unworthy soever, as long as he was not contumacious, of his* "pensio mixta" or "congrua sustentatio," inalienably attached to the Title of his Ordination, or rather to the dignity and sanctity of the sacerdotal order, which is the foundation and efficient cause of all the strict legislation of the Church, regarding the Title of Ordination. As the ANALECTA JURIS PONTIFICII justly remarks: "*The Church never abandons the members of the clergy to mendicancy.*" This canonical axiom the Sacred Congregation of the Propaganda sustains most emphatically when it affirms: "Ut quicumque in ecclesia Dei ad Sacros Ordines essent promovendi, eisdem de congrua perpetuaque substentatione provideretur." Instr. *de Tit. Ord.*

According to the universal practice of the Church, founded on the legislation of the Council of Trent, every one receiving Sacred Orders must be ordained to a Title. This Title gives him the assurance of an honest subsistence during his lifetime, and a right to the same. This legislation regarding the Title is suggested, and based upon, and imperatively demanded by the honor and reverence due to the sacerdotal character and dignity. It is the Priesthood which requires an honest subsistence, so that it may not be degraded by mendicity or secular employments in the person of any one who bears it on his soul. The Title simply shows whence the "congrua sustentatio" must come, either from a Benefice or other canonical arrangement; or in this country, from the mission or diocese to which a priest is canonically attached.

But even when a priest has lost his Title, so that his Benefice or Mission is of no service whatever to him, to enable him to live as becomes a priest, his priestly character remains,—this cannot be taken away from him,—and as in the mind of the Church, this is the foundation and efficient motive of the Title itself, the inalienable right remains to him as long as he is not contumacious, of receiving an honest subsistence from the Church, through him who is his immediate lawful ecclesiastical superior. The reason why a contumacious priest has no right to even "congrua sustentatio" comes from the very nature of things. He voluntarily puts himself beyond the reach of the Church's clemency, or, as St. Liguori puts it: "Non debet ab ecclesia subveniri ei qui voluntarie ecclesiæ disciplinam vilipendit, cum libere possit a sua contumacia recedere." *Tom. 7. lib. 7. c. 3. de Susp.* St. Liguori, therefore, intimates that as soon as he submits to ecclesiastical discipline, "debet ab ecclesia subvenire."

Though the Title of the Mission and the other canonical Titles in the Church are widely different in many respects, yet they are primarily and essentially the same as to their end, viz.: "congrua perpetuaque substentatio." Now, as every canonical Title confers ever and always, even on the unworthy if not contumacious, an honest subsistence, *a pari* does the Title of the Mission confer the same; nay, in one sense, it confers it *a fortiori ;* for, if the right to an honest subsistence is possessed by priests though unworthy, but not contumacious, having Benefices, whose labors comparatively are light and easy, how much stronger does not the consideration of the sacrifices and hardships of a priest ordained to the Title of the Mission, and more exposed to danger, make this right, which moreover is essentially attached to his Title, as long as he is not contumacious? Who will be bold enough to assert that the former must be provided for, and the latter thrown helplessly on the world to beg, or starve; or that our holy and tender hearted mother, the Catholic Church, would approve such unjust discrimination, or crying injustice?

It is evident, therefore, from the whole tenor of the "Instructio" *de Tit. Ord.*, addressed to the bishops of the United States, that the Title of the Mission, to which secular priests in this country are ordained, in its primary and essential end, has the same meaning as that attached to Benefice, Patrimony, or Pension of which the Council of Trent speaks, and which, according to all canonists without an exception, signifies the assurance for life of an honest subsistence, and which gives the right thereto.

It is only sophistry to say, that a priest ordained "ad Titulum Beneficii," has a greater, or stronger right to "congrua sustentatio" than he who has been ordained "ad Titulum Missionis." The former has a right to a becoming support, even though unworthy, as long as he is not contumacious, *only because he possesses a legitimate Title, and is in Holy Orders.* What motive under the heavens can deprive a secular priest in the United States of "congrua sustentatio," *under the selfsame circumstances?* He is in Holy Orders, and he possesses likewise a legitimate Title, *of which the Holy See alone can deprive him.*

CHAPTER X.

REASONS OF THE TITLE OF ORDINATION.

In the two preceding chapters, I proved that it is repugnant to the priestly character and dignity, for a clergyman to be obliged to beg, or engage in secular pursuits to gain a livelihood, and that the Church, in consequence, has wisely provided against the possibility of such, to him, humiliating contingency, by legislating that every one of her sacred ministers be ordained to a Title, which gives him the assured means of subsistence during his lifetime, and an inalienable right to it, as long as he is submissive to her discipline, and does not, by contumacy, place himself beyond the reach of her merciful ministrations. All that I have already said, or will yet say of the possession of this right by even an unworthy priest not contumacious, will, I think, be vastly strengthened by exposing more in detail the motives actuating the heart of the Church in this wise and humane legislation.

The motives impelling the Church to require every one receiving Sacred Orders to be ordained to a Title, which assures him of an honest subsistence during his lifetime, and gives to him an inalienable right to the same, are chiefly three: 1. A motive of justice and gratitude on the part of the Church towards her ministers, who renounce every means of gaining a living, to devote themselves irrevocably to her service. 2. A motive of prudence, to cut off from the clergy all occasions of avarice. 3. Above and before all other motives, is that of reverence and veneration for the sublime dignity and august character of the Priesthood itself.

I. In requiring every cleric receiving Sacred Orders to be ordained to a Title, which secures to him a becoming support during his lifetime, the Church is moved by a motive not only of gratitude, but of justice likewise. He who dedicates himself to her service in the holy Priesthood, must necessarily make many and great sacrifices. True, he makes them for a noble, grand, sublime end,—the incomparable honor of becoming a priest; of being able to offer the Clean Oblation of the New Dispensation, the Unbloody Sacrifice of the Christian Altar; of preaching to men the Word of God, "that enlighteneth every man that cometh into this world;" of pouring over them the regenerating waters of life; of loosing their souls from the bonds of sin, and freeing them from the slavery of Satan; of nourishing and strengthening them with the Bread of Life: in one word, of being "another Jesus Christ," "going about doing good," man's best friend in life, and who surrounds his death-bed with those divine consolations which the Catholic priest alone has power to communicate,—consolations which, in that dread and trying hour, bring peace and confidence, and sometimes even a glimpse of heaven, and a foretaste of the joys of a happy eternity. Oh! it is indeed, a high, a noble, a sublime calling, that of the Catholic priest! Any sacrifice, how great soever, to attain it, must appear paltry and insignificant, to one whose mind and heart are imbued with Christian principles, and feelings, and sentiments, and who is capable of appreciating the grand, the sublime and the beautiful. Yet, humanly speaking, viewing the matter in the light of sober reason, and as the great majority of men view it, the young man who is called to the Priesthood must necessarily make many and grave sacrifices. He must, like Abraham of old, hearken to the voice of God, inspiring him to leave all things else for his sake. In obedience to that voice whispering to his heart, he goes forth from his country, and his kindred, and his father's house, to prepare himself by years of rigid discipline to become a soldier of the Cross. He must have a true vocation to endure the ten or more years of restraints and exact discipline of a well regulated ecclesiastical collegiate and seminary life: the early rising and early retiring; the exercises of piety, penance and mortification; the continued study and the constant and punctual fidelity to rule. - No worldling would undertake it for the same length of time, were he rewarded with the wealth of a state; and therefore, as he nears the goal of his holy ambition, he sees the faint-hearted—or rather those whom God does not call to the Priesthood—drop behind him one by one. But he is supported and strengthened and buoyed up by the grace of God and many interior consolations, for to him whom God calls to the Priesthood is given the "hidden manna" that makes duty a pleasure, and prayer and penance and mortification full of consolation.

Nevertheless, the whole collegiate and seminary course

of ecclesiastical discipline implies many sacrifices, much self-denial, constant application to prayer and study. In a word, it supposes assiduous and unremitting efforts to train the heart to virtue, and store the mind with knowledge to fit the ecclesiastical student to become a successful and efficient laborer in our dear Lord's vineyard. And yet, at the close of his seminary course, when called to Sacred Orders, his sacrifices are then only to begin. As he steps forward to be enrolled in the ranks of the Priesthood, he is called upon to make new and heroic ones, to take upon himself arduous, weighty obligations, which will cease only with his last breath.

The young acolyte, prostrate on the sacred pavement of God's holy temple, before that altar which he is soon to ascend as a "priest of the most high God, according to the order of Melchisedech," is the very picture of heroic sacrifice, and complete self-immolation. He not only renounces the world, its pomps and its vanities as the simple Christian, but he casts behind him forever all worldly ambition and pursuits, riches, honors, pleasures, family ties,—all, in a word, that makes life enjoyable and attractive to the most part of men, to devote himself irrevocably to the service of God's Church. In the very beginning of his manhood, when the world smiles brightly upon him, and invites him to select a sphere of life that may bring him wealth, or honor, or both, he forsakes everything: the hope of earthly emoluments and dignities; the consolation and comforts that cluster around the family hearth; yea, he sacrifices even the hope of making a living by any cunning of hand or work of brain, except the material or intellectual labor attached to the priestly office, that he may be enabled to dedicate his whole being, and for his whole lifetime, to the furthering of the interests of the Church, and of the salvation of immortal souls.

The Catholic Church, like her Divine Founder, God Himself, will not be outdone in generosity. Therefore, in consideration of the sacrifices her sacred ministers necessarily make to serve her, *renouncing even the means of acquiring by secular pursuits, that material support necessary for their very existence, which they do by receiving Sacred Orders*, the Church is moved by a motive of justice and gratitude, to positively forbid that they who have made such sacrifices for her sake, should ever be obliged to beg, or follow secular employments to make a living, "aut mendicatis subsidiis, aut ex sordido quæstu ea quæ ad victum necessaria sunt, sibi comparare cogantur," and furthermore, she has made her prohibition effective, by providing for their honest subsistence during life: "Nemo ignorat ab antiquissimis inde temporibus cautum fuisse, ut quicumque in ecclesia Dei ad Sacros Ordines essent promovendi, eisdem de congrua perpetuaque substentatione provideretur." Instr. *de Tit. Ord.*

II. The second motive we may assign for the Church's legislation, that those who have made the above sacrifices for her sake, and have been ordained her consecrated ministers, should be secured a becoming subsistence for life, is one of consummate prudence, viz.: To preclude the danger of the sin of avarice in the clergy.

Avarice is one of the most dangerous and incorrigible of all the passions to which the poor, weak heart of man is exposed. It is most insidious and crafty in its inception and growth, and often gets possession of its victim before he is aware of it: nay, the victim himself is the only one who is seemingly unconscious that he is the slave of the insatiable demon of avarice, and that every faculty of his soul is bound up in the chains of this remorseless tyrant. Like the ivy, slowly but surely creeping up the walls and buttresses, spires and pinnacles of the stately cathedral, insinuating itself into every nook, and corner, and crevice, and hiding alike from view the rough foundation, the beautifully chiselled cornice, and the medallioned window, so the vice of avarice imperceptibly, but slowly and surely sometimes grows up around the most beautiful temple of this lower creation, a masterpiece of divine omnipotence and love,—the soul of a priest,—taking root in his heart, entwining itself around every fibre thereof, and in the end, choking the love of God and every generous aspiration and holy inspiration.

To cut off this dangerous enemy from the clergy, the Church has made provision for them. By the Title of their Ordination, she gives them the assurance of a life-long support becoming the dignity of their order, and thus effectually removes the germ of avarice, solicitude for the future. For they know, where the laws of the Church are observed, that as long as they are her obedient children, though they should even be stranded on the shoal of human infirmity, they will not be left to the mercy of the winds and of the storm, but will most certainly find a refuge and a shelter within her port of pity and mercy. By the Title of Ordination, which gives the assurance of an honest subsistence for life, and the right to it, the chief incentive to avarice—the providing for the wants of the future, or of old age—is entirely taken away from the clergy, for the sustenance their Title secures them is not only "congrua" but "perpetua." Every motive and incentive, therefore, for hoarding up money or goods, is thus taken away from them, and consequently, every proximate occasion of the vice of avarice.

The wisdom of the Church's legislation concerning the Title, which, as we have just seen, removes the occasion of avarice, is seen from the fact, that where this legislation is ignored, or not carried out, there the vice of avarice is found to a greater or less degree making inroads among the clergy. It can scarcely be otherwise. For, after all, when a clergyman looks the matter squarely and fairly in the face; when he knows, from the practice of the country in which he lives, that his Title has no significance whatever, and that should he make a *faux pas*, in vain will he plead in its name for a mouthful of bread or a roof to shelter his head; when he knows well from the many sad experiences of others, that should he become disabled or incapacitated for active duty, by any of the many accidents to which life is subject, his only hope of subsistence is in the charity of the public, in the wards of some free hospital, or in the poor-house, no one will, or can blame him, for making some provision for the future,—at least, he has grave reasons to make sure for himself that "congrua sustentatio" which the wise laws of the Church, where they are observed, have already secured to him. To that end he begins by laying aside a little. It is not long before the transition is made from saving a little to hoarding and piling up much; and that poor man, whose motive in the beginning was good, or at least in the present unprotected state of the clergy in the United States, hardly censurable, sometimes ends in—*becoming a miser*, to the scandal of the flock and the robbing of the poor of Jesus Christ, and perhaps to his own perdition.

I may here add for the information of our venerable prelates, that in our day there is a feeling among many clergymen, that, in our present unsettled state of ecclesiastical discipline, it is only a dictate of ordinary prudence for them to amass sufficient capital whose interest will secure them "congrua sustentatio," or purchase a farm upon which they can live, should they ever come in conflict with their bishops, and be abandoned by them. No one but will confess, from what I have said, that there is some foundation for holding such a sentiment, neither will any one deny that it is one fraught with danger to themselves and injury to the Church. It is a sentiment that has arisen in consequence of the utter disregard of the *right* to "congrua sustentatio" given by the Title of Ordination, and shows that no law of the Church can be set aside and violated with impunity. Sooner or later fruits of evil and death will follow. My advice in this matter to every clergyman would be, to labor faithfully and disinterestedly in our dear Lord's vineyard, garnering a harvest of souls for eternity, with no view to any earthly reward, but moved solely by the love of Jesus Christ, the salvation of souls, and the immortal crown of glory which will be his recompense. *His bishop may, but God will not abandon him.* Let him have no undue solicitude for the wants of declining and enfeebled age, but leave all in the hands of that merciful and loving Providence, Who "feeds the birds of the air and clothes the lilies of the valley," and Who will not care less for him, His anointed Minister.

It must, however, be confessed, that the insecurity in which priests in the United States are placed, who, though having a *right* by their Title of Ordination to "congrua perpetuaque substentatio," are nevertheless morally certain they will not receive it, when perhaps they may need it most, is calculated to give occasion to this most terrible, and insidious, and irradicated of all the human passions,—avarice, or the inordinate love of money,—and encourage it in the hearts of the clergy. In their helpless, unprotected and unprovided condition, they cannot but feel and know, from the experience of others, that should sickness or any other unforeseen accident overtake them, their own pockets are their best and sometimes only friend. The neglect, therefore, to carry out to their full extent the laws of the Church connected with the Title of Ordination, or utterly disregarding the right it gives to "congrua perpetuaque substentatio," IS THE HAND THAT HAS PLANTED, AND IS

STILL PLANTING THE GERMS OF AVARICE IN THE HEART OF MANY A PRIEST IN THE UNITED STATES.

Instead of the wise provisions of the Church securing by his Title to every priest not contumacious, a becoming support from the revenues of the diocese, which, supplying only the necessaries of life even to several priests, would not expose it to bankruptcy, clerical Benevolent Associations have sprung up in some dioceses of the United States. But they are exclusive. They are only intended to relieve the necessities of priests in good standing who have lost their health, and of these latter, only those who have regularly contributed to the fund. From what I have seen and heard of these " Associations," there is not a particle of charity in them, and often little justice. They are not, nor can they be, superior to the legislation of the Church, which, for *the honor due the priestly character and dignity*, gives by right of his Title of Ordination even to the delinquent clergyman, not contumacious, the same right to a maintenance as to his brother broken down by bodily infirmities or enfeebled by old age, as I shall conclusively demonstrate further on.

III. But beyond and above that of gratitude, injustice, generosity, and prudence, the Church is animated by a more exalted and holier motive, when she legislates that every one in Sacred Orders must have a Title, and be thereby secured "congrua perpetuaque substentatio." That motive is the sublime, the august, the ineffable dignity of the Priesthood itself. This is the first and the last, the great, the primary, the final motive, the one to which all others must yield in importance, which is paramount to every other, in her legislation in the matter of the Title of Ordination. In fact, it is the only one which she gives herself for determining her action therein: "Cum indecorum omnino sit, atque a clericorum qui in Sacris Ordinibus constituunter *dignitate prorsus alienum,*" and "*Cum ordinis dedecore,*" as the Council of Trent expresses it.

It would be only presumption on my part to attempt, with my feeble pen, to depict the grandeur, and sublimity, and beauty, and glory, and power of the sacerdotal character. No created intelligence can adequately compass the greatness and the magnitude of the power bestowed by the Sacrament of Order upon the humblest, or even the most unworthy Christian, and no words can therefore describe it, so as to make it known and understood in all its magnificent proportions.

"No tongue
So vast a theme could equal, speech and thought
Both impotent alike."—*Dante.*

The power of a priest is nothing less than the power of changing the simple elements of bread and wine into the Body and Blood of Jesus Christ,—of offering up to the Eternal Father His only Begotten Son in Sacrifice, a Sacrifice as true, and as real, and as perfect,—for it is essentially the same Sacrifice,—as that once offered on Mt. Calvary. If the Royal Prophet, contemplating the wonderful and admirable goodness of God displayed in the creation, could justly cry out: "Quid est homo quod memor es ejus, aut filius hominis quoniam visitas eum? Minuisti eum paulo minus ab angelis, gloria et honore coronasti eum, et constituisti eum supra opera manuum Tuarum," with how much more reason cannot a priest, filled with astonishment and admiration at God's ineffable goodness and condescension towards him, utter with more profound gratitude the same sentiments of thanksgiving, seeing that as a *priest* he has been exalted *above* the angels!

Great indeed is the power and dignity of the priestly character! " Grande mysterium," says the Imitation of Christ, "et magna dignitas sacerdotum, quibus datum est quod angelis non est concessum! Soli namque sacerdotes rite in Ecclesia ordinati, potestatem habent celebrandi et Corpus Christi conficiendi." St. Augustine, contemplating the sacerdotal power and dignity, exclaims: "O veneranda sacerdotum dignitas, in quorum manibus Dei Filius, veluti in utero virginis incarnatur!" Hom. 2 *in Ps.* 37 ; and again, " O venerabilis sanctitudo manuum! O felix exercitium! Qui creavit me (si fas est dicere), dedit mihi creare Se: et Qui creavit me, sine me, Ipse creavit Se, mediante me!" Ib. St. Ephrem *de Sacerd.* calls the Priesthood a stupendous miracle of Divine power: "Miraculum est stupendum; magna, immensa, infinita sacerdotii dignitas!" Cassian, *in Catal. Glor.*, speaks thus : " O sacerdos Dei, si altitudinem cœli contemplaris, altior es: si dominorum sublimitatem, sublimior es: solo Deo et Creatore Tuo inferior es!" St. Lawrence Justinian, *in Serm. de Euch.*, says of the sublime and august power of the Priesthood: "O maxima potestas! Ad eorum (sacerdotum) pene libitum, Corpus Christi de panis transubstantiatur materia; descendit de cœlo in carne Verbum, et altaris reperitur in mensa! Hoc illis erogatur ex gratia, quod nusquam datum est Angelis. Hi assistunt Deo: illi contrectant manibus, tribuunt, et in se suscipiunt!"

In such and like magnificent strains and exalted eulogy, do the fathers of the Church, and saints and holy writers, speak of the sacerdotal dignity! But who understands it better than the Church herself? Therefore is it that in all ages, she has ever sedulously protected the august character of the Priesthood in all, how remotely soever they were connected with it.

In the Sacred Orders are numbered deaconship and sub-deaconship, and the law of Title consequently reaches those receiving these orders. Even the tonsured clerk is protected by the Church, because he is a clergyman and destined for the priestly office and dignity. With her dread and terrible *Anathema* does she strike him, who would dare offer malicious violence to such a one. The nearer he approaches the altar; the closer he comes in contact with the tremendous mystery of the Holy Eucharist; as he ascends, step by step, towards the priestly office and dignity, the more lovingly and securely does the Church gather about him the mantle of her protection. And when at length, arrived at the goal of his high and holy aspirations, his hands have been anointed with the holy oils of consecration, and he is empowered to mingle his voice with the angelic choirs around the Throne of God, chanting the endless refrain, "Sanctus, Sanctus, Sanctus Dominus Deus Sabaoth,"—nay more, can give more honor and glory to the Triune God by celebrating one mass in which is immolated "the Lamb slain from the foundation of the world," than all the heavenly host can throughout endless ages—then it is, that the Church guards and protects him with the most thoughtful solicitude, then is it that she throws around the sacred and august character with which she has invested him, her maternal and powerful protection.

It is, therefore, chiefly and primarily the knowledge of the high dignity of the Priesthood, and the reverence due to it, that influences the Church in her legislation, that every one receiving Sacred Orders should possess a Title or the means of subsistence. The Priesthood of Jesus Christ is reflected in every priest,—in fact, Jesus Christ is the only priest: all others are but His vicegerents, and act in His name and by His authority. It is to shield His Priesthood in the person of her ministers that she forbids them to beg, or engage in secular pursuits, a prohibition which she makes easy of compliance, by bestowing upon them a Title, or letter of credit, which secures them all that is necessary for their honest subsistence.

But back of the Title is the priestly honor and dignity which are its efficient cause and foundation. This is clearly seen from the fact, that even when there is no Title whatever, the Church insists upon a clergyman receiving a proper and becoming support, as I will prove in the following chapter by many decisions of Sacred Congregations, and as is also apparent from the Council of Lateran under Innocent III., *cap. cum secun. de Proeb.*, where it is decreed that a bishop ordaining without a Title, would incur the obligation of supporting the clergyman thus ordained at his own expense, thus clearly demonstrating that it is the sacerdotal character and dignity which is the efficient motive of the Title and the reason of "Congrua perpetuaque substentatio."

Having proved that it is repugnant to the spirit and letter of the teaching of the Catholic Church, for any one in Sacred Orders to be ever necessitated to beg or to engage in secular employments for a living, which latter, moreover, are forbidden to them under the most dreadful penalties; and having shown, that to remove the possibility of such a humiliation and degradation of the sacerdotal character, the Church wisely ordains them to a Title which secures to them the means of subsistence for life; and having, moreover, exposed the motives actuating the Church in this wise and beneficent and salutary legislation,—motives of justice and gratitude towards her ministers for their sacrifices in her behalf, besides the cutting off of all occasions and incentives to avarice, but above all, the motive of the sublime dignity and sacred character of the Priesthood itself,—I will now proceed to prove that the Church includes in her legislation for the becoming subsistence of the clergy, erring clergymen not contumacious, as well as those in good standing.

CHAPTER XI.

EVEN AN UNWORTHY CLERGYMAN, NOT CONTUMACIOUS, HAS A RIGHT TO A BECOMING SUPPORT.

A clergyman who may have had the misfortune to stray away from the strait path of ecclesiastical discipline, and who possesses a patrimony, or an annuity sufficient for his wants, could not with propriety burthen the diocese with his support. But the greatest number of secular priests in the United States are poor, and should sickness or any other unforeseen accident overtake them, they are, as a rule, entirely helpless to provide for themselves. I hold under these circumstances that as long as they are not contumacious, they are entitled to a becoming subsistence. This the honor and reverence due the priestly character demand. It is a shame and a disgrace, as the Church expresses it, even for them to beg, or engage in secular pursuits for a living. No bishop would throw his golden chalice, which has become unfitted for use, in a heap of discarded clothing and broken crockery. *A fortiori*, should he abstain from casting forth *a priest* unfit for use, into the midst of the unanointed, to mingle with them and be undistinguished from them. He may take from the chalice its sacred character, and make of it a common vessel that will suffer no indignity from being mingled with other rubbish, though its gilding and precious material will probably secure for it a better fate ; but he cannot rub out from the hands of the priest the oil of consecration, nor take from him his priestly character, "Juravit Dominus et non pœnitebit eum, tu es sacerdos in æternum secundum ordinem Melchisedech." Therefore, because of this sublime character, and for the honor of the Priesthood of Jesus Christ indelibly imprinted on his soul, a priest, though unworthy, if not contumacious, must receive a becoming subsistence. This I will now prove by authorities that cannot be gainsaid.

The priest who, through human frailty, or even malice, may have fallen, is nevertheless a priest. For all time, and so will it be for all eternity, he bears ineffaceably impressed on his soul, the sublime character of the Priesthood of Jesus Christ, the primary and the final motive of the law of the Church, which requires all in Sacred Orders to be provided with a becoming support during their lifetime. This character no sin can efface, no misconduct can obliterate. There is but one offence which can cause the Church to turn away momentarily from an erring clergyman, and even deprive him of "congrua sustentatio," and that is the sin of contumacy. But even then, it is not the Church which abandons him, it is not she who turns her face of mercy from him : it is he who abandons her, turns his back upon her, and openly rebels against her authority. For privation under these circumstances of "congrua sustentatio," he can blame only himself, not the Church. Like the Prodigal, he leaves the shelter of the paternal roof, and goes beyond the reach of the father's care and protection.

But like the Father of the Prodigal, the Church again receives him with open arms and heartfelt rejoicings, as soon as he returns humble and penitent to her protection, and submits himself to her laws and discipline.

If the Church had reference to priests of good standing only, when she proclaims the impropriety of clergymen being obliged to beg, or to follow some secular avocation to gain a livelihood, and meant that they alone had the right to an honest subsistence, and that in consequence, unworthy priests might be dismissed from their dioceses, abandoned by their bishops, thrown helplessly on public charity, and consigned to penury and infamy, then the efforts of the Church to protect the honor of the priestly character, and to shield it from insult and degradation, would be completely paralyzed, and her voice, forbidding the humiliation of the Priesthood by mendicancy, or by engaging in secular employments, would be only as the echoes of the mountain. For, contempt and infamy, humiliation and degradation, are brought on the Priesthood by any and every priest, who is forced to live in a manner unbecoming his sacred character, which is ever and always the case when he is dismissed from his diocese without the means of an honest subsistence.

That the Church includes all priests, the frail and erring, as well as those in good standing, in her legislation concerning the Title of Ordination, is clear from her own words. She does not say, Cum non deceat eos qui *digni* sunt, etc., or, Cum indecorum omnino sit atque a clericorum *dignorum* prorsus alienum, etc., but, "Cum non deceat *eos qui* Divino ministerio adscripti sunt," etc., *i. e., omnes clericos* divino ministerio adscriptos, and, "Cum indecorum omnino sit atque a *clericorum* qui Sacris Ordinibus constituuntur prorsus alienum," etc., *i. e., omnium* clericorum in Sacris Ordinibus constitutorum. "Ubi lex non distinguit, nec nos distinguere debemus."

Before I adduce the many, and grave, and unexceptionable authorities which prove that even an unworthy priest, not contumacious, has a right to an honest subsistence, if he has not the means to live as becomes the priestly character and dignity, I will first meet here on the very threshold of the question, the objection that may be, and probably will be brought against me, viz.: that the Plenary Council of Baltimore asserts the very contrary of what I advance, when it says: "Nullum jus habent (sacerdotes suspensi) ad sustentationem." These words are found in N. 77 in the following sentence: "Sacerdotes quibus per Ordinarii sententiam, sacerdotii exercitium interdictum fuerit, nullum jus habent ad sustentationem ab eo petendam, cum ipsi, se, sua culpa, missionibus operam navandi incapaces reddiderint."

I scarcely know how to speak of the above extract from the II. Plenary Council of Baltimore. It does not indeed invalidate my proposition, that an unworthy priest not contumacious, and not having the means to live as becomes his character, has a right to an honest subsistence, for this proposition is supported and proved by such an overwhelming number of authorities of the greatest weight, viz.: by the authority of Roman

Pontiffs, Decisions of Sacred Congregations, etc., that no mere Provincial or even Plenary Council can overthrow it.

My reluctance to speak of the above extract, comes from the sentiments of reverence and veneration I entertain for the venerable assembly whence it emanated. I would much rather not be obliged to take exception to any thing coming from such a source. I cannot comprehend how such a sentiment as that contained in these words, "Nullum jus habent ad sustentationem," so opposed as I will show it to be to the spirit and letter of the highest and most venerable authorities in the Church, could ever have been inserted in the *Acta et Decreta* of the Council, except by some strange and unaccountable oversight on the part of the venerable Fathers thereof.

I thought at first of interpreting these words of the Council, " Nullum jus habent ad sustentationem," according to the forty-ninth Rule Juris in Sexto, " In pœnis benignior est interpretatio facienda," by making them signify, that the Fathers of the Council meant simply to make a formal statute depriving a suspended priest of the "pensio ecclesiastica" only given for services in the ministry, to cut off from malicious priests all occasions of lawsuits, and that these words, therefore, did not exclude the "pensio mixta" which has reference only to the bare means of subsistence.

But such an interpretation I found untenable. For, it would be only folly to frame a statute to deprive a priest of what he is already deprived by the very fact of his suspension. Again, the words are, "*Nullum* jus habent ad sustentationem." Now "congrua sustentatio," is a "jus" given by the Title of Ordination, attached to the honor of the Priesthood, and of which suspension alone cannot deprive a priest not contumacious. But this right is evidently excluded by the "nullum" of the Council of Baltimore in the text quoted, which is absolute and unequivocal. Finally, the words "*ab eo petendam*," show clearly that the Statute or Decree has not reference to the "pensio ecclesiastica" alone, but includes likewise the "pensio mixta" or the bare means of subsistence, which is denied by the "Nullum jus" of the Council of Baltimore, thus proving that the "benignior interpretatio" of which I spoke could not be applied to this strange text.

Not being able then to make the wording of this sentence, "Nullum jus habent ad sustentationem ab eo petendam," agree with this "benignior interpretatio," and moreover, finding it utterly impossible to reconcile such interpretation with the palpable and well known fact of priests in the United States being so frequently thrown homeless and penniless on the charity of the public, I leave it to some one else to say how these words became incorporated in N. 77 of the II. Plenary Council of Baltimore, what they do mean, and to reconcile them with the Decisions of Rome, and other venerable authorities that I will adduce in this and the following chapters.

This premised, I will now prove, and I invite the attention of my readers, especially of the clergy, to the weight and solidity of the authorities I shall bring forward to prove, that even an unworthy clergyman, without the means of subsistence, and. not contumacious, *i. e.*, not wilfully disobedient to any lawful summons, or judicial order of the regularly constituted ecclesiastical court of his diocese, has a right to the means of subsistence.

The only authority I can find for the opinion that an unworthy clergyman has not the right to "congrua sustentatio" is that of J. B. Bouvier. In his theology, *Trac. de ord.*, cap v., art. 2., No. 9, ed. 1856, the following words are found: "Sicut autem episcopus sustentare non tenebatur clericum cum debita diligentia ordinatum, cujus titulus deprehendebatur fictitius, aut casu perierat, *ita nunc, alere non tenetur eum qui propria culpa munere ecclesiastico se constituit indignum*, nec eum qui aliunde sibi providere potest," etc. This is identically, though expressed in different words, the same proposition as that enunciated in N. 77, II. Plenary Council of Baltimore, scil. "Sacerdotes quibus per ordinarii sententiam, sacerdotii exercitium interdictum fuerit, *nullum jus habent ad sustentationem ab eo petendam, cum ipsi, se sua culpa missionibus operam navandi incapaces reddiderint.*" The refutation of the one therefore necessarily implies the refutation of the other.

I am even spared the trouble of collating the authorities which show the falsity of the teaching expressed in the above extract from Bouvier, whose opinion seems to have been followed by the Council of Baltimore, since the latter expresses precisely the same sentiment, as any one can see by comparing the sentence from the Council with that of Bouvier, both of which I have just given. Another has shown clearly, and most satisfactorily, how antagonistic this opinion of Bouvier and of the II. Plenary Council of Baltimore is to the teaching and practice of the Church. I refer the reader to the ANALECTA JURIS PONTIFICII, published at ROME, 9th series, 1867.

In this work is found a Treatise "On Ecclesiastical Tribunals," in which the author refutes conclusively the opinion expressed by Bouvier, and conveyed in the "nullum jus habent ad sustentationem," of the Council of Baltimore. He proves clearly and beyond the shadow of doubt, that even an unworthy priest, not contumacious, has the right to an honest subsistence if he has not the means to live as becomes a priest. This Treatise from which I quote in support of this proposition, has been sanctioned by the two following *Imprimatur:* 1. "*Imprimatur.* Fr. Hieronymus Gigli Ord. Præd. S. P. Apostolici Magister." 2. "*Imprimatur.* Petrus Castellacci Villanova, Arch. Pet. Vicesgerens." With these two distinguished *Imprimatur* no priest or bishop in the United States, I hope, will doubt its orthodoxy. I may remind my readers, moreover, that the work in which the Treatise is found was published in ROME, the centre of Truth and Unity.

Commenting on the very words of Bouvier quoted above, the author of the "Treatise on Ecclesiastical Tribunals," Col. 455, N. iii., speaks as follows:

"A senseless, horrible principle (une maxime insensée et horrible), is expressed by certain authors, especially by *Bouvier* in his Theology. They say that a clergyman who behaves badly, renders himself unworthy of all compassion, and has no right to receive the means of subsistence (pension alimentaire)."

I may here with propriety remark, that this alimentary pension of which the learned author speaks, is the same as the "pensio mixta," or "congrua sustentatio," corresponding to the "alere" in the text of Bouvier, and to "sustentationem" in that of the Council of Baltimore, the denial of which the author denominates "A SENSELESS AND HORRIBLE PRINCIPLE."

The author of the Treatise above indicated then continues: "The holy Canons assimilate the denial of the alimentary pension to the PAIN OF DEATH. A parish priest should not be deprived of his alimentary pension, *although he be deposed even for great crimes.* Without doubt, he has no right to receive a pension from his parish, *but his right to an alimentary pension remains intact.* THE CHURCH NEVER ABANDONS THE MEMBERS OF THE CLERGY TO MENDICANCY."

I would kindly call the attention of the learned author of *Notes* on the Second Plenary Council of Baltimore, to the above extract from the ANALECTA JURIS PONTIFICII. The former, page 236, says: "This right (of congrua sustentatio) may be forfeited by criminal conduct." The ANALECTA JURIS PONTIFICII affirms and proves by the highest and most venerable authorities, which I will presently reproduce, that, "a parish priest should not be deprived of his alimentary pension, although he be deposed even for great crimes." Smith says: "No bishop is obliged to support a priest whom he has been compelled to suspend on account of bad conduct." The

ANALECTA says: "Without doubt he has no right to receive a pension from his parish, but his right to an alimentary pension remains intact. The Church never abandons the members of the clergy to mendicancy." In another place of the same article it says: "The obligation to furnish the means of subsistence is stricter, when there is question of suspension *ex informata conscientia.*"

The ANALECTA JURIS PONTIFICII then gives the authorities which prove what it advocates, viz.: that even a delinquent clergyman, not contumacious, and not having the means of living, has a right to a becoming maintenance. From it I extract the following:

"In a case in which there was suspicion of the complicity of a parish priest in a homicide, which required his removal from his parish, the Sacred Congregation prescribed that means of support should be assigned to him: 'Episcopus procuret assignamentum pro congrua parochi, et habito, injungatur eidem exilium a loco commissi delicti.'" Die. 20 Dec. 1675.

"Confirming the sentence of deposition against a parish priest, the Sacred Congregation enjoined on the bishop to furnish him with the means of subsistence, otherwise it would assign him a pension from the parish. Of this the following Rescript sent to a bishop in 1714 is in evidence: 'The cause of Bernard C., the parish priest of Gambola, has been treated anew. He begged to be re-instated in his parish, and asked for some other favors. The most Eminent Cardinals have confirmed again the sentence of the episcopal court, as regards the article of deposition. But, *they are unanimously of the opinion that your lordship is absolutely obliged to furnish the means of subsistence to this priest in want*, so that he may be able to live in a manner becoming the priestly character, and that he may not be obliged to beg. If this is not done, the Sacred Congregation itself will assign to him a pension from the parish ; for, *if it was just to deprive him of his parish on account of his wrong-doing, it is also just that he have the means of subsistence.*' " Rome, July, 1714.

In the above we have an explicit and clear Decision of Rome proving what I assert, that even an unworthy priest, not contumacious, ought to receive the means of subsistence, if he is unable to support himself becomingly. The clergyman of whom there is question in the above Decision had indeed committed no slight fault, since he was deposed from his office of Pastor. The sentence of deposition pronounced by the episcopal court, from which he had appealed, the Sacred Congregation confirms. But it does not make of him a helpless outcast on the world. It informs his bishop that he is absolutely obliged to furnish the means of subsistence to the deposed clergyman, that he may be enabled "to live in a manner becoming the priestly character, and that he may not be obliged to beg." Note here that the reason assigned by the Sacred Congregation for obliging his bishop to furnish this priest in want with a becoming support is the sacerdotal dignity, "that he may be enabled to live in a manner becoming the priestly character," another proof of what I have more than once remarked, that it is the honor and reverence due the Priesthood which is the principal and efficient motive, as well as the foundation of the law of Title, or "congrua sustentatio."

I continue to quote from the ANALECTA JURIS PONTIFICII: "The Sacred Congregation, A. D. 1717, sent the following despatch to the Apostolic Nuncio at Madrid: 'The pension for the payment of which you have been charged by the Sacred Congregation, is due Don Joseph Cornezo here imprisoned, even though his offence deserved no compassion whatever.'"

The author whom I have been quoting then proves, from Acts of the Sacred Congregation of Rome, that a priest condemned to the *ergastulum*, or House of Correction for clergymen, has a right to his subsistence; that poor ecclesiastics have a right to receive the benefit of the law *gratis*, and a lawyer for their defence during their trial; that those even who are *contumacious* are deprived of their maintenance, *only as long as they persist in their contumacy*, as can be seen from the following Rescript: "The parish priest of N. having spontaneously chosen the city of Rome for his residence, instead of his prison, has a right to receive out of the revenues of his parish, his pension not only for the time to come until tried, but even for the two years past in which he was contumacious." Rome, 29 May, 1761.

The same author likewise proves by a Roman Decision, that a parish priest appealing to the Holy See against suspension *ab officio*, must receive the means of support.

The article whence I have taken the above extracts, concludes thus: "The ordinary contracts special obligations towards clergymen ordained without a Title. For if the parish priest, DESERVING TO BE DIVESTED OF HIS TITLE OF ORDINATION, HAS, NEVERTHELESS, A RIGHT TO HIS LIVING, with much more reason has the clergyman whom the bishop ordains without a Title. All canonists agree that a bishop contracts for himself and his successors in office, the obligation of providing for the maintenance of such a clergyman from the revenues of the bishopric. The obligation to furnish the means of subsistence is stricter when there is question of suspension *ex informata conscientia*. THE PRINCIPLE SET FORTH BY BOUVIER IS OPPOSED TO THE SPIRIT AND LETTER OF THE HOLY CANONS." That principle is precisely and identically the same as that put forth in the extract quoted above from N. 77 of the II. Plenary Council of Baltimore, and is therefore opposed to the spirit and letter of the Holy Canons, and—untenable. I need not remind the most of my readers of the great weight the Declarations and Decisions of Sacred Congregations possess as authorities. Though not unalterable, they have the force of law for the cases which they decide, and are a sure guide of action for all parallel cases. Speaking of them Konings, N. 173, says: " Quam vim habeant SS. Congregationum Declarationes et Decreta? Resp. 1. Inspecto fonte, ex quo derivantur, *eandem vim habent ac si a S. Pontifice immediate processissent*, dummodo tamen, sint authentica, *i. e.*, subscripta a respectivæ Congregationis Præfecto et Secretario, ac ejusdem sigilla munita. 2. Vim illam habent, etsi a S. Pontifice non explicite confirmantur. 3. Infallibilia tamen non sunt, nisi a S. Pontifice eoque ex cathedra loquente, confirmentur."

The Sacred Congregations of 1675, 1714, 1717, and of other years, which prescribed, decreed and commanded the means of subsistence to be given delinquent clergymen, not contumacious, and unable to support themselves, would not most assuredly have given the opposite of such decisions in 1866, or subsequently.

It is clear, therefore, from the authorities given above, that an erring priest not contumacious and not having the means of subsistence, cannot be thrown helplessly on public charity, but from his benefice, or the revenues of the diocese or bishopric, must receive a suitable living. Though I will bring other authorities to prove this, yet those which I have just adduced for this purpose are even more than sufficient. They are of the first rank and speak to the point.

I am aware that some will bring the objection that these Decisions do not hold in the United States,—that there is no Canon Law here. Allow me to say to such as these, that although Canon Law does not exist in its entirety in the United States, nor would it be practicable to promulgate the whole of it, yet the *spirit* of Canon Law should exist *everywhere* in the Church, regulate the principles of action, and animate the conduct of all bishops and priests in their relations towards each other. If times and circumstances change, the Catholic Church and the principles of justice never change. Her spirit is ever the same, not indeed the spirit of tyranny, nor a spirit of selfishness, and cruelty, and hardheartedness, but the spirit of a loving, tender, compassionate, just and merciful mother, whose heart yearns towards even the erring, who would lovingly fold them penitent in her arms, pardon them, and cleanse them, and present them purified and sanctified by her sacraments, to her Divine Spouse, Jesus Christ, as the fruits and victory of his most precious Blood. Not only this, but for the honor of the Priesthood throughout the entire world, that it may not be exposed to insult and contempt,—which would be the case if priests were necessitated to beg, or engage in secular avocations to gain a livelihood,—the Church has ever and always cared even for their temporal necessities, and has legislated for their becoming support as long as they submit to her discipline, which is replete with mercy, even when justice demands that she make use of the rod of correction and punishment.

Moreover, in depriving an unworthy priest, not contumacious, and not having the means of subsistence, of the support becoming his sacred character, or in other words, in dismissing him uncanonically from his diocese, and making of him a homeless and penniless wanderer on the face of the earth, the canons of Justice and Charity, Religion and Humanity are grievously violated. Who will say that these latter are not as binding in the United States as in the countries of Europe? And it is upon the principles of Charity, Justice, Religion and Humanity that the Decisions of Sacred Congregations just quoted are founded, as much as upon the Canon Law of the Church. These principles are binding everywhere, at all times, and amongst all Christian people.

But let those who so flippantly fall back on this senseless argument that there is no Canon Law in the United States, and use it to bridge over every difficulty, and sometimes even to palliate, or justify evident wrong and injustice, cast aside this delusion, *for there is Canon Law in the United States.* True, there is not much of it, and the little there is is scarcely observed. Nevertheless it exists in the statute books. There is a law which positively forbids any bishop to dismiss a priest from his diocese, until he has secured another bishop. THIS VERY LAW (N. 122 of the II. Plenary Council of Baltimore) INCLUDES ALL THAT I HAVE BEEN CONTENDING FOR IN THIS CHAPTER, viz.: that no priest not contumacious, can be helplessly thrown into the streets to beg or starve, but must receive a becoming support from his diocese, a proposition abundantly proved by the venerable authorities I have cited.

I cannot understand this argument of the non-existence of Canon Law in the United States, sometimes used to justify *uncanonical* proceedings. It seems to my humble judgment, that the Decisions of Roman Pontiffs and Sacred Congregations, ought in like circumstances to be law for every bishop and priest in the world. When he has a case to decide, identical in all its circumstances and bearings with one that Rome has decided, is it not a sound principle to be guided in his action by this safe authority? Is he not much more secure in taking the decisions of the Church for his guide, than in following his own fallible judgment? There is not a true Catholic bishop or priest in the world, who would dare violate the expressed wish of our Holy Father, the Supreme Pastor of the Church. Is not his will and ruling expressed in the Declarations and Decisions of the Sacred Congregations of Rome? Konings says of them: "*Eandem vim habent ac si a Romano Pontifice immediate processissent,*" nay, "*etsi a S. Pontifice non explicite confirmentur.*" If it were only observed, we would be amazed at the amount of Canon Law we possess in the United States. That there is little or none observed, *concedo*; that none exists, *nego*.

The reason, as I have more than once remarked, why the Church allows even an unworthy priest, not contumacious, an honest and becoming subsistence, is the sacred character and dignity of the Priesthood. The sacerdotal character was as indelibly imprinted on the soul of Judas, as on that of Peter. The former became a reprobate; the latter, having wept over his fault and been reconciled to his Saviour, was made Head of the Church. "Tu es sacerdos in æternum secundum ordinem Melchisedech," is as true of an unworthy priest as of the greatest saint that ever offered up sacrifice. The unworthy priest would degrade the Priesthood in the eyes of men, and bring it into contempt, if he were obliged to beg for his sustenance, or gain it by "sordid" employments, as well as the priest in good standing. Therefore has the Church made provision that all her clergy in Sacred Orders receive "congrua perpetuaque substentatio."

There is not, and there ought not to be a distinction made between priests in this country, and in those countries where Canon Law is observed. If either were deserving of any special favors, the priest in the United States, exposed to greater dangers, and subject to greater hardships, could justly lay claim to them. Tell me not that Canon Law protects the priest in Europe and cries out against the wrong of privation of "congrua sustentatio," whilst a priest in this country, who makes greater sacrifices and has less comforts, is liable to be dismissed from his diocese, abandoned by his bishop and reduced to want and misery. The Catholic Church is the same Catholic Church in the United States as it is in Europe. The clergy are as devoted here as there. The Catholic Priesthood is the same the world over. And everywhere is that Priesthood worthy of protection, whether he who bears it on his soul is a saint, or a sinner. As the ANALECTA JURIS PONTIFICII says: "*A priest should not be deprived of his alimentary pension, although he be deposed even for great crimes. Without doubt he has no right to receive a pension from his parish, but his right to an alimentary pension remains intact.* THE CHURCH NEVER ABANDONS THE MEMBERS OF THE CLERGY TO MENDICANCY."

CHAPTER XII.

EVEN AN UNWORTHY CLERGYMAN, NOT CONTUMACIOUS, HAS A RIGHT TO A BECOMING SUPPORT.—
Continued.

Among the Decrees of the Council of Bordeaux, held A. D. 1624, is the following: " Regulares promoti ad ordines, si quando ab hujusmodi superioribus, pro criminis exigentia puniri conveniat, et si urgeat necessitas, non possunt tamen habitu religionis privari, ita ut, extra monasteria *in contemptum Ecclesiæ dejiciantur mendicaturi*, sed intra eorundem monasteriorum septa detineri, puniri et *sustentari*, et ad illud prædicti Superiores per Ordinarios compellantur." Con. Burd., *c*. 6, *n*. 4.

The Fathers of this Council, as we gather from the above decree, legislated, that the Ordinary of the diocese compel religious Superiors to punish their delinquent subjects within their monasteries, and at the same time support them. This *modus agendi* those bishops certainly followed in the treatment of their own delinquent clergy. It is not probable that they violated, in the treatment of their own subjects, the rules they so rigidly enforced on the Superiors of religious orders, and we can therefore justly infer, that they cared for, and protected their own delinquents. In this legislation, the Fathers of this Council were influenced by the same motive that actuated the Fathers of Trent, in enacting the law of the Title, viz.: the sanctity and dignity of the Priesthood, and the reverence due to it: " Ne in contemptum Ecclesiæ dejiciantur mendicaturi."

Sixtus V., to prevent those who left the Jesuits after having received orders, from suffering want, as can be seen in Pyrrhus Corradus, *lib.* 4 *de Dispens. Apostol., c.* 7., *n.* 37, 38, approved the following declaration of the Sacred Congregation of Cardinals: "Quoad Jesuitas, cum post sacerdotium exire non possint, nisi a Superioribus dejiciantur, *prævideatur illis de reditu quadraginta aureorum nummorum ex bonis religionis.*"

In this Declaration of the Sacred Congregation, approved by the Pope, there is question of unworthy clergymen, "a Superioribus dejiciantur." Yet the Sacred Congregation requires that they be provided with a pension for their decent support, "'Provideatur illis de reditu quadraginta aureorum nummorum ex bonis religionis." The above declaration of Rome is sufficiently clear and to the point, to prove that it is the spirit and wish of the Church that an unworthy clergyman, not contumacious, should not be abandoned to mendicity, but be provided for from the revenues of the diocese or bishopric, if a secular, or if a religious, by his order, "ex bonis religionis."

In the ANALECTA JURIS PONTIFICII, 12th series, Col. 145, is found a Decree of the Sacred Congregation of Bishops and Regulars, by order of His Holiness Pius VI., "cum jussu Sanctitatis Suæ Pii VI.," which has reference to a Spanish priest who had committed a grievous crime, for which he had *ipso facto* incurred irregularity. The case was referred to Rome. As its solution and settlement by that august authority show the merciful spirit of the Church,—as it clearly bears me out in the assertion that no priest, how criminal soever, who is not contumacious, can be thrown helplessly on the world, but must receive a suitable maintenance from the Church,—I will here transcribe a goodly portion of the Decree itself.

The delinquent of whom there is question in this Decree was Michael Philip de Tabalza, "qui longe aliter, quam instituti sui ratio ferebat, nihil antiquius habuit, quam arma tractare, ac satellitum more armatus incedere, unde jurgia, et rixas frequenter aucupabatur, propterea necem per illum illatam villico Joanni de Tabalza, non casu aliquo fortuito, sed ejusdem culpa et pravitate accedisse neutiquam est dubitandum." His crime was aggravated still more by the injury it inflicted on others, "Itaque cum Beatissimus Pater, ex relatu nostro, audisset perpetrati criminis reum sacerdotem, qui ad curam animarum præpositus, exemplum lenitatis esse debebat, non potuit valde non commoveri, eo vel maxime, quod ob eam villico mortem, uxor superstes ac septem teneræ ætatis nati, egerrimam vitam modo ducere coguntur in summa inopia atque egestate."

Let us now consider the punishment the Holy Father inflicts for this enormous crime, attended with such sad circumstances of injury and misery to the helpless and innocent. "In hoc rerum statu, Sanctitas Sua, secum animo pervolutans, quid fieri oporteret, Michaelem Philippum (sacerdotem) ab exercitio muneris parochialis perpetuo arcendum esse voluit, neque aliter dispensandum quam ut pro nunc extra diœcesim sacrum peragere illi permittatur. Verum, cum procul a sua regione exul et profugus Romam usque perrexerit, stipemque modo emendicare cogatur, Beatissimus Pater, cum rigore justitiæ temperandam esse pietatem ratus, illius egestati satis consulere existimavit, si ex parochiæ fructibus *sexaginta ducati argentei, eidem in singulos annos rependantur*, ita tamen, ut villici uxori superstiti ac septem natis, quoad Michael vixerit, centum quinquaginta reales annuatim persolvi possint." Romæ, dec. oct, Kal Jan., 1776.

If ever there were circumstances justifying the making of an erring clergyman a hopeless outcast on the world, they are those found in the above Decree emanating from His Holiness, Pius VI. And yet the Holy Father does not condemn him to such a fate. As to Adam fallen from grace, God held out the hope of a Redeemer, and through Him, pardon and reconciliation, so the Pope held out to this unfortunate man the hope of peace, and of even happiness to a certain extent in the future. He exiles him, it is true, from his diocese, a penalty which he most justly deserved, and debarred him ever after from assuming any parochial charge, but he tempers with mercy this sentence so just. He sweetens the bitterness of his exile, with the assurance that he will again be permitted to say Mass: "ut pro nunc extra diœcesim sacrum paragere illi permittatur." Not only this, but he decrees that he receive a pension for his material necessities, " sexaginta ducati argentei eidem in singulos annos rependantur."

The ANALECTA JURIS PONTIFICII, commenting upon the above decree issued by the Sacred Congregation, *with the explicit approbation of Pius VI.*, remarks, that *whatever be the crime an ecclesiastic is guilty of, his alimentary pension* (" congrua sustentatio"), IS NEVER DENIED HIM BY THE CHURCH. It is, of course, understood, that he does not rebel against her authority by becoming contumacious, but humbly submits himself to her discipline.

In the Thesaurus Resolutionum, *Tom.* 69, p. 79, is related another case which bears directly on the point I am discussing. It is that of a parish priest named Boletta. His bishop, *ex informata conscientia*, suspended him *a divinis et ab officio.* He appealed to Rome. The Sacred Congregation, whilst confirming the sentence of suspension, decided that he should be supported " ex reditibus parœciæ : sin minus prout de jure."

It may possibly be objected that the above decisions are old. The same objection might be made against the Church herself and her venerable Priesthood. But to satisfy even those who foolishly might not be inclined to give much heed to decisions made one or two hundred years ago, or even in a more remote age, I will adduce one of recent date bearing on the subject, which has come under my observation. The S. C. Concilii gave the decision I will presently quote, on Aug. 12, 1865. This decision has reference to a priest who had been suspended by his bishop. The sentence of suspension, on an appeal made to the Holy See, was confirmed by it. After this, " suspensione violata, in irregularitatem (sacerdos supradictus) inciderat." On the question assuming this new phase, it was again submitted to the consideration of the S. C. Concilii. The latter (1) Affirmed and maintained the suspension and irregularity. (2) To the question, "An et quomodo sit locus depositioni sacerdotis a parœcia in casu, ob gravem aversionem parœchinorum et relativam inidoneitatem parochi?" the same Sacred Congregation answered, "Esse locum deputationi administrationis parœciæ in spiritualibus et temporalibus, *assignata favore sacerdotis, donec de beneficio ecclesiastico provideatur, pensione libellorum 400.*"

The unfortunate priest of whom there is question in the above decision had behaved very badly indeed. "Ob flagrantem contumaciam," or disobedience to the bishop and to the Holy See, he had been suspended, and "suspensione violata in irregularitatem inciderat." Notwithstanding, the Sacred Congregation of the Council imposed on him only the following comparatively light penance before being absolved from censure and irregularity: " Peractis per decem dies spiritualibus exercitiis in aliqua domo religiosa ab episcopo designanda, esse locum absolutionis a censuris et dispensationis ab irregularitate," and besides assigned for his becoming support a pension of " libellorum 400," until such time as he could be provided with an ecclesiastical benefice.

This Decision of Aug. 12, 1865, is based on the same principle for the protection of the honor of the Priesthood, as far as "congrua sustentatio" is concerned, as that of St. Pius V. three hundred years before. In his Constitution *Quanta Ecclesiæ*, 1 Apr., 1568, this great Pontiff speaks thus: " Beneficia" may be resigned by those, "qui ob capitales inimicitias, nequeunt, vel non audent, in loco beneficii residere secure." But he adds:

"*Sed nec horum ullus sacro ordini mancipatus, nisi Religionem ingressurus, valeat ullo modo beneficium vel officium ecclesiasticum resignare ; nisi aliunde ei sit quo in vita posset commode sustentari.*" Here we have Rome of three centuries ago, and Rome of to-day, consistent with itself, uttering the same sentiments of justice, mercy and clemency as she always does.

Nor can the senseless objection be brought against the authorities I have quoted, that there are no benefices in this country, whence " congrua sustentatio " could be drawn. The Religious within the jurisdiction of the bishops that composed the Council of Bordeaux, A. D. 1216, had no benefices. Yet if any of them erred, their superiors were not permitted to let them wander around, "in contemptum Ecclesiæ mendicaturi," but were obliged to support them in their own monasteries, " intra eorumdem monasteriorum septa puniri et sustentari compellantur." This legislation shows the spirit of the Church in the thirteenth century.

The Jesuits had no benefices. Yet Sixtus V. required that, in case any of them were expelled from the Order, they should receive a pension for their honest subsistence, " Provideatur illis de reditu quadraginta aureorum nummorum ex bonis religionis."

Moreover, as we have already seen, the " Titulus Missionis" confers, essentially, the same right to "congrua sustentatio" as " Titulus Beneficii," or any other regular canonical Title in the Church.

Besides, in providing a suitable support for an erring priest, not contumacious, the diocese to which he belongs consults its own honor and interest, as well as the honor of the Church and of the Priesthood. In face of the authorities I have quoted, and will yet bring forward, it is, in my mind, a humiliating reflection both on the diocese, and the one who presides over it, to find any one of its priests wandering from place to place, and subsisting on the charity of the clergy and faithful. It is not saying much to assert, that there ought to be enough of *beneficence* at least, if not charity and justice, amongst the bishop, priests and faithful of a diocese to provide the necessaries of life for one or another clergyman belonging to it, who for any cause whatever may become unfitted for duty.

Finally, it is not true that "congrua sustentatio" is given in Europe only to those possessing benefices. The case of a bishop ordaining without a Title is an instance. In such circumstances, as we have already seen, the bishop is bound to support him at his own expense. Moreover, we have many instances of priests possessed of no Title whatever, and yet Rome decided that they should receive an alimentary pension or the means of subsistence. "The Church never abandons the members of the clergy to mendicancy."

To the above Decisions and Declarations of Roman Pontiffs and Sacred Congregations, so clearly and conclusively proving that even an unworthy priest, not contumacious, ought to be provided for in some way, and not thrown helplessly on the charity of the public, I will add the testimony of theologians, of such weight and authority that they cannot be gainsaid.

St. Liguori, of whom the Church now sings, "O Doctor optime, Ecclesiæ sanctæ lumen," whose teaching has been positively sanctioned by Rome, as is evident from the following twofold decision, blended in one, of the Sacred Penitentiary: "Tutum esse S. Theologiæ Professorem, ac non esse inquietandum confessarium, qui omnes Sancti Alphonsi sententias sola ipsius auctoritate ducti, sequuntur,"—St. Alphonsus Liguori, *in Tom.* 7, *lib.* 7, *c.* 3 *de Surp.*, has the following: "Dubit. I. An suspensus a beneficio, si sit pauper, possit fructus sibi retinere? Respondetur affirmative, si suspensio est lata in pœnam criminis omnino præteriti, secus, si fuerit lata ob contumaciam, quia non debet ab Ecclesia subveniri ei qui voluntarie Ecclesiæ disciplinam vilipendit, cum libere possit a sua contumacia recedere. Ita Suarez et alii."

The Summa S. Thomæ, by F. C. R. Billuart, a theologian of the very first rank, a new edition of whose work, in 8 vols., was published as late as 1873, and whose Theology had the honor of being constantly on the tables of the august assembly of the Vatican Œcumenical Council (Billuart, ed. Leodi 1751, Vol. xiv., p. 371) says: "Suspensus totaliter a beneficio, non potest gerere ejus administrationem, nec percipere ullos fructus, sive quotidianos, sive principales, nisi in quantum sunt necessaria ad victum, si tamen ab eo non pendeat ut absolvatur, alioquin (contumacia) sibi imputet."

Daelman, Professor in the University of Louvain, and Rector of the same, in his Theology, printed at Antwerp, A. D. 1735, *trac. de Sacrm.*, p. 139, has the following: "Dicet aliquis: si clericus totaliter suspendatur a beneficio: ergo, interim, debebit talis mendicare, vel esurire? Resp. Si talis aliunde non habeat unde se sustentet, et suspendatur ad annum, aut aliud tempus definitum, tunc ei debet sufficiens assignari sustentatio."

In Theologia Practica, by J. B. F. Vernier, in note *b* to N. 660, the following sentence is found: "Juxta multos, suspensus (saltem in pœnam delicti commissi, et non ob contumaciam) potest sibi de fructibus retinere ad vivendum, si pauper sit." Vernier's standing as a theologian is, " Probabilior ista in doctrinis practicis versatus, sed sæpius severioris ethices sectator."

No one could desire any thing clearer, or more to the point, than the language of the above theologians in support of the position I am advocating, that even an unworthy clergyman, not contumacious, has a right to the means of an honest subsistence.

I will draw this chapter to a close by citing an historical incident of great weight, in confirmation of the above quoted Decrees of Sovereign Pontiffs, Decisions of Sacred Congregations and teachings of theologians. It will, moreover, show the mercy, and charity, and humanity of the Church towards the clergy, and carrying us back centuries,—almost to the beginning of Christianity,—will prove that her spirit then was the same as that set forth in the authorities I have already, or will yet cite, and which prove so clearly, so conclusively and so unequivocally, that no priest, how unworthy soever, and not contumacious, should ever be abandoned by his bishop to helpless want and unspeakable misery, which is done, as a rule, when he is uncanonically dismissed from his diocese.

The historical fact to which I have reference, is related in the Acts of the Holy and Œcumenical Council of Chalcedon, held A. D. 451: "Residentibus universis ante cancellos sancti altaris, Maximus Reverendissimus Episcopus Antiochiæ dixit: Deprecor magnificentissimos et gloriosissimos judices, et sanctam hanc universalem synodum, ut humanitatem exercere in Domnum, qui fuit Antiochiæ Episcopus dignemini, et statuere ei certos sumptus de Ecclesia quæ sub me est. . . .

"Universa Sancta Synodus vociferata est: Laudabiles merito sunt benevolentiæ Archiepiscopi: omnes cogitatum ejus laudamus: hic decet ejus existimationem hujus cogitatus Pontificis." Con. Chal., *prt.* 2, *act.* 10 *in fine.*

Domnus, the bishop who is here spoken of, was deposed from the See of Antioch. What a noble example of Christian charity and sacerdotal friendship, did not the sainted Maximus display to the assembled Council, when, rising from his seat, he begged the Fathers to provide for his deposed predecessor, "statuere ei certos sumptus de Ecclesia quæ sub me est." And grander still, and even more worthy of admiration, was the reply of the venerable Fathers of the Council, bursting forth spontaneously, in one grand shout of Christian charity: "Universa Sancta Synodus vociferata est: Laudabiles merito sunt benevolentiæ Archiepiscopi."

Here we have, I might say, an Œcumenical Council deciding the proposition I am advocating in these humble pages, or at least most unequivocally supporting it, by proclaiming the justness and propriety of giving to a delinquent clergyman, not contumacious, a becoming support when he has not means of his own. But such has ever been the spirit of the Catholic Church from the very beginning. She knows the dignity of the sacerdotal character, and adequately understands the honor and veneration due to it. Therefore has she so persistently, by Decrees of Councils, by Decisions of her Sacred Congregations, and by rulings of her Supreme Pontiffs, protected that sacred character, even in him who had lost sight of the honor due to it in his own person by falling into open sin or crime. Not even such a one does she allow to be deprived of a becoming subsistence, lest he might bring shame and dishonor on the Church and the Priesthood, by being obliged to beg or have recourse to secular pursuits to gain a livelihood. " Nemo ignorat, ab antiquissimis inde temporibus cautum fuisse, ut quicumque in Ecclesia Dei ad Sacros Ordines essent promovendi, eisdem de congrua perpetuaque substentatione provideretur, cum indecorum omnino sit atque a clericorum qui Sacris Ordinibus constituuntur, dignitate prorsus alienum, ut ipsi, aut mendicatis subsidiis, aut ex sordido quæstu, ea quæ ad victum necessaria sunt, sibi comparare cogantur." Instr. S. C. de P. F. *de Tit. Ord.*

CHAPTER XIII.

EVEN AN UNWORTHY CLERGYMAN, NOT CONTUMACIOUS, HAS A RIGHT TO A BECOMING SUPPORT.—
Concluded.

As this is an important question in its practical bearing and consequences, I will adduce yet other authorities to sustain what, I am sure, I have already clearly demonstrated in the two preceding chapters, viz.: that even an unworthy clergyman, not contumacious, cannot lawfully be dismissed from his diocese, and abandoned to public charity, but that, according to the spirit and letter of the Church's teaching, and the Decisions of her Sacred Congregations, he must receive the means to live as becomes his sacred character.

The same Œcumenical Council of Chalcedon, of which I spoke in the preceding chapter, also enacted that a pension, "Nutrimenti gratia et consolationis, annis singulis, solidos aureos ducentos," should be given to two bishops, Bassian and Stephen, who had intruded themselves into the See of Ephesus, and who were removed therefrom. The words of the Council are: " Removebuntur equidem a Sancta Ephesinorum Ecclesia Bassianus et Stephanus Reverendissimi: habeant autem dignitatem episcopi: et ex reditibus memoratæ sanctissimæ Ecclesiæ, nutrimenti gratia et consolationis, annis singulis solidos aureos ducentos accipiant." And all the venerable Fathers of the Council answered unanimously: " Hæc justa sententia: hæc justa forma: hæc bene habent." Con. Chal., *Act.* 12 *in fine.*

St. Gregory the Great prescribed that a pension be given to Agathon, a bishop who had been deposed on account of his bad life, and who had no means of subsistence. The following are the words of this great and holy Pontiff: " Postquam in Agathonem, quondam episcopum, juxta qualitatem excessuum, districtione canonica est vindicatum ; *necesse est humanitatis intuitu quemadmodum sustentari possit disponere.* Propterea, paternitas tua ad Liparitanam Ecclesiam in qua supradictus Agatho sacerdotis gessit officium, festinet dirigere eique ad præsens exinde quinquaginta solidos, qui in ejus possent proficere victum, transmittas; NAM, NIMIS EST IMPIUM, SI ALIMENTORUM NECESSITATI POST VINDICTUM SUBJACEAT." S. Greg. Magn., *lib.* 2, *Ep. ind.* 11, *Epist.* 53.

I cannot, here, refrain from making a brief commentary on the text of St. Gregory the Great, just quoted. None can dispute, with these words of that illustrious and immortal Pontiff before his eyes, that an unworthy priest, not contumacious, ought to be provided with the means of an honest subsistence. None can deny, that this proposition is clearly and forcibly upheld by the above quoted words of this bright light and glory of the Church, St. Gregory the Great.

The bishop Agatho had been deposed for his great excesses, 'juxta qualitatem excessuum districtione canonica est vindicatum." Then, on the score of *humanity*, St. Gregory required that some provision be made for his maintenance, "Necesse est humanitatis intuitu, quemadmodum sustentari possit disponere." Having directed how this should be done, he concludes with these forcible, but most truthful words, than which none more pointed or vigorous have fallen from my humble pen, in speaking of the same matter: "NIMIS EST IMPIUM SI ALIMENTORUM NECESSITATI POST VINDICTUM SUBJACEAT." If I had no other authority than these words of St. Gregory the Great, to prove the propriety and justice of giving even to an unworthy clergyman, not contumacious, a suitable living, they would be more than sufficient.

Nor will it be objected, that the culprits in these three cases, as well as in the one related in the previous chapter, were bishops. The circumstance that a delinquent clergyman belongs to the episcopal order, does not, in the estimation of mankind in general, or in the judgment of the Church, palliate his crime; on the contrary, it rather aggravates it, and renders the criminal less worthy of pity and compassion. If, therefore, according to St. Gregory the Great, it is wrong and even inhuman and impious, to deprive an unworthy bishop of the means of an honest subsistence, together with making him suffer the punishment of his crimes, is it not likewise wrong, inhuman and impious, to treat an unworthy priest in the same manner?

. It is not I, therefore, but the great St. Gregory, who so worthily filled the chair of Peter, that reproves, in no gentle speech either, those ecclesiastical superiors who not only punish a clergyman by suspending him from his office, but who, moreover, cruelly deprive him of every means of subsistence; and oftentimes, by uncanonically dismissing him from his diocese, reduce him, a priest of God, to the condition of a helpless mendicant, to want, to misery, to beggary and to rags. I need not offer any apology whatever, for stigmatizing this inhuman conduct, when I have been obliged to allude to it, in the mild and truthful terms I have employed, when I put my expressions side by side with this utterance of the renowned St. Gregory the Great: "NIMIS EST IMPIUM SI ALIMENTORUM NECESSITATI POST VINDICTUM SUBJACEAT."

The last authority I will cite in favor of my thesis, that a delinquent clergyman, not contumacious, and not having the means of subsistence, has a right to "congrua sustentatio," is drawn from the reply of the Sacred Congregation of the Propaganda to the suggestion made through the II. Plenary Council of Baltimore by the Rt. Rev. John Henry Luers, D. D., Bishop of Ft. Wayne, Indiana, to whose merciful soul may the God of mercy grant peace and eternal rest.

I know not, nor have I the means of ascertaining, what was in the text of Nos. 345, 346 and 357 (see II. Plen. Coun. Balto., p. cxxxix., No. 14), which numbers, by order of the Sacred Congregation, were suppressed altogether, nor do I know what was the precise wording of No. 347; but what I find in the note to No. 15 (see II. Plen. Coun. Balto., p. cxl.) is amply sufficient for my purpose.

According to this note, Rt. Rev. J. H. Luers made the suggestion contained in the following words: " Ordinarii locorum, in quibus ejusmodi (scil. pauperes ac infirmi titulo missionis ordinati) sacerdotes, annuale quoddam stipendium ad eorum decentem sustentationem sufficiens, ab illis congregationibus, seu districtibus missionariis, in quibus prius operam impenderunt exigant, iisdemque sacerdotibus statis temporibus distribuant. Sed cum haud raro sit pertimescendum, ne hæc provisio, vel sit insufficiens, vel haud facile executioni dari possit, ideo decernimus insuper ut per Ordinarios fundus quidam specialis ex taxis singulis, uniuscujusque Diœceseos Congregationibus pro rata et æque imponendis constituatur, unde sacerdotes, de quibus est sermo, victum competentem habere possint. Modus autem fundum hujusmodi colligendi et administrandi a respectivis Diœcesanis Synodis ordinetur. Prædicti vero sacerdotes plena gaudeant libertate utendi pecunia modo hic exposito recepta, ubicumque illis magis commorari placuerit, modo in omnibus, uti Sacerdotalem decet dignitatem, sese gerant. Quinimo, ex eodem fundo, Ordinarii judicio, poterunt saltem aliquatenus, sustentari illi etiam Sacerdotes, QUI QUIDEM SUNT VEL RECENTER FUERUNT INDIGNI, sed de quibus spes effulgeat illos ad meliorem frugem esse reducendos."

To the above *Postulatum* of the merciful hearted bishop of Ft. Wayne, the Sacred Congregation of the Propaganda (see II. Plenary Council of Baltimore, p. cxxxix., No. 15) replied as follows : " Cum vero EE. PP. diligenter expendissent additionem, quam Episcopus Wayne castrensis textui No. 347 inserendam proposuit, circa jura Missionariorum ex titulo ordinationis acquisita, nec non circa modum eis satisfaciendi, illius quidem sententiam admittere noluerunt ; PLACUIT TAMEN IPSIS, UT PER HANC EPISTOLAM INSTITUTIO PRO SACERDOTIBUS PAUPERIBUS SUSTENTAN-

DIS, A WAYNE CASTRENSIS PRÆSULE INSINUATA, AMPLITUDINI SUÆ CÆTERISQUE EPISCOPIS COMMENDARETUR."

Although the above answer of the Most Eminent Cardinals of the Sacred Congregation of the Propaganda to the *Postulatum* of the lamented bishop of Ft. Wayne, is sufficiently clear, to any one reading it with that attention required for understanding the answers of Rome, in which not one word is wanting, and none are superfluous, yet it will not be out of place to make a few comments thereon, and show how evidently it supports, what I think I have already satisfactorily proved, that a priest who is not contumacious, and not having the means of subsistence, should receive the same from the Church.

In the first place, the Sacred Congregation did not coincide with all the views of the bishop of Ft. Wayne, as expressed in his *Postulatum* "circa jura Missionariorum ex titulo ordinationis acquisita, nec non circa modum eis satisfaciendi, illius quidam sententiam admittere noluerunt." They do not state, explicitly, the reasons of their dissent. This, in fact, was unnecessary, for in the previous No., viz.: 14 (see II. Plenary Council of Baltimore, No. 14, p. cxxxix), they promised to all the bishops of the United States a Document which would treat *ex officio*, of the rights of missionary priests and the mode of satisfying them, and which, in fact, was sent to them Apr. 27, 1871,— I mean the " Instructio " of the Propaganda concerning the Title of Ordination, from which, in Chap. xi., I made several extracts, to show that the Title of the Mission gave the right to an honest subsistence as validly as any other Title in the Church.

But one thing is clear, and certain, and beyond the shadow of a doubt, and that is, that the Sacred Congregation approved of the " Institutio " itself suggested by the kind hearted bishop of Ft. Wayne, or, if they found any fault with it, it was because it did not determine more explicitly and boldly the right of priests " qui quidem sunt vel recenter fuerunt indigni," to participate *de jure*, equally with priests " pauperes ac infirmi," in the benevolent fund that was proposed to be raised. This is evidently seen from the very answer itself of the Sacred Congregation. In the answers of Roman Congregations every word is fraught with meaning. Nothing is useless; nothing is wanting. The words "pauperes ac infirmi" were *conspicuous* in the *Postulatum* of the pious bishop of Ft. Wayne, and the greater part of it had reference to such clergymen. It was only in the end that he timidly suggested, that priests " qui sunt vel recenter fuerunt indigni," might sometimes, at the option of the Ordinary, participate in the benevolent fund to be raised chiefly for " sacerdotes pauperes ac infirmi."

Now in the answer to the *Postulatum* of the bishop of Ft. Wayne, Rome discarded entirely the word " infirmi," which was so prominent and conspicuous therein, and recommended an " Institutio pro sacerdotibus pauperibus sustentandis," thus giving to the two classes mentioned in the *Postulatum*, scil.: " Sacerdotes pauperes ac infirmi," and those " qui sunt vel fuerunt indigni," an equal right *de jure* of benefitting by the benevolent fund which was suggested to be raised in each diocese. Accordingly, the Most Eminent Cardinals APPROVE and

SANCTION and COMMEND an " INSTITUTIO PRO SACERDOTI-
BUS PAUPERIBUS," whether they are " pauperes ac infirmi,"
or "qui sunt vel recenter fuerunt indigni," as their words
plainly show: " PLACUIT IPSIS UT PER HANC EPISTOLAM
INSTITUTIO PRO SACERDOTIBUS PAUPERIBUS SUSTENTAN-
DIS, a Wayne castrensis præsule insinuata, AMPLITUDINI
SUÆ, CÆTERISQUE EPISCOPIS COMMENDARETUR."

Hence Rome, in commending the " Institutio " of the
lamented, just and merciful bishop of Ft. Wayne to all
the prelates of the United States, gave them distinctly to
understand that delinquent priests, not contumacious,
ought not to be abandoned to poverty and want, but
provided at least with the necessaries of life.

After the many and unexceptionable authorities I have
adduced to prove this proposition, that any priest not
contumacious and not possessing the means of subsistence,
has a right to receive a becoming support, I need not
dwell on it any longer. I have proved it conclusively
and beyond the shadow of doubt. I do not anticipate
that there is a bishop or priest in the Church who will or
can call it in question. If we had not the authority of
St. Gregory the Great, of Sixtus V., and of Pius VI.; of
theologians such as St. Liguori, Billuart and Suarez; of a
great number of decisions of Sacred Congregations—the
highest authority in the Church of God, after an
Œcumenical Council, or the Pope speaking *ex Cathedra*—
to support this proposition, it would be amply sustained
on the ground of the honor and reverence due the Priesthood of Jesus Christ, on the principles of Christian

charity alone, and not to speak at all of justice, on the broad principles of our common humanity.

What is it, in fact, to refuse even an unworthy priest "congrua sustentatio," a right given him by the Title of his Ordination, and of which he should at least reap the advantage, above all other times, when he is in extreme need? It is to reduce him to a condition which "the Holy Canons assimilate to the pain of death;" it is to drag him down into want and misery, so that he is unable "to live in a manner becoming the priestly character;" it is to throw him helplessly on the charity of the public, "in contemptum Ecclesiæ mendicaturus;" it is to make of him generally, "procul a sua regione exul et profugus;" and it is, as St. Gregory the Great expresses it, inhuman and "nimis impium." To dismiss even an unworthy priest from his diocese, and refuse him "congrua sustentatio," is to reduce him to poverty and want, thence to beggary and rags; it is to drive him to despair, desolation and ruin; it is to bring infamy on the Priesthood of Jesus Christ, and shame and dishonor on His Immaculate Spouse, the Church; it is to give cause for sorrow and tears to the faithful, of sadness to the angels of heaven, and of grief to the Sacred Hearts of Jesus and Mary; whilst the infidel, and irreligious, and all the enemies of God's Church rejoice and are glad, and the very demons of hell shout for joy, for they know well the fruits of evil, of sin and of scandal, that attend the making of any priest a helpless outcast on the world.

As no priest is permitted to gain his livelihood, "ex sordido quæstu," vel "ex mendicatis subsidiis," amply proved by the many authorities I have quoted ; and since even an unworthy priest can bring dishonor on the Priesthood in general, and scandal and disgrace on the Church, when he is helplessly dismissed from his diocese, abandoned by his bishop, and denied that honest subsistence which the Title of Ordination requires, it follows that it is a solemn obligation, incumbent on every bishop, to place such a priest in a position that will preclude the necessity of begging, or engaging in secular employments, and which, at the same time, will take from him the occasion or opportunity of giving scandal. *It is a bishop's duty, therefore, to provide for him a home or a refuge of some kind, no matter how unworthy soever he may be, as long as he is not contumacious.* There can be no other conclusion drawn from the many authorities I have adduced. There is not a particle of doubt that such is the spirit and practice of the Church, clearly evident from the same authorities. How unworthy soever he may be, he is nevertheless a priest. The priestly character, as I have already noted, is the exalted motive actuating the Church in her reiterated prohibition, which debars him from all secular employments, and in declaring that once he has received Sacred Orders, he must receive "congrua perpetuaque substentatio." All this is done to protect the honor and dignity of the Priesthood. And so determined is the Church to protect the priestly character from being exposed to insult and infamy, that when she finds any of her ministers incorrigible, who wilfully and persistently violates his obligations as a priest, and thereby gives scandal and dishonors to the Priesthood, she encloses him, where she has the power, within the precincts of her "ergastula," or Houses of Correction for Clergymen. This she does, not only for his own individual benefit and correction, but to protect the honor and dignity of the Priesthood, of which he is, though unworthy, a member.

The same solicitude for the honor and dignity of the sacerdotal character, ought to animate the heart of every bishop in the Catholic Church. Hence the instructions and admonitions of the Council of Trent to bishops; hence the importance and necessity of every priest having a Title, which secures him a becoming support; hence, too, the prohibition of the II. Plenary Council of Baltimore forbidding the dismissal of any priest from his diocese before he has secured another bishop. All these laws and regulations are intended to throw around a clergyman that protection which will save him even from himself, if necessary.

A secular priest must always have his bishop to whom he owes obedience, and who is bound by his office to care for him always, unless by contumacy he cuts himself loose from the Church's mercy and clemency. As a priest cannot, of his own will and pleasure, leave his bishop to go where his inclinations or fancy may suggest, neither can a bishop, of his own will and pleasure, lawfully dismiss a clergyman from his diocese, and abandon him to his own resources, or throw him helplessly on the charity of the world. He was ordained for one or another diocese, or regularly affiliated to it. The bishop of that diocese is the father and protector whom the

Church has given him. Hence the words of the Council of Trent, " tanquam fratres et filios diligant." What kind of a father would he be, who would cast forth from under his roof even an unworthy child, to famish of hunger or die by the wayside? He would certainly not deserve the sweet name of Father, but would rather be looked upon by the community as a monster.

A bishop, therefore, should govern his clergy with the firm but kind hand of a father. It is his duty to admonish any of them forgetful of their high and holy calling; to exhort and advise them, to expostulate with them, to pray for them: in a word, to employ all the means the Church has placed in his hands, and a father's heart suggests, to correct and reform them, but *never* is he allowed to abandon them as long as they are not contumacious; *never* is he permitted to place them in the sad alternative, either to beg or starve. This, I think, has been abundantly proved in the preceding chapters. Besides, it is cruel in the extreme, if we look at it calmly, and consider it in itself, and in all its frightful, and sometimes irreparable consequences of evil. " Nemo ignorat, ab antiquissimis inde temporibus cautum fuisse, ut quicumque in Ecclesia Dei ad Sacros Ordines essent promovendi, eisdem de congrua perpetuaque substentatione provideretur, cum indecorum omnino sit, atque a clericorum qui Sacris Ordinibus constituuntur, dignitate prorsus alienum, ut ipsi, aut mendicatis subsidiis, aut ex sordido quæstu, ea quæ ad victum necessaria sunt, sibi comparare cogantur. " Instr. S. C. de P. F. *de Tit. Ord.*

CHAPTER XIV.

SPIRIT OF ROME TOWARDS THE CLERGY.

After the many Decisions of Roman Pontiffs and Roman Congregations given in the preceding chapters, it seems almost superfluous to speak in a special chapter of the spirit of Rome towards the clergy. For from these Decisions, her spirit is apparent. It unmistakably shines forth in its true colors, in all the *Acta et Gesta S. Sedis*, and is proved to be in perfect accord with the spirit of the Church, or rather is the spirit of the Church, the spirit of Jesus Christ Himself, which is pre-eminently a spirit of charity, mercy and forgiveness.

The spirit of Rome towards the clergy is exemplified by a thousand facts. It is shown in the solicitude she manifests that every priest be ordained to a legitimate Title, which gives him the right to a becoming subsistence, and in her desire that, in this country, the extraordinary Title of the Mission be superseded, as soon as possible, by the regular canonical Titles in use for ages, to the end that this "becoming subsistence" may be secured the more successfully. Her spirit of charity, mercy and forgiveness, is seen in all her decisions in criminal causes. It is manifest in the case I mentioned above, where a clergyman was accused of homicide. Though justice demanded a severe punishment, Rome nevertheless blends mercy with judgment, and orders the bishop to provide for his material wants, "Episcopus procuret assignamentum pro congrua parochi et habito." It is evident, in another case, where a priest was deposed for his offences. Whilst Rome wields the sword of justice, and confirms the sentence of deposition against him, she tempers, however, the sentence with mercy, for she writes to the bishop: "Your lordship is absolutely obliged to furnish the means of subsistence to this priest in want, so that he may be able to live in a manner becoming the priestly character, and not be obliged to beg," at the same time informing him that if he does not comply with this injunction and his obligation, she will take the means of having the order executed, adding these words, worthy of special note: "It it is just to punish him for his crime, it is also just that he receive the means of subsistence." The clemency of Rome again is seen in the case I related, of a clergyman who had been guilty of flagrant contumacy, by disobeying his bishop and the Holy See, and who, "suspensione violata," had incurred irregularity. Yet the Sacred Congregation imposed on him the following penance only, to be relieved of suspension and irregularity, "Peractis per decem dies spiritualibus exercitiis in aliqua domo religiosa ab episcopo designanda, esse locum absolutionis a censuris et dispensationis ab irregularitate," having also allowed him a pension for his maintenance. Again, the spirit of Rome's mercy and clemency is apparent in the answer of Pius VI. to a case in which the priest was guilty of "Necem illatam, non casu aliquo fortuito, sed ejusdem culpa et pravitate." The venerable Father of the faithful laments indeed, that he who ought to have been an example of meekness, "exemplum lenitatis," should have so far forgotten the law of God, his priestly dignity, and the promptings of humanity itself, as to commit the heinous offence he did, yet believing, "cum rigore justitiæ, temperandam esse pietatem," he extends to him the consolation, " ut pro nunc extra diœcesim sacrum peragere illi permittatur," and assigns him "congrua sustentatio." Rome's mercy, and clemency, and spirit of forgiveness are proverbial. A thousand or more instances could be adduced in evidence of it.

Many people, alas, in our day, are imbued with that pharisaical spirit which looks only at outside appearances. They possess, more or less without knowing it, of the spirit of false righteousness, which on the one hand raises the cry of condemnation and reprobation against the poor unfortunate whom dire necessity compels to wander hither and thither in search of employment, or the distracted father who takes a loaf of bread to keep his wife and children from starvation, whilst on the other hand, that same spirit of external probity condones the most enormous crimes committed "respectably," fawns and smiles on the heartless thief who openly, but legally, robs widows and orphans, and lauds the sleek-tongued and smiling hypocrite, who considers that he is at liberty to commit every crime in the catalogue of iniquity, provided he can do so without imperilling his "reputation." Seeing this spirit of false righteousness manifested on every side of them, and for the multitude forming the rule of judging and acting, even "the children of light" sometimes unconsciously fall into the snare and habit of passing sentence on their brethren, according to false, worldly principles, instead of those of the Gospel. In consequence, they may be almost scandalized, or at least much surprised, at the wonderful leniency of Rome, who shows mercy and clemency to sinners, and pardons those whom some may consider almost, if not altogether unpardonable.

But the spirit of Rome is not that of the world or of worldlings. It is the spirit of Truth, not the spirit of error. In dealing with the erring, it is a spirit of impartial justice, ever and always blended with mercy. Rome follows to the letter the admirable instructions of the Council of Trent, Sess. xiii., c. 1 *de Refor.*, quoted in a previous chapter, and directed to all the bishops of the Catholic Church. Her sovereign Pontiffs and Sacred Congregations ever show towards the clergy the solicitude of true Pastors, and treat them with paternal kindness and consideration, even when forced to use the rod of correction. When obliged to punish, "tunc cum mansuctudine rigor, cum misericordia judicium, cum lenitate severitas" is the Rule Rome invariably follows, "*ut qui correcti fuerint, emendentur.*"

"*Ut emendentur.*" That the erring may be corrected and amend their lives, is the great object of Rome in all her punishments, as it should be the end of every ecclesiastical superior. As the father punishes the disobedient child through a sense of duty, and for its own greater good, so does Rome punish her erring children; only she joins the mother's tenderness with the father's love, and blends the justice and firmness of the latter with the mercy and compassion of the former. In so doing, she only imitates the example of Jesus Christ, an example that has been copied by all bishops of the Church who have been enrolled in her catalogue of saints, as well as by all holy prelates of all climes and of all ages who take Him for their Model, and the admonitions and instructions of His Spouse, the Catholic Church, for their guide of conduct.

That Rome's spirit of clemency, is the same in this year of grace 1882, as it was in 1714, or in 1658, and during all the centuries back to the very days of Peter, as ecclesiastical history abundantly proves, I will produce a few decisions of Roman Pontiffs and Sacred Congregations in evidence. Of several practical cases, I select first the following, which is *ad rem*, and of recent date. I find it in the ANALECTA JURIS PONTIFICII, 13th series, 1874. Whilst it tells its own sad story, it shows at the same time the clement and merciful spirit of Rome. It is in the form of a letter written to a bishop by the Sacred Congregation, to whom the Holy Father had committed the matter. It reads as follows:

ORDINARIO:

Presbyter Petrus Paulus N., hujus Culmensis Diœcesis, in quem ejus episcopus nuper defunctus aliquibus pœnis animadverterat, ad Apostolicam Sedem confugit, ut apud eam appellationem contra ordinarii sui decreta prosequeretur. Re ex SSmi. D. N. mandato, ad Sacram Congregationem Episcoporum et Regularium delata, eadem S. C. controversiam componere curavit, ne ex una parte Ordinarii auctoritas in discrimen et ex alia *orator in des-*

perationem adduceretur, præsertim cum ipse omni spe destitutus victum non sine sacri caracteris dedecore quasi mendicare cogeretur. Cum igitur ipse, monitis ei datis obtemperans, appellationi apud S. Sedem interpositæ renunciaverit, prout ex adnexa copia apparet, ea spe fretus, ut ab ordinario recipiatur, sibique aliquod munus conferatur, ex quo proventus ad vitam necessarios habeat, eadem S. Congregatio præfatum presbyterum ad te remittit, illum charitati tuæ enixe commendans, ut benigne excipias ac de congrua sustentatione provideatur, quo fiet, ut diuturnæ controversiæ ex qua gravia poterant scandala oriri, finis imponatur. Hæc tibi significanda erant, cui interea fausta omnia adprecor a Domino." Romæ, die 13 Aug., 1857.

It seems that the clergyman of whom there is question in the above, was ordained without a Title, as the ANALECTA gives the case in the Index under the heading of "Priests ordained without a Title." This Declaration of Rome therefore is another proof of what I have already said, that it is not the Title itself, but the sacerdotal character, which in the mind of the Church, requires "congrua sustentatio," the Title simply showing the source whence it must come.

In the following letter written by Cardinal Cadolini in 1845 to the Sacred Congregation, is clearly manifested the spirit of Rome and of her bishops towards clergymen, which is to protect them and to care for them and not to abandon them to ruin and desolation.

" To recall some ecclesiastics of my diocese to a sense of their duty, and to put an end to talk and scandal, the duty of my pastoral charge frequently obliges me to punish them for their correction, and sometimes the offence requires a formal trial.

"Not having any special place of confinement for ecclesiastics, nor a place that would serve the purpose, my predecessors sent delinquents and those against whom charges were made, to religious communities for the purpose of amendment, or to await there the judicial proceedings necessary to clear up the accusations brought against them. Indeed, to cite but one example, my immediate predecessor, Cardinal della Gonza, in 1840 sent to the convent of the Capuchins at Ferrara, Rev. Antony N., who remained there more than two years to atone for his fault. *I myself have done the same in three cases, and have sent some priests for correction to the convent of the Capuchins, or to the Priests of the Mission, and even to the convent of the Barefooted Augustinians.*

"These communities now inform me that they have received orders from their Superiors not to receive such priests henceforth, and for this reason excuse themselves for not being able to grant my just desire. What shall I do in so afflicting a situation? Must I transfer such ecclesiastics to the public prisons, to the great dishonor of the sacerdotal character? To avoid this painful extremity I earnestly pray your Eminence to induce the Sacred Congregation to kindly order that the Rev. Capuchin Fathers of Ferrara would henceforth receive into their convent, as it is one of the most rigorous observance, and most convenient, the ecclesiastics whom I

shall send there. All expenses will be punctually paid either by the clergymen themselves, *or by myself.*"
"CARD. CADOLINI.
"Ferrara, 23 June, 1845."

To the above letter, the S. C. Ep. et Reg. answered: "Scribatur P. Ministro Generali Capucinorum ad mentem," *i.e.*, let the Father Minister General of the Capuchins be written to on the subject, to the effect that the Capuchin Fathers of Ferrara accede to the just request of Cardinal Cadolini. (Rome, 8 Aug., 1845.)

This method of acting—so full of true charity and mercy, blended at the same time with justice—indicated in the above letter of Cardinal Cadolini, who in this only imitated, as he says, his predecessors, sufficiently shows the spirit and practice of Rome towards clergymen. We see therein exhibited the paternal solicitude of a true, Christian bishop. Does the Cardinal think for a moment of abandoning those of his clergy who failed in their duty; or of refusing them the means of subsistence which would force them to become mendicants? From the tenor of his letter, we infer that such a thought never for a moment entered his mind. He knew too well the laws and spirit of the Church, to burden his conscience with such a sin. And when the Capuchin Fathers, at the bidding of their superiors, declined to receive delinquent clergymen into their house, he earnestly begs the Sacred Congregation to write to them, and to prevail upon them to accede to his just and merciful desire.

Such is the spirit, such the practice of Rome in her treatment of the clergy. In fact, a well authenticated case of the abandonment by Rome of any priest not contumacious, is not on record. Nor, indeed, have I ever heard of its being done in any country in the world, ours only excepted. In other countries where the laws of the Church are observed, no one ever hears of a priest roaming through the country without a home or a refuge. An asylum of some kind is afforded him, a pillow upon which to lay his head, a bite to eat, and if he is without censure, an altar at which he can feed and strengthen his soul with the Bread of life. It is only in the United States that a priest is often made homeless and penniless, and for whom the words of the Psalmist have neither joy nor significance, " Introibo ad altare Dei, ad Deum Qui lætificat juventutem meam," though he may be a true penitent, and in God's holy grace.

The spirit of Rome, that no priest should be deprived of an honest subsistence, is seen moreover from the following Decisions of Roman Congregations, concerning the secularization of Religious. I extract them from the ANALECTA JURIS PONTIFICII, 17th series, A. D. 1878.

To priests of Religious Orders, applying to Rome to be secularized, an indispensable condition is, the securing by them of a bishop, as we infer from the answer of Rome to a Capuchin priest asking to be secularized: " Inveniat episcopum benevolum receptorem, et dein providebitur." Romæ, 19 June, 1853.

Upon the same clergyman applying a second time for secularization, he received the same answer, and was again informed that a necessary condition for secularization was first to find a bishop who would receive him.

This shows clearly that Rome *never permits any priest to be cut off from his legitimate superior, until he has placed himself under another.* The same principle is embodied in Decree 122 of the II. Plenary Council of Baltimore.

A case very similar to the above is mentioned (ibid. Col. 443), that of Ambrose Arnon, who had obtained an indult of perpetual secularization, but which could not be executed, because he had no patrimony, or means of subsistence. The very Rev. General of the Carthusians, however, having taken upon himself the obligation of furnishing him every year with stipends for masses to the amount of 360 francs, besides a title to 100 francs annually, the Sacred Congregation of Bishops and Regulars authorized the bishop of Frani to execute the indult of secularization, as the clause, "dummodo provisus sit" was deemed sufficiently complied with, by the obligation assumed by the very Rev. General of the Carthusians.

In Col. 717 we find the following Decree of the S. C. Ep. et Reg.:

"The long and deplorable difficulty between a Barnabite priest and his superiors, renders it necessary that he should be secularized. This is granted " in forma gratiosa," *i. e.*, without commission, he being only required to present it to the Ordinary with his Title of Patrimony. At the same time, the Ordinary is authorized to absolve him, even through a delegate, from all censures and ecclesiastical penalties, to relieve him of any irregularity he may have incurred, as well as to diminish the amount required for his patrimony." Romæ, 8 Jul., 1848.

Again, the same S. Congregation writes to a superior as follows:

"Although the S. C. Ep. et Reg. rarely permits a religious to lay aside his habit and reside outside of his convent, before securing an Ordinary willing to receive him, nevertheless, considering the peculiar circumstances in the case of Father Antonio Armano, the S. Congregation authorizes you to permit this religious to lay aside his habit and leave his convent, to the end that he may procure a patrimony, and the execution of the indult of secularization granted to him the 7th of May last. If in this he does not succeed within six months, *he is obliged to return to the cloister, under the penalties decreed against apostates, and* HIS ORDER CANNOT REFUSE TO RECEIVE HIM." Rome, 23 Jun., 1841.

These Decisions are irrefragable proofs that Rome wishes no priest to be cut loose from his lawful superior, and thus left without the means of subsistence. We have a confirmation of this in the "Instructio" *de Tit. Ord.*, where we read: "Quod si amisso titulo generatim, aut etiam titulo missionis, alter ei non substituatur, sacerdos haud propterea remanet suspensus, sed Ordinarii tenentur compellere ad alterius tituli subrogationem, prout sacris canonibus consultum est." Such, too, is the end and aim of N. 122, of the II. Plenary Council of Baltimore : "Nullum harum Provinciarum sacerdotem dimittendum, nisi certo constet eum ab alio episcopo recipiendum." Alas, and alas! the day of judgment alone will reveal the amount of sin and misery caused by the violation of this wholesome, and merciful, and orderly spirit of the

Catholic Church by many ecclesiastical superiors in the United States, both secular and regular!

What I have said in this chapter of the spirit of Rome receives a signal confirmation from the noble conduct of Leo XIII. towards the erring but penitent Mgr. Kupelian, who had been the Schismatic Patriarch of Constantinople. For the honor of our beloved Holy Father, who by this generous act has gained still more in the affections of his children,—for it places him before them in that beautiful and lovely character of the "Good Shepherd,"—as well as for the confirmation of all I have said in the preceding chapters, I give entire the touching narrative of this grand act of mercy, nobility of soul and Christian forgiveness of the venerated Head of Christendom, as taken from the N. Y. Freeman's Journal of May 10, 1879.

RETRACTION OF MGR. JEAN KUPELIAN,
Late Patriarch of the Neo-Schismatic Armenians.

On April 18th, His Holiness, Pope Leo XIII., surrounded by a number of Cardinals belonging to the Congregation of the Propaganda for Affairs of the Oriental Rite, deigned to admit into his august presence Mgr. Kupelian, who, in a loud voice and in the presence of all, read the following letter of retractation, which he had addressed to the Holy Father immediately on his arrival in Rome:

"MOST HOLY FATHER: I am one of your Holiness' stray sheep, who, becoming disobedient and disregarding the warnings and censures of the Apostolic See, wandered away from the bosom of our holy Mother, the

Catholic Church; who adhered to the new Armenian Schism of Constantinople, and who dared to receive, contrary to the laws of the Roman Catholic Church, the episcopal order and the title of Catholic Patriarch. To-day, with contrite heart, coming in person to the feet of your Holiness, I humbly beseech of your paternal clemency, pardon for all my offences and errors.

"Most Holy Father, desiring to repair all the injury and scandals caused by my illegitimate Patriarchate, before leaving Constantinople, I officially tendered my resignation of it to the Sublime Porte from which I had received it. I acknowledged my grave offences, de-claring before the same Sublime Porte the innocence of His Most Rev. Excellency, Anthony Peter IX., the lawful Patriarch, and proclaiming his sacred rights and those of the Holy See.

"And now, in compliance with the oath taken at my ordination, I renew my vow of obedience to the Apostol-ic See, and I sincerely profess this doctrine of the Roman Catholic Church taught me from my earliest infancy, that the Roman Pontiff is the successor of the Apostle St. Peter, the Vicar of Jesus Christ, the Head of the Univer-sal Church by divine right, and that he has, in matters of faith, as well as in morals and discipline, the immediate authority received from Jesus Christ to teach, to feed, to rule and govern the whole Church, in general and speci-ally, and each nation and each individual, whether of the Eastern or Western Rite.

"In here renewing, Most Holy Father, the foregoing profession, I humbly implore your Holiness to receive me again into the bosom of the Holy Catholic Church, after having absolved me from all the censures and irregularities I have incurred. With this object I sincerely retract all I have said, written, and done against the Holy Roman Apostolic See. I pray your Holiness to give me permission to retire for a few days in holy exercises and in penance for the grave scandals and unlawful acts I have been guilty of.

"For this favor I will always continue to be a grateful servant and a most faithful child of your Holiness. I call upon Almighty God, and the divine and apostolic authority of your Holiness, to witness the sincerity of the sentiments I have given utterance to.

"In the confidence of obtaining at the earliest moment from your Holiness' paternal clemency the favor asked for, I prostrate myself with sentiments of distinguished respect, of sincere gratitude and of profound veneration to kiss your sacred foot, and to implore your Apostolic Benediction. Your Holiness, etc."

THE POPE'S REPLY.

The Holy Father, after permitting Mgr. Kupelian to kiss his hand and foot, and receiving him with the greatest kindness, addressed him as follows:

"It is sweet and consoling to a father to embrace, to press to his heart a son he thought to have been lost; it is a great joy to a shepherd to see his long strayed sheep returning repentant to the fold he had forsaken.

"It is this joy, this consolation, that fills our heart today, on seeing you, beloved and long expected son, returning to the pale of the Catholic Church, and removing from among the Armenian Catholics the seeds of a most fatal division.

"And this holy joy is all the greater and more keenly felt because we have every reason to believe in the sincerity and constancy of your conversion. We find evidence of it in the courage and firmness with which you have undertaken and carried out so holy a resolution. We see assurances of it in the circumstances and good purposes that accompany it; such as the sincere humility which led you to promptly lay down the episcopal insignia, to make a long and fatiguing journey to Rome to make in person and spontaneously a just reparation to the Apostolic See, and which, the better to dispose you to receive the benefits of absolution, has counselled you, first to seek the retirement of holy and spiritual retreat.

"We find assurance, above all, in the noble sentiments of repentance for past errors and the absolute acceptance of Catholic faith you have just made in our presence.

"From the very bottom of our heart we thank God most clement, Who, working efficaciously in you by His grace, has vouchsafed to rejoice our Pontificate by so happy an event. We at the same time thank Him for you, who, through His mercy, have the courage to perform an act so noble and so honorable to your person. *Indeed, to humbly acknowledge one's fault, to confess it, to detest it publicly, and to make honorable amends for it, is assuredly, the most difficult of virtues; and this, according to the infallible judgment of Divine wisdom, instead of humbling and degrading, ennobles and elevates the soul of him who has been able to achieve such a victory. In the face of such a brilliant example, all remembrance of past faults is wiped out, and you, well beloved son, by this act gain imperishable glory before God and man.*

"We, who, although without any merit of our own, represent God here below, remembering the boundless charity of Jesus Christ, Who not only granted pardon to the penitent sinner, but honored him still further by signs of true predilection, cannot withhold from pouring upon you all the clemency of our paternal heart. Still, by the act through which we grant you full and entire pardon, we propose to make of you, of our own spontaneous will, an exception to the general rules of ecclesiastical discipline, by bestowing upon you the titles, the insignia and the honors of episcopal dignity, wrongfully conferred upon your person by some prelates, deserters from Catholic unity.

"Animated by the same spirit of charity and Christian love, we are ready to receive and embrace all those who by a great misfortune live outside of the true Church of Jesus Christ, if they will only return to her with a contrite heart like yours.

"Oh, how dear are the Oriental Churches to us! How much do we admire their ancient splendors! How happy would we be to see them shine out in their pristine grandeur! To this end, in the humility of our heart, we most ardently pray the Prince of Shepherds, that He vouchsafe to cause His divine light to shine upon the minds of so many of His stray children in the East, and inspire them with the noble courage, which, after your example, would lead them to return once more to the only fold of Christ, and to recognize the sovereign authority of the only Supreme Pastor of the whole Church.

"In the meantime, as an earnest of our forgiveness and of the special affection with which we have received you within our pale, we bestow upon you from the bottom of our heart, beloved son, and to all Armenian and Oriental Catholics, the Apostolic Benediction."

Benedictio Dei, etc.

CHAPTER XV.

RECAPITULATION.

As far as the chief end I had in view in writing these pages is concerned, I might now bring them to a close, as I have attained that end, viz.: to prove that it is unlawful and unjust, and contrary to the spirit and letter of the Canon Law of the Church, to dismiss uncanonically from his diocese any clergyman not contumacious, and thus abandoning him to helplessness and to want, place him in a position in which he is in great danger of losing his own soul, of bringing dishonor on the Priesthood, and of inflicting much injury on religion. In proving the uncanonicalness of this proceeding, I have, within a brief space, adduced a superabundance even, of authorities of the greatest weight and importance, from reason itself, justice, charity and humanity, to the voice of the Church made clear and unmistakable through the Decisions of her Sovereign Pontiffs and Sacred Congregations. The dismissing, therefore, uncanonically from his diocese of any clergyman, being wrong and unjust, contrary to the spirit of the Catholic Church, and opposed to her Sacred Canons, it is scarcely possible to imagine how the evil can continue to exist.

Before I speak of how a clergyman who may have lapsed from the path of rectitude should be treated, which is but the complement of the preceding chapters, it will not be out of place to make a brief recapitulation of the authorities I have cited, and which prove beyond a shadow of doubt, and leave no room for cavil, that it is a grave de-ordination and a monstrous evil, to abandon altogether him upon whose soul is impressed the sacred and august character of the Priesthood of Jesus Christ, though he should have grievously and even repeatedly erred. as long as he is not a rebel to authority. But there would be little danger of repetition of error, if delinquents were canonically punished, as I shall show hereafter.

In starting out to prove the thesis which I have advocated throughout these pages, I first laid down as a solid foundation the fact that there exists in the Church a wise and comprehensive system of *law*, intended to promote the welfare of her subjects, and regulate their relations with each other. The Catholic Church has ever abhorred absolute and arbitrary power, within her own realm, and moreover, has consistently and persistently opposed it in all Christian rulers. It is owing to her unceasing efforts in the cause of *right* against *might*, it is due to her divine principles of Christian charity for the whole human race, and of impartial justice to all men, upon which her wise and salutary laws are founded, and which is their inspiring and animating motive, that we owe the civilization and liberty which have blessed the earth in modern times. Being the stanch friend, and incorruptible advocate, and fearless champion of law and order, we are not surprised to find, that within the ranks of her own officials and ministers, she never countenances absolute.

much less arbitrary power. Such power she has not entrusted even to her Supreme and Infallible Pontiff, not to speak of her inferior ministers. In the Catholic Church all are subject to law : all are governed by law: none are excepted from its sway.

Having laid down these facts and principles, I then alluded to our anomalous condition of ecclesiastical government, which, no one will deny who is conversant with it, has approached nearer to the absolute or rather to the arbitrary than to any other known form. "Sic volo, sic jubeo, stat pro ratione voluntas," expresses concisely yet truthfully its very nature such as it has been administered so often in the United States. As a missionary country we were necessarily subjected to exceptional legislation, though no exceptional form of ecclesiastical government in any part of the world is lawless, or ever sanctions the exercise of absolute, much less arbitrary power, which is ever and always reprehensible. But no longer can the United States with propriety be considered a missionary country. This is, I think, conceded by all. In consequence, we need a fixed and determined ecclesiastical discipline for the government of the Church in these States, especially in all that regards the relations of the clergy with their bishops.

Among the many evils resulting from our anomalous condition of ecclesiastical government, not the least is that of dismissing clergymen uncanonically from their dioceses, and thus abandoning them as a rule to poverty and want, exposing them to spiritual, temporal and eternal ruin, besides bringing opprobrium on the Church.

The magnitude of this evil and of others that follow in its train I touched upon. They are all briefly summed up by St. Pius V., in these words: "Ut per sæculum vagantes (sacerdotes), vel mendicare, vel sordidum quæstum exercere, non sine ipsorum dedecore, et ordinis vilipendio, et quamplurimorum Christifidelium scandalo." Bulla *Rom. Pon.*, 1568.

I then proved that it is unlawful and uncanonical to abandon any clergyman not contumacious, by authorities of such weight and moment, that I do not think there is a bishop or priest in the world, who will, or can deny it.

1. *No Law of the Church, no Statute or Decree of Council, no Bull, Brief, or Encyclical of Pontiff, no Decision of Rome or of her Sacred Congregations, no Principle of Morals,*—and, with the exception of Bouvier, from whose theology this should have been expurgated as were so many other inaccuracies and even errors, *no teaching of Theologian, Canonist or Sacred Writer can be adduced to justify it. It is a pure, simple, unadulterated act of arbitrary power, and, therefore, most unjustifiable and most reprehensible.*

2. I showed the magnitude of this evil of helplessly dismissing from his diocese any clergyman not contumacious, from the untold miseries it inflicts on the individual thus dismissed. Looking at it in this light, humanity alone, apart from any other consideration, condemns it. I exposed the magnitude of this evil from the injury it inflicts on the Church and on the Christian Priesthood. For this religion reprobates it.

3. I cited the authority of the Council of Trent, Sess. xiii., C. 1 *de Refor.*, which utterly condemns it, and the au-

thority of the Second Plenary Council of Baltimore, which positively forbids it: "Censent Patres nullum harum Provinciarum sacerdotem a proprio episcopo dimittendum, nisi certo conset eum ab alio episcopo recipiendum."

4. I proved that Charity and Justice both forbid it. Charity imposes an obligation *sub gravi* upon every bishop of succoring his subject, even at the risk of his life, who is placed in grave spiritual and temporal necessity. *A fortiori* does Charity forbid a bishop to actually place his subject in grave spiritual and temporal necessity, which he undoubtedly does when he abandons him altogether, and helplessly dismisses him from his diocese.

"Episcopus tenetur, etiam cum magno suo damno temporali, procurare magnam utilitatem spiritualem subditi." Suarez.

"Si proximus sit in gravi necessitate, sive spirituali, sive temporali, nemo ei *per se* tenetur succurere cum gravi incommodo," sed, "teneretur etiam cum periculo vitæ, qui ad id obligaretur vel ratione officii, ut animarum pastores." Konings, N. 279.

Now he is in extreme or grave necessity, who "nisi adjuvetur ab alio difficillime effugere valet periculum animæ, vel vitæ corporis, alteriusve gravis mali." Ib., N. 278. That a priest, uncanonically dismissed from his diocese, and abandoned altogether by his bishop, is, as a rule, placed in such grave necessity, both spiritual and temporal, no one I think can or will deny.

Justice forbids it on several counts, of which it is sufficient here to recall two: 1. The violation of Decree N.

122 of the II. Plenary Council of Baltimore. 2. The disregarding a priest's right to "congrua sustentatio," which his Title of Ordination gives him.

5. I clearly proved that the Church abhors that any clergyman in Sacred Orders should be reduced to the condition of a beggar, or be obliged to have recourse to secular employments to make a living. For proof of this I needed only to quote her own words: "Cum indecorum omnino sit atque a clericorum qui Sacris Ordinibus constituuntur dignitate prorsus alienum, aut mendicatis subsidiis, aut ex sordido quæstu, ea quæ ad victum necessaria sunt sibi comparare cogantur." Instr. *de Tit. Ord.*

Now, to dismiss a priest uncanonically from his diocese, is to oblige him, as a rule, to disregard this injunction of the Church; for as the natural law forbids him to commit suicide by starvation, he has no other alternative but to act in opposition to her commands, either by begging, or engaging in some secular pursuit to make a living.

6. I proved from the Council of Trent, Sess. xxii., C. 11 *de Refor.*, and from the "Instructio" of the S. C. de P. F. *de Tit. Ord.*, that the Title of Ordination gives a strict right to an honest subsistence, and therefore, that a bishop is not justified—in fact, sins against justice—in disregarding this right, by uncanonically dismissing any clergyman from his diocese and abandoning him to public charity.

7. I then dwelt on the reasons which of themselves were calculated to strengthen the preceding arguments which went to show that the Church has provided, by means of the Title of Ordination, for the honorable support during life of her Ministers in Sacred Orders.

These reasons are: 1. Gratitude and justice on the part of the Church towards her ministers, who voluntarily made such great sacrifices for her sake. 2. Prudence, to cut off from them every danger, temptation, and occasion of avarice. 3. The honor, respect, and veneration the Church has for the priestly character and dignity.

8. I then demonstrated by unexceptionable and incontrovertible proofs from authority, that even an erring priest, not contumacious, has a right to receive an honest subsistence, if he has not the means of supporting himself. All these authorities prove likewise, as a necessary consequence, that a bishop cannot lawfully rob him of this right, or in other words uncanonically dismiss him from his diocese and abandon him to want and poverty. These authorities, which I gave at length, may be summed up as follows:

The ANALECTA JURIS PONTIFICII, 9th series, ROME, 1867, calls the teaching of those few who, with Bouvier,—whom the II. Plenary Council of Baltimore seems to have followed,—contend that an unworthy priest has no right to receive the means of subsistence, and consequently, that he may be helplessly dismissed from his diocese, and abandoned to his own resources,—this eminent authority denominates such teaching "A SENSELESS AND HORRIBLE PRINCIPLE."

"The Holy Canons assimilate the denial to a priest of his alimentary pension TO THE PAIN OF DEATH. A parish priest SHOULD NOT BE DEPRIVED OF HIS ALIMENTARY PENSION, ALTHOUGH HE BE DEPOSED EVEN FOR GREAT CRIMES. Without doubt he has no right to receive a pension from his parish, BUT HIS RIGHT TO AN ALIMENTARY PENSION REMAINS INTACT. THE CHURCH NEVER ABANDONS THE MEMBERS OF THE CLERGY TO MENDICANCY."

A Sacred Congregation, 20 Dec., 1675, decreed a pension in favor of a clergyman convicted of a serious crime: " Episcopus procuret assignamentum pro congrua parochi et habito."

A Decree of July, 1714, confirming the sentence of deposition against a clergyman, speaks thus: " But they (the most Eminent Cardinals) are unanimously of the opinion, that your lordship is absolutely obliged to furnish the means of subsistence to this priest in want, so that he may be able to live in a manner becoming the priestly character, and that he may not be obliged to beg."

A Sacred Congregation, A. D. 1717, informs a dignitary of his duty to pay the alimentary pension of a certain clergyman, "even though his offence deserved no compassion whatever."

The ANALECTA JURIS PONTIFICII, same series, speaking of priests ordained without a Title, says: " If the parish priest, deserving to be divested of his Title of Ordination, HAS NEVERTHELESS A RIGHT TO HIS SUBSISTENCE, with much more reason has the clergyman whom the bishop ordains without a Title: *All canonists agree that the bishop contracts for himself and his successors in office, the obligation of providing for such a clergyman from the revenues of the bishopric. The obligation of furnishing the means of subsistence is* STRICTER WHEN THERE IS QUESTION OF SUSPENSION EX INFORMATA CONSCIENTIA." Have not all the suspensions heretofore in the United States been *ex informata conscientia?*

The Council of Bordeaux, held A. D. 1624, has the following Decree:

"Regulares promoti ad ordines, si quando ab hujusmodi superioribus pro criminis exigentia puniri conveniat, et urgeat necessitas, non possunt tamen habitu religionis privari, ita ut extra monasteria in contemptum ecclesiæ dejiciantur mendicaturi, sed *intra* eorundem monasteriorum septa, detineri, puniri et sustentari, et ad illud prædicti superiores per Ordinarios compellantur."

Sixtus V. made the following regulation with regard to Jesuits expelled from their Order:

"Quoad Jesuitas, cum post sacerdotium exire non possint, nisi a superioribus dejiciantur, provideatur illis de reditu quadraginta aureorum nummorum ex bonis religionis." Pyrrh. Corrad. *l.* 4. *de Disp. Apos., c.* 7., *n.* 37 *and* 38.

The following provision was made in favor of a clergyman who had committed a most grievous crime, for which he was punished and banished: "Beatissimus Pater (Pius VI.)... secum animo pervolutans, quid fieri oporteret... Michælem Philippum (sacerdotem), ab exercitio muneris parochialis perpetuo arcendum esse voluit, neque aliter dispensandum quam ut pro nunc extra diœcesim sacrum peragere illi permittatur. Verum..... cum rigore justitiæ temperandam esse pietatem ratus, illius egestati satis consulere existimavit, si ex parochiæ fructibus, sexaginta ducati argentei, eidem in singulos annos rependantur." Romæ 18 Kal., Jan., 1776.

In the Thesaurus Resol., tom. 69, p. 79, is related a case where a Sacred Congregation decided in favor of a priest who had been suspended *a divinis et ab officio*, that he should receive the means of subsistence: "Ex reditibus parœciæ sin minus prout de jure."

The Sacred Congregation of the Council, 12 Aug., 1865, settled as follows the case of a clergyman who had erred very grievously: "Peractis per decem dies spiritualibus exercitiis in aliqua domo religiosa ab episcopo designanda, esse locum absolutionis a censuris et dispensationis ab irregularitate," and that he might not suffer want the same Sacred Congregation likewise decreed a pension in his favor: "Assignata favore sacerdotis, donec aliter de beneficio ecclesiastico provideatur, pensione libellorum 400."

St. Liguori, Suarez, Billuart and others teach, that an erring priest, not contumacious, and unable to support himself, has a right to receive the means of subsistence. "An suspensus a beneficio, si sit pauper, possit fructus sibi retinere? Resp. Affirmative. Ita Suarez et alii." St. Liguori.

"Suspensus totaliter a beneficio non potest gerere ejus administrationem, nec percipere ullos fructus, sive quotidianos, sive principales, nisi in quantum sint necessaria ad victum." Billuart.

"Si clericus totaliter suspendatur a beneficio, ... et aliunde non habeat unde se sustineat, et suspendatur ad annum, aut aliud tempus definitum, tunc ei debet sufficiens assignari sustentatio." Daelman.

"Juxta multos, suspensus, saltem in pœnam delicti

commissi, et non ob contumaciam, potest sibi de fructibus retinere ad vivendum, si pauper sit." Vernier.

The Holy and Œcumenical Council of Chalcedon, held A. D. 451, made provision for several bishops who for crime had been deposed from their Sees. See Con. Chal., *par.* 2, *act* 10 *in fin.*, *and act* 14.

The following words of the immortal St. Gregory the Great bear directly on the point of helplessly dismissing a priest from his diocese and abandoning him to poverty and want: " Postquam in Agathonem quondam episcopum, juxta qualitatem excessuum districtione canonica est vindicatum ; necesse est, humanitatis intuitu, quemadmodum sustentari possit disponere. Propterea, paternitas tua ad Liparitanam Ecclesiam, in qua supradictus Agatho sacerdotis gessit officium, festinet dirigere, eique ad præsens exinde quinquaginta solidos, qui in ejus possint proficere victum transmittas ; NAM NIMIS EST IMPIUM, SI ALIMENTORUM NECESSITATI POST VINDICTUM SUBJACEAT."

Rome, in our own day, most earnestly recommended all the prelates of the United States to protect and make some provision for the sustenance of priests " qui sunt vel fuerunt indigni," as can be seen from the explicit answer of the Sacred Congregation of the Propaganda to the merciful *Postulatum* of the sainted and much lamented bishop of Ft. Wayne, Rt. Rev. J. H. Luers, D. D.: " Placuit ipsis (EE. PP. Cardinalibus), ut PER HANC EPISTOLAM INSTITUTIO PRO SACERDOTIBUS PAUPERIBUS SUSTENTANDIS AMPLITUDINI TUÆ CŒTERISQUE EPISCOPIS COMMENDARETUR."

Finally, I adduced the example of our Most Holy and venerated Father Leo XIII., who has proved himself in the eyes of all nations to be the Good Pastor. How benign, compassionate, and merciful was not his conduct towards the penitent Mgr. Kupelian, a schismatic Patriarch of the East! He had scandalized a nation, I might even say the whole Catholic world. He had erred most grievously. And yet when he came, an humble penitent, to the feet of the Holy Father, did he refuse to see him? Did he close his doors against him? Did he reproach him with bitterness for his unworthy conduct and send him forth to expiate it as an outcast and a wanderer on the face of the earth? Ah, no. No true bishop, no true pastor, no father would treat a penitent child thus, and our revered and beloved Holy Father, Leo XIII., is all these. He receives with open arms the penitent bishop, he treats him with all the heartfelt demonstrations of joy, with all the clemency, paternal affection and spirit of forgiveness of his prototype of the Gospel, the father of the Prodigal, and sends him back to his country with his Apostolic blessing, to edify in the future by his exemplary life those whom, in the past, he had scandalized by his bad conduct.

No more beautiful or illustrious example than this have I recorded in these pages, of the spirit and practice of Rome, and of the Catholic Church. In the face of it, how any bishop can spurn from his feet his poor, penitent priest, mercilessly close his doors against him, and abandon him to helpless misery, to poverty and want, to insult, humiliation and infamy, to spiritual, temporal and—

as much as in him lies—to eternal ruin, is something which I cannot understand. And yet this has been done, times without number, in these United States. It is in sad contrast with the spirit and practice of Rome, which I have illustrated by many authentic examples, of which that of the now venerated Head of the Church, Leo XIII., is not the least striking.

Having proved that no clergyman can be uncanonically dismissed from his diocese and abandoned by his bishop, I will now proceed to show how he ought be treated. The general and common law of the Church is, that every clergyman accused of any fault must be canonically tried and canonically punished if found guilty. Naturally, therefore, the next chapters, as the complement of the preceding, will treat of Canonical Procedure.

CHAPTER XVI.

DOCUMENTS PERTAINING TO CANONICAL TRIALS.

The general and common law of the Church rigorously requires that a clergyman accused of any crime be canonically tried by a canonically constituted ecclesiastical court.

The decree of Innocent III., to which the Fathers of the Council of Trent refer in Sess. xxiv., C. 5 *de Refor.*, which they there formally and explicitly sanction, and the observance of which they enjoined upon all, is found in *Lib.* 5. *Decret. tit.* I. *de accus. et denunt.*, *C.* 24, and is as follows:

" Qualiter et quando debeat prælatus procedere ad inquirendum et puniendum subditorum excessus, ex auctoritate novi et veteris testamenti colligitur evidenter, ex quibus postea processerunt canonicæ sanctiones, sicut olim aperte distinximus, et nunc sacri approbatione Concilii confirmamus. Legitur enim in Evangelio, quod villicus ille, qui diffamatus erat apud dominum suum quasi dissipasset bona ipsius, audivit ab illo: Quid hoc audio de te? Redde rationem villicationis tuæ; jam enim non poteris villicare. Et in Genesi Dominus ait: Descendam, et videbo, utrum clamorem, qui venit ad me opere compleverint. Ex quibus auctoritatibus manifeste comprobatur, quod non solum cum subditus, verum etiam cum prælatus excedit, si per clamorem et famam ad aures superioris pervenerit, *non quidem a malevolis et maledicis*, sed a providis et honestis; nec *semel* tantum, sed *sæpe* (quod clamor innuit, et diffamatio manifestat), debet coram Ecclesiæ senioribus veritatem diligentius perscrutari: ut, si rei poposcerit qualitas, canonica districtio culpam feriat delinquentis, non tanquam sit auctor et judex, sed quasi deferente fama, vel denuntiante clamore, officii sui debitum exequatur. Licet autem hoc sit observandum in subditis, diligentius tamen observandum est in prælatis, qui quasi signum sint positi ad sagittam. Et quia non possunt omnibus complacere, cum ex officio teneantur non solum arguere sed etiam increpare; quin etiam interdum suspendere, nonnunquam vero ligare, frequenter odium multorum incurrunt, et insidias patiuntur: ideo sancti patres provide statuerunt, ut accusatio prælatorum non facile admittatur, ne concussis columnis, corruat ædificium; nisi diligens adhibeatur cautela, per quam non solum falsæ, sed etiam malignæ criminationi janua præcludatur. Verum ita voluerunt providere prælatis, ne criminarentur injuste, ut tamen caverent, ne delinquerent insolenter, contra morbum utrumque invenientes congruam medicinam; videlicet, ut criminalis accusatio, quæ ad diminutionem capitis (id est, degradationem) intenditur, nisi legitima præcedat inscriptio, nullatenus admittatur. Sed cum super excessibus suis quisquam fuerit infamatus, ita ut jam clamor ascendat, qui diutius sine scandalo dissimulari non possit, vel sine periculo tolerari, *absque dubitationis scrupulo, ad inquirendum et puniendum ejus excessus, non ex odii fomite, sed charitatis procedatur affectu*, quatenus si fuerit gravis excessus, *etsi non degradetur ab ordine*, ab administratione tamen amoveatur omnino: quod est secundum Evangelicam sententiam, a villicatione villicum amoveri, qui non potest villicationis suæ dignam reddere rationem. DEBET IGITUR ESSE PRÆSENS IS CONTRA QUEM FACIENDA EST INQUISITIO, NISI SE PER CONTUMACIAM ABSENTAVERIT: ET EXPONENDA SUNT EI ILLA CAPITA, DE QUIBUS FUERIT INQUIRENDUM, UT FACULTATEM HABEAT DEFENDENDI SE IPSUM. ET NON SOLUM DICTA, SED NOMINA IPSA TESTIUM SUNT EI, UT QUID, ET A QUO SIT DICTUM APPAREAT, PUBLICANDA: NEC NON EXCEPTIONES ET REPLICATIONES LEGITIMÆ ADMITTENDÆ, NE PER SUPPRESSIONEM NOMINUM, INFAMANDI, PER EXCEPTIONUM VERO EXCLUSIONEM DEPONENDI FALSUM, AUDACIA PRÆBEATUR. Ad *corrigendos* itaque subditorum excessus, tanto diligentius debet prælatus assurgere, quanto damnabilius eorum offensas deserere incorrectas: contra quos, ut de nostris excessibus taceatur, etsi tribus modis possit procedi, per accusationem videlicet, denunciationem et inquisitionem eorum, ut tamen in omnibus diligens adhibeatur cautela, ne forte per leve compendium ad grave dispendium veniatur; sicut ACCUSATIONEM LEGITIMA PRÆCEDERE DEBET INSCRIPTIO, SIC ET DENUNCIATIONEM CHARITATIVA ADMONITIO, ET INQUISITIONEM CLAMOSA INSINUATIO PRÆVENIRE: ILLO SEMPER ADHIBITO MODERAMINE, UT JUXTA FORMAM JUDICII, SENTENTIÆ QUOQUE FORMA DICTETUR. Hunc tamen ordinem circa regulares personas non credimus usquequaque servandum, quæ, cum causa requirit, facilius et liberius a suis possunt administrationibus amoveri."

I thought it proper to give the above Decree of Innocent III. in full, because it is not only a venerable Document in itself, full of information and instruction on the manner of conducting canonical investigations, but also, because it shows the spirit of impartial justice that animates the mind and heart of the Church, and because, moreover, it is the model and foundation of all canonical procedure.

The Council of Trent positively and explicitly confirmed the above Decree of Innocent III. See Sess. xxiv., C. 5 *de Refor.* Having in the chapter just indicated, made a special enactment for the trial of " causæ criminales graviores contra episcopos," they take occasion of this exceptional legislation to promulgate anew the Constitution of Innocent III. above given : " Constitutio sub Innocentio III. in Concilio Generali, quæ incipit *Qualiter et quando*, quam sancta synodus in præsenti innovat, AB OMNIBUS OBSERVETUR."

The Council of Trent, besides approving and promulgating anew the Decree *Qualiter et quando* of Innocent III., enacted the following, which will also throw light upon ecclesiastical trials, and show·their importance and the spirit with which they should be conducted:

" Quoniam, ob malitiosam petentium suggestionem, et quandoque ob locorum longinquitatem, personarum notitia, quibus causæ mandantur, usque adeo haberi non potest ; hincque interdum judicibus non undequaque idoneis, causæ in partibus delegantur: statuit sancta synodus, in singulis consiliis provincialibus, aut diœcesanis, aliquot personas, quæ qualitates habeant, juxta Constitutionem Bonifacii VIII., quæ incipit *Statutum*, et alioquin ad id aptas designari, ut, præter ordinarios locorum, iis etiam posthac causæ ecclesiasticæ, ac spirituales, et ad Forum Ecclesiasticum pertinentes, in partibus delegandæ committantur. Et, si aliquem interim ex designatis mori contigerit, substituat ordinarius loci cum consilio capituli alium in ejus locum usque ad futuram provincialem, aut diœcesanam synodum : ita ut habeat quæque diœcesis quatuor saltem, aut etiam plures probatas personas, ac ut supra qualificatas, quibus hujusmodi causæ a quolibet legato, vel nuntio, atque etiam a Sede Apostolica committantur ; alioquin post designationem factam, quam statim episcopi ad Summum Romanum Pontificem transmittant, delegationes quæcumque aliorum judicum, aliis, quam his factæ, subreptitiæ censeantur. Admonet dehinc sancta synodus tam ordinarios, quam alios quoscumque judices, ut terminandis causis, quanta poterit brevitate, studeant ; et litigatorum artibus, seu in litis contestatione, seu alia parte judicii differenda, modis omnibus, aut termini præfixione aut competenti alia ratione occurrant." Sess. xxv., C. 10 *de Refor.*

As intimated in the above decree of the Council of Trent, the Constitution of Boniface VIII. *Statutum* gives the qualification required in the "Judices Causarum." This Constitution is found in Sexto Decret., *lib.* 1, *lit.* 3 *de Rescrip., c.* xi., and is as follows:

"Statutum, quod circa judices a Sede Apostolica deputandos nuper edidimus, cum quædam contenta in eo, quæ pro communi utilitate credebantur inducta (sicut experientia docuit) tendere dignoscantur ad noxam, sanctione præsenti, quam irrefragabiliter observari mandamus, suadente utilitate, in melius duximus reformandam. Sancimus igitur, ut nullis nisi dignitate præditis, aut personatum obtinentibus, seu ecclesiarum cathedralium canonicis, causæ auctoritate litterarum Sedis Apostolicæ, vel Legatorum ejus, de cetero committantur; nec audiantur alibi quam in civitatibus, vel locis insignibus, ubi possit commode copia peritorum haberi."

To come down now to the present time, Gregory XVI., June 23, 1832, prescribed a form of trial for clergymen, and for other canonical causes, to be observed in all the dioceses of the Pontifical States, which is still in force. This form is perhaps the most perfect that has ever been devised.

The ecclesiastical court instituted by this great Pontiff, Gregory XVI., is composed of five judges; or if it be impossible or impracticable to have this number, of three only. One of the judges is always the bishop, or his vicar-general, who, however, has but one vote. The other four, or two, as the case may be, are chosen not permanently, but for each case by the bishop, who is thus enabled to select judges unobjectionable to the accused. This is a most commendable feature, for an enemy for example of the one who is to be tried, would not, in his case, be a suitable person to sit in judgment over him. A sufficient sign of hostility to disqualify one from sitting as judge in a trial would be, "si signum benevolentiæ. ipsi (accusato) deneget, quod aliis ejusdem conditionis et status hominibus exhibere solet." This fact shows the extreme solicitude of the Church, that no obstacle should be permitted to the rendering by her tribunals of justice, of a fair, just and impartial sentence. There are many other reasons which might justify the accused in excepting to one or more of his judges, as is evident, the chief of which I will give further on. In this, therefore, that in the ecclesiastical tribunal erected by Gregory XVI. the accused can have judges whom he feels will be just to him, does its perfection consist. In every ecclesiastical court, however, the accused has the right of objecting to any of his judges, if he can bring sufficient evidence to prove that he has good reasons for believing that one or more of them is unduly prejudiced against him.

In the Tribunal established by Gregory XVI., the majority always decides. The bishop or vicar-general presiding, has but one vote like the rest. All sentences against clergymen without this form of judicature are null and void.

Finally, the II. Plenary Council of Baltimore framed, or rather adopted and promulgated the following Decree on ecclesiastical trials. It is found marked 77 in the Acta et Decreta:

"Demum, ex eorundem Consultorum numero, si episcopo videatur, selegantur Judices Causarum, qui sacerdotes criminis postulatos in prima instantia, ex episcopi delegatione, judicent; juxta normam quæ in Concilio Provinciali Sancti Ludovici, anno 1855 habito, a Sancta Sede recognitum, præscribebatur, quamque legis esse communis statuunt hujus Plenarii Concilii Patres.

"Sacerdotes quibus per Ordinarii sententiam sacerdotii exercitium interdictum fuerit, nullum jus habent ad sustentationem ab eo petendam, cum ipsi se sua culpa missionibus operam navandi incapaces reddiderint."

This last appendage (if it means that a suspended priest, not contumacious, has no right to an honest subsistence from his diocese, or to the "congrua sustentatio" given to him by the Title of his Ordination, and that, consequently, he may be abandoned to poverty and want and helpless misery) is untenable, as I have proved by the most eminent and unassailable authorities.

Decree N. 77 of the II. Plenary Council of Baltimore then continues:

" Ut autem, omnis causa querelarum tollatur, censent Patres omnino expedire, ut Ordinarii, in causis criminalibus clericorum aut presbyterorum, servent certi judicii formam, quæ ad illam a Concilio Tridentino præscriptam quam proxime accedat; scilicet, ut Episcopus, seu ejus Vicarius Generalis, de ipsius Commissione, duos ejusdem episcopi Consultores, nec semper eosdem eligat, qui ei presbyterum criminis postulatum judicaturo, coram Notario tamen ipsius episcopi assistant. Unum autem sit utriusque votum, possitque alter episcopo accedere. Quod si ambo ab Episcopo, seu ejus Vicario, discordes fuerint, tertium tunc ex prædictis suis Consultoribus ipse eligat, et juxta eam partem, cum qua tertius convenit, causa terminetur. Si autem contigerit omnes Consultores, ab Ordinario electos, ab ejus sententia discedere, tunc ad Metropolitanum causa referri debet, qui sententiarum motiva expendet, et judicium feret. Quando autem quæstio erit de subdito Metropolitani criminis postulato, et omnes Assessores Metropolitani ab ejus sententia dissenserint, tunc appellatio fiat ad seniorem episcopum

CHAPTER XVII.

COMPENDIUM OF IMPORTANT PRINCIPLES AND DECISIONS OF SACRED CONGREGATIONS CONCERNING CANONICAL TRIALS.

The following compendium I compile from a treatise on diocesan officialties, found in the ANALECTA JURIS PONTIFICII, 13th series, 1874. I select only those decisions which I judge to be of more importance, or which may be even of practical utility in determining questions that may arise in judicial, or quasi-judicial investigations. At least, they will be of great interest to my clerical readers.

Moreover, these decisions and principles will be of service in aiding many of the clergy who have not had the time or the opportunity of studying much Canon Law, to understand the various criminal processes, of which I will presently speak. They will also throw light on the proper understanding of the late "Instructio" *Quamvis* of the Sacred Congregation of the Propaganda, regarding the method now to be pursued in the United States, " in definiendis causis criminalibus et disciplinaribus clericorum."

TITLE I.—*Ecclesiastical Judicature.*—The author indicates the proofs of the Judiciary power of the Church, as found in Holy Writ, Tradition, History, etc.

TITLE II.—*Ecclesiastical Offences.*—"The offences an ecclesiastic may commit are either purely ecclesiastical, or purely civil, or mixed.

"The purely ecclesiastical offences are: 1. Occult or public heresy. 2. Schism. 3. Apostasy. 4. Simony. 5. Blasphemy. 6. Personal or Local Sacrilege.

"The purely civil offences are: 1. Homicide. 2. Arson. 3. Theft. 4. Perjury. 5. The Forging or Falsifying of Pontifical Letters. 6. Libel and Slander. 7. Conspiracy, Sedition, or Rebellion against the temporal power.

"The mixed offences are those injurious to religion or the social order, as adultery, etc.

"Clergymen are under the jurisdiction of their diocesan officials for all offences they may commit, even for those purely civil."

TITLE III.—*Canonical Penalties.*—"Ordinaries have the power to proceed extra-judicially, when there is question of inflicting a paternal punishment only, or a light correctional penalty. A canonical trial is rigorously required for grave corrections, and for any public spiritual penalty. This principle of canonical legislation is absolute. Suspension *ex informata conscientia* does not derogate from it, and is no exception to it.

"Ecclesiastical penalties must be communicated by writing. Suspension, interdict and excommunication cannot be inflicted by word of mouth. Decision 5 Sept., 1803.

"A clergyman cannot be condemned to a disgraceful penalty (such as being committed to the *ergastulum*, or confined in a place of penance) without a canonical trial, in which he was legally convicted of his misdeeds. Decision 7 July, 1823.

"An extra-judicial information cannot form a legal

basis for the deposition of a parish priest. Decision 20 June, 1831.

" A regular canonical trial is required for the deposition of an immovable parish priest. Decision 9 May, 1834.

" It is not permitted to inflict an indeterminate and indefinite suspension without a canonical trial, for such suspension would have the same effect as deposition and degradation. Decision 3 Feb., 1852.

" The procedure *ex informata conscientia* cannot be employed to inflict a public suspension for crimes that are not occult. In such cases, it is necessary to have recourse to a canonical trial. Decision Mar., 1858.

" A clergyman who has resided several years in another (not his own) diocese, cannot be dismissed from that diocese without a canonical trial. Decision Mar., 1846."

TITLE IV.—*Essential Rules for Trials.*—" The Natural Law itself prescribes all the essential formalities of trials. These fundamental rules are: that the judge admits the complaint or accusations and hears the defence ; that he grants the necessary time for a thorough investigation of the accusation, and for the examination of all the evidence in favor of, or against the accused, who should be granted every opportunity of defence; that, finally, he deliberates on the case and pronounces sentence.

" The other formalities of a trial are of positive law.

" The essential formalities of Summary Trials (Processus Summarius), according to the Clementine " Dispendiosam," are: 1. The citation and examination of the accused. 2. The copy of the complaint, or petition of the public prosecutor in the trial. 3. The examination of the parties to the trial, and of their witnesses as far as equity requires. 4. The appointing a time to hear the proofs of the prosecution sustaining the charge, and those of the defence, rebutting it. 5. The citation 'ad sententiam.'

" The other formalities in the judicial order for Summary Trials may be employed, if the parties do not object, but they are not rigorously required."

I may add here that whatever is said in the following Principles and Decisions on Appeals (Appellationes) and Exceptions (Recusationes), according to Canon Law, is applicable to the Summary Trial.

TITLE V.—*Juridical Precepts.*—" When there is question of crimes against morality, such as seduction, adultery and other sins, in which those who were wronged lodge a formal complaint, the Ordinary must proceed immediately to an investigation.

" In ordinary cases the discipline of the Church requires that a precept or admonition should precede a canonical trial.

" The precept is either paternal or juridical. The paternal precept is kept secret. It is given directly by the bishop, who can require the delinquent to sign it, so that he cannot afterwards deny having received this correction. The juridical precept is preceded by several warnings which require at least extra-judicial information. Thus, there is the precept *de bene vivendo; de non conversando cum quibusdam, etc.*

" These precepts are sanctioned by penalties incurred

by the simple fact of their violation. To declare and apply these penalties *in foro externo*, a juridical information, citation and defence are requisite.

"He whom the juridical precepts do not induce to enter into himself to the amending of his life, is inexcusable, and deserves to experience the severity of the law."

TITLE VI.—*The Public Prosecutor.*—"He who prosecutes the offence is named in Canon Law 'Promoter Fiscalis,' or Public Prosecutor.

"The clerk or chancellor cannot discharge the functions of the public prosecutor. Decision Apr., 1827."

TITLE VII.—*Summoners.*—"Ordinaries have the power to appoint Summoners for the service of their ecclesiastical courts. Citations are forwarded and sentences are notified through them."

TITLE VIII.—*Examining Judge.*—"The Council of Trent reserves criminal causes to the bishops themselves. The vicar-general, therefore, must receive special faculties from his bishop to institute a criminal information. This power is generally given with the official document constituting him vicar-general.

"A layman cannot hold the office of examining judge, for *Canon Law does not concede jurisdiction to a layman over clergymen, not even should he have been delegated by the bishop.* Decision 30 June, 1832.

"Except for spiritual causes, and criminal matters against clergymen, bishops may make use of the services of lay magistrates. Decision 24 Nov., 1832.

"The examining judge cannot claim indemnity for

travelling expenses, or a change of venue. Decision June, 1701."

TITLE IX.—*The Clerk.*—" Ordinaries have the power of appointing Clerks or Chancellors for their courts. The accused is allowed to take exception to the chancellor, if he fears the latter will be unjust to him. If there is any evidence or presumption that such is the case, the Ordinary must appoint another clerk to write the remaining acts of the information. Decision 2 Aug., 1804."

TITLE X.—*Detention of the Accused before Trial.*—" As a rule the accused retires to a religious house whilst subject to the examination of the official charged with this duty. If he leaves the religious house and does not put in an appearance, the trial is nevertheless continued to the sentence exclusively. Decision 13 Apr., 1818.

" After the lapse of ten years, he who has been condemned for non-appearance, will be no longer permitted to purge himself of contumacy except through a dispensation from Rome. Decision May, 1715.

" They who are cited and do not appear before the judge, are deprived of their subsistence, or alimentary pension. This pension, however, is restored to them with all arrears, as soon as they put in an appearance and are willing to lay aside their contumacious spirit. Decision 29 May, 1761."

TITLE XI.—*The Citation.*—" The citation of the accused to appear, is an essential formality of a canonical trial. If omitted, the proceedings are entirely null and void. Decision 22 Sept., 1741.

" The citation of the accused is an essential part of the

procedure, even when the sentence is declaratory only, which is the case when there is question of censures, or penalties incurred *ipso facto*. Then, the guilty party must be summoned *ad dicendam causam*, etc. He must appear to show any cause which might prevent the declaration *in foro externo*, of the censures incurred *ipso facto*. Decision 22 Sept., 1741.

" The acts of the judicial proceedings, the substance of the offence (corpus delicti), the examinations, etc., must be written in the language of the country where the trial is held. Pius VII., Bulla *Post diuturnas*, A. D. 1800."

TITLE XII.—*Examination of the Accused.*—" The reader may here recall what was said under TITLE X., of the retirement of the accused to a religious house, and the consequences of his leaving the same and not putting in an appearance.

" The examination of the accused is made by the official who is legally charged with it (Juge d' Instruction, or Judge of Information, or Examining Judge), assisted by the clerk or chancellor.

" It is peremptorily forbidden to administer an oath to the accused when under examination in his own case. The oath under such circumstances was abolished in 1725 by a Decree of the Roman Council. The judge must confine himself to a serious admonition to the accused, to tell the truth in the matters upon which he may be interrogated. *Notification*, 24 Apr., 1728.

" An oath, however, may be administered to the accused, when he is called upon as a witness against others. *Notification*, 24 Apr., 1728.

"Every examination in which the accused was obliged to take an oath, when testifying in his own case, is, *ipso jure*, null and void; and the judgment rendered on such evidence is equally null and void."

The following are the words of Benedict XIII., as found in *Tit.* 13, *c.* 2 of a Roman Provincial Council, held A. D. 1725 : " Nec juramentum hujusmodi (nempe de veritate dicenda) nullatenus a reis iisdem (nisi tamen ut testes quoad alios examinentur) in futurum per quoscumque judices et ministros, sub quovis pretextu, causa et quæsito colore, volumus exigatur; alias examen sive constitutum, ac acta omnia nulla sint eo ipso et irrita, omnique caveant contra reos effectu."

I have heard of bishops administering an oath to clergymen accused of crime, which is evidently forbidden by the above Decree ; but does it not likewise forbid clergymen from administering an oath to any of their parishioners, or placing them upon their knees before the Blessed Sacrament, or the Crucifix, and conjuring them to tell the truth, an act which I consider a very solemn oath ?

Although the above enactment of Benedict XIII. was made through a Provincial Council, yet it is so well grounded on reason, propriety and justice, and so unanimously observed in practice, that it has become a part of the *jus commune*, and is regarded as common law by all recent canonists.

"The accused who does not answer the questions of the examining judge, exposes himself to have his silence regarded as an admission of guilt. Decision 6 Sept., 1713.

"A criminal trial must be terminated within two years. If it is not, the accused is then considered re-instated, provided the delay is not imputable to him."

TITLE XIII.—*Witnesses.*—"No one should prevent witnesses from making their depositions before the ecclesiastical judge. The Decretals allow even censures to be employed against such as hinder them from appearing.

"In default of clergymen, lay persons may be witnesses in the criminal causes of ecclesiastics. Decret. Venerabilis *ad tit. de testibus.*

"Each and every witness must sign his deposition Another must sign for those who cannot write. Decision 20 July, 1815."

TITLE XIV.—*Confrontation of the Accused and the Witnesses.*—"In capital causes an ecclesiastical tribunal has the power to grant the personal confrontation of the accused and the witnesses. Constitutio *Post diuturnas.*

"In ordinary trials which do not involve the pain of death, the personal confrontation of the accused and the witnesses is not admitted in ecclesiastical tribunals. The depositions are communicated to the accused, so that he may reply to them. They must be read conformably to the text, and indicate the name of each witness. This is called verbal confrontation, or legitimation of the proceedings.

"This legitimation of the trial is so essential that, without it, the entire proceedings, and the judgment, or sentence based thereon, are entirely null and void, so that all has to be begun *ex integro.* Decision 17 Dec., 1852.

"The right of lawful defence would be violated, if the accused were left in ignorance of the names of the witnesses who deposed against him, and had not the means or the opportunity of taking exception to them, or to their assertions."

TITLE XV.—*Making Known the Result of the Examination.*—" The examination of the accused being finished, and the formality of legitimation having been observed, the proceedings must be made known. A copy of the same transcribed and authenticated by the clerk, must be transmitted to the accused and his lawyers, so that they can prepare for the defence. Decision 27 July, 1759.

"The accused and his lawyers must possess a copy of the examination in its integrity. Decision 15 Mar., 1817.

"All the acts of the canonical procedure are given gratuitously to poor clergymen. Decision Aug., 1721.

"The space of two days *ad probandum* is too short a time for the accused to prepare himself for his defence. Want of sufficient time for this purpose may be enough to annul the proceedings. Decision 20 Aug., 1681."

TITLE XVI.—*Advocate of the Accused.*—" The Holy Canons require that a poor clergyman be defended gratuitously, by advocates designated for that purpose. Every ecclesiastical tribunal, therefore, must appoint a Defender of the poor. Decision 23 May, 1823."

TITLE XVII.—*The Tribunal.*—" An ecclesiastical tribunal with one judge only, exhibits something odious. For this reason Gregory XVI. enacted that in the Pontifical States, the ecclesiastical court should be composed of the Ordinary and four judges. Decision 23 June, 1832.

"The judges of the episcopal court must be clergymen. The judgment passed by them being an act of jurisdiction over the accused, laymen are not allowed to take part in it. Ordinaries cannot call upon lay magistrates to act as judges.

"Although the vicar-general may have made the judicial examination or inquiry, or may have taken part therein, he can nevertheless preside over the episcopal court, and cast his vote with the other judges. Decision 18 June, 1855.

"Two brothers cannot act at the same time as judges in an ecclesiastical court. Decision 12 May, 1852.

"The bishop, or vicar-general who presides at the sitting of the ecclesiastical court, casts his vote, and signs the sentence as the other judges. Even cardinals, presiding over the ecclesiastical courts of their dioceses, do not possess a preponderating vote. Decision 27 Aug., 1852.

"The accused has the right to take exception to the judges of the ecclesiastical court before which he is tried. In case he does, a delay of proceedings is granted, to enable him to give his reasons for the exception before the superior judge of the court. During the vacancy of the episcopal see, the right of deciding upon an exception taken against the vicar-capitular belongs to the chapter."

TITLE XVIII.—*Session of the Court.*—" Though ecclesiastical courts do not hold any formal and public sessions, yet it is rigorously required that the accused be called 'ad sententiam.' He must appear before the court, as well as his lawyers or advocates, who have then the right to speak independently of his pleading, which he has had previously printed and presented to the judges.

" The accused appears, therefore, before the ecclesiastical tribunal accompanied by his lawyers, but the witnesses are not called. If a personal confrontation of the latter and the accused is deemed necessary, it takes place in the presence of the examining judge. Decision 4 Sept., 1834.

" The public prosecutor is present in court and makes his address. The lawyer of the accused has always the right of replying, and the privilege of speaking last.

" The court does not close the debate, and commence to deliberate in view of a verdict, until the lawyer of the accused declares that he has nothing more to say.

" The sentence is determined by a majority of votes. All the judges of the ecclesiastical court must sign it.

"*The sentence is null and void, if it does not state the grounds, jure et de facto, upon which it rests.* The Sacred Congregations alone have the privilege of withholding the motives or grounds of their decisions.

" Bishops have not the power to remit the punishment decreed by an ecclesiastical criminal court. Decision 8 Jan., 1858."

TITLE XIX.—*The Acquittal.*—" The acquittal of the accused is decreed in various ways. 1. Acquittal 'ex quo satis,' which means, that the accused is sufficiently punished by the fact of his trial. 2. When the judges bring a verdict of 'not found guilty.' The clause ' tanquam non repertus culpabilis' is not a declaration of innocence. The accused remains under censure of irregularity, in consequence of the defamation he sustained from the indications and presumptions of guilt, which hardly ever takes place, except in cases of homicide. Decision 11 Sept., 1804. 3. Acquittal 'ex capite innocentiæ,' when the judges fully recognize the innocence of the accused.

" The declaration of innocence involves as a necessary consequence, the suppression of the judicial examination and trial. All documents concerning it must be torn up and burned. Decision 4 Apr., 1775."

TITLE XX.—*Appeals.*—"An appeal must be taken within ten days after notification of sentence. The Sacred Congregation having informed the Ordinary that it admits the appeal, the case must be proceeded with. The bishop and the appellant send their documents to Rome within twenty days after such notification. Circular 22 Feb., 1851.

" The appeal is *suspensiva* when there is question of deposition. The installation of a new canon, or of a new parish priest, before the judgment on appeal is rendered, constitutes contempt of authority. Decision 23 May, 1681.

" In matters regarding morality, the appeal is not *suspensiva*, but *devolutiva*; for the sentence of the Ordinary must be temporarily executed, unless there be question of irreparable acts, as deposition, or consignment to the 'ergastulum.' Decision 20 July, 1742.

" Suspension is *suspensiva*, when the suspension of the lower tribunal does not take effect, or is suspended, until the superior tribunal to which the appeal is taken, renders judgment. It is *devolutiva* when the suspension does take effect pending the decision of the superior tribunal.

"Whenever the condemned appeals, he does not pay the expense of the new trial, unless it is so stated in the appeal."

I may here very properly add the general rules governing appeals. They are:

I. An appeal can be taken from any judge who has passed sentence, except:— 1. From the sentence of the Pope to a General Council, and *a fortiori* to any other tribunal. 2. From the sentence of a General Council legitimately assembled and united to its head. 3. From the sentence of all the College of Cardinals, and from the final sentence of the Roman Court (Rotæ Romanæ). 4. From the sentence of arbitrators, where the parties bind themselves to abide by their decision, but not from the sentence of arbitrators *juris*. In these four cases no appeal can be taken.

II. The judge, from whom the appeal is made, must be notified of the same.

III. Aside from an appeal to the Pope, the appeal must be made from the inferior judge, to his immediate Superior, thus: from the vicar general or bishop to the archbishop, from the latter to the primate, from the primate to the patriarch, and from the patriarch to the Pope. To appeal to a Roman Congregation, is the same as to appeal to the Pope.

IV. Passing by all intermediate tribunals an appeal can be made directly to the Pope.

N. B. 1. If an appeal is taken, the judge yet sitting on

the bench, it can be made *viva voce*, by simply saying
"I appeal." 2. Should it be taken afterwards it must be
made in writing, and within ten days after notification of
sentence.

TITLE XXI.—*Alimentary Pension.*—"A parish priest
appealing to the Holy See against suspension, must
receive an alimentary pension from the revenues of his
parish, until the cause is judged. Decision 13 Feb., 1856.

"When a parish priest has been deposed after a canonical trial, he must receive the means of subsistence, or be granted a pension from his parish. Decision July, 1714.

"A clergyman condemned to retirement in a house of penance must receive an alimentary pension. Decision Apr., 1718.

"A parish priest, condemned to perpetual supension and exile from his diocese for 'homicidium,' must nevertheless receive an alimentary pension. Decision 28 Dec., 1776.

"THE HOLY CANONS LOOK UPON THE DENIAL OF THE ALIMENTARY PENSION" (or in other words, the means of subsistence) "AS A CONDEMNATION TO DEATH. WHENEVER A PARISH PRIEST IS DEPOSED, A PENSION FROM THE REVENUES OF HIS PARISH IS RESERVED."

CHAPTER XVIII.

Ecclesiastical Procedure.—Trial Ex Notorio.

We have only to reflect for a moment to see that the legislation of the Church, granting to clergymen a judicial enquiry into any crime of which they are charged, is but a promulgation of what the Natural Law itself teaches. Independently, therefore, of any positive law, the Natural Law demands that any one accused of crime be given an opportunity of proving himself innocent of the charge, or of showing the existence of circumstances that may extenuate, or lessen his guilt. In a word, the Natural Law gives to every one the right of defending himself, and of not being condemned until he is proved guilty. The Church, therefore, in legislating for ecclesiastical tribunals of justice, has given the sanction of her authority to that which the Natural Law imperatively demands.

In our present state of fallen nature, in which the heart of man is prone to evil, and his mind is more or less clouded by ignorance and biased by human passions, Superiors and subjects being equally liable to err,—a sad inheritance from our first Father Adam, "Ecce enim in iniquitatibus conceptus sum et in peccatis concepit me mater mea,"—it is an absolute necessity that some means should exist, which will effect that the subject, on the one hand, be justly punished when he deserves it, and on the other, that the Superior may be restrained from abusing his power by inflicting punishment on the innocent, or exhibiting undue severity towards the guilty. This thought, as well as the one conveyed in the preceding paragraph, is well expressed by Bouix, *trac. de jud. eccl., par.* 1, *p.* 15, in the following words:

"Ex jure naturali, debet in omni societate completa, judiciorum proprie dictorum institutio induci. Nam, ea est in præsenti naturæ lapsæ statu hominum conditio, ut multæ lites et delicta perpetuo tum in societate ecclesiastica, tum in civilibus præcipue societatibus exoriantur. Necessarii inde multi magistratus qui et delicta coerceant et lites dirimant. *Iterum autem ob prædictam naturæ humanæ ad delinquendum proclivæ conditionem, nisi ordinarie et regulariter dicti magistratus adstringantur in jure dicundo, ad eas formas servandas quæ de substantia judicii sunt, persæpe ex negligentia, errore, aut partium etiam studio, in transversum agentur, et a justitiæ transite aberrabunt. Dictat ergo recta ratio et bonum publicum aperte postulat,* ut *in omni societate completa,* id est, *sive in Ecclesia, sive in qualibet temporali republica, tribunali constituantur;* et judices teneantur conditiones ad proprie dictum judicium necessarias, ordinarie saltem, in facienda justitia observare."

To punish crime, correct disorder, and enforce ecclesiastical discipline, on the one hand, and on the other, to prevent Superiors from acting through impulse, anger, error, hatred, malice, or other unjust motive, ecclesiastical tribunals have been established in the Church. They protect the innocent, and mete out just punishment to the guilty. Every clergyman, charged with crime, or serious infraction of discipline, has a right therefore not only by the positive law of the Church, but by the Natural Law, to a canonical investigation of his offence, or an ecclesiastical trial.

The conditions necessary for a trial properly so called are found in the definition of Ecclesiastical Procedure *in Foro Externo,* or of *Judicium Forense,* given by the same learned author, Bouix: "Judicium Forense est, judicis de jure ab actore contra reum præmissa disceptatione, sententia," a definition with which all canonists agree.

Ecclesiastical Criminal Procedure is divided into: 1. Ordinary, or full Criminal Procedure (Processus Criminalis Ordinarius, seu Plenarius). 2. Extraordinary Criminal Procedure (Processus Criminalis Extraordinarius).

The first of these, or the Ordinary Criminal Process, is threefold: 1. By way of Accusation (per viam Accusationis). 2. By way of Denunciation (per viam Denunciationis). 3. By way of Examination or Inquisition (per viam Inquisitionis).

But as all these ordinary trials are clothed with such a multiplicity of legal formalities and solemnities, and as in the United States, at least, they are impracticable, I have no need to enter into any details concerning them. What is of interest now, and of practical utility for us, will chiefly occupy my attention, and these are the Extraordinary Criminal Proceedings.

Of these latter, the following only I consider of immediate interest, viz.: 1. The trial *Ex Notorio* (Proces-

sus Criminalis Ex Notorio). 2. The Summary Trial
(Processus Summarius). 3. Sentences of suspension *ex
informata conscientia.*

In this chapter I will speak briefly of the first, or of
Procedure *Ex Notorio.* It will at least show the spirit
of strict and impartial justice which exists in the Church,
and the fear she has of punishing even the notoriously
guilty beyond their deserts. In the two following chapters, I will speak respectively of the Summary Trial, and
suspension *ex informata conscientia.*

The importance and necessity attached by the Church to
a canonical trial for clergymen charged with any violation of law, shine forth most clearly from the fact, that
according to canonists, when a crime is notorious,
even then, a clergyman cannot be lawfully condemned,
without formal proceedings against him. Hence the
procedure, or trial *Ex Notorio.*

The procedure *Ex Notorio* can be employed only, when
the offence is notorious *notorietate facti, i. e.,* when there is
no possibility of concealing, or denying it, when at the
same time, the culpability is so evident, that there is no
possibility of excusing, extenuating, or palliating it; in
fine, when the offence is perpetrated in the presence of,
or under the eyes of as many witnesses as the law, custom, or judge requires for notoriety in similar circumstances.

That the culpability must be such as I have described,
viz.: that it must be so evident that there is no possibility
of excusing, extenuating, or palliating it, is clear from
Cap. Sua. 8, *Tit.* 2, *lib.* 3 *Decretalium,* and the teaching of

all canonists. See Schmalzgrueber, cited by Bouix *in tit.* 1, *lib.* 5 *Decret.*, especially Nos. 9, 10 and 14. The other conditions mentioned above are *per se* evidently necessary that a crime be justly considered notorious.

In the criminal process *Ex Notorio*, the judge should proceed with great caution. He should not admit the crime as notorious, although many assert it to be so, until he is perfectly convinced of it, by the deposition of eye-witnesses. Nay, even when the delinquent is taken in *flagrante delicto*, and brought immediately to the judge, the latter should take the evidence of the witnesses, which should be written down by the clerk, or notary. He should ask the culprit whether he pleads guilty, or has any thing to say in his defence. If the former, the lawful penalty is inflicted for the crime; but if the latter, the privilege of pleading his cause is given him, and a time appointed to enable him to prove any extenuating circumstances which may lessen his guilt. He is condemned only according to the *probata*, or the evidence.

Nay, more, if the crime be committed under the very eyes of the judge, he can, it is true, punish the culprit without any trial, or further proofs, but even then it is better and more prudent to ask him if he acknowledges his guilt. If he does not he takes the evidence of the witnesses, confronting the latter with the culprit. Otherwise he might expose himself to censure for prosecuting one against whom there was no evidence, which would be the case if the culprit denied having committed the offence, and the witnesses thereto could not be found.

According to Canon Law, the following formalities

may sometimes be dispensed with in trials *Ex Notorio;* nevertheless, as they must be employed in certain cases, it will be generally, not to say always more prudent to make use of them, viz.: 1. Citation " ad dicendam causam," or the defence of the guilty. This is rigorously required, when there is any doubt to be cleared up, or when the culprit may be enabled to plead extenuating circumstances, to the lessening of the grievousness of his fault. 2. Citation "ad sententiam." This is always required, unless the delay would be injurious to the public welfare. 3. Pronouncing sentence, at least declaratory.

There is no appeal from the sentence *Ex Notorio*, except when the notoriety of the crime is not expressed in the sentence. Also, no exception can be taken against the judge, unless the penalty is not determined by law and custom, but subject to his ruling alone, in which case, the just exceptions allowed by Canon Law, and indicated in the next chapter, hold.

CHAPTER XIX.

THE SUMMARY TRIAL.

The ordinary ecclesiastical trial, as I have already remarked, being attended with such a multitude of formalities and solemnities, all of which are insisted upon as necessary, and the omission of any of which may vitiate and annul the entire proceedings, it often occupies, of necessity, a more or less protracted period of time. The Summary Trial, or "Processus Criminalis Summarius," is in contradistinction to the ordinary trial. It is called Summary, because though amply sufficient for all the ends of justice, it is brief in comparison with the ordinary trial, being confined to a narrower compass of legal forms, and restricted, in consequence, to a shorter space of time for the expediting thereof. This cutting off of the many formalities of ordinary trials, and thus making them summary, is tersely expressed by Boniface VIII. in his Constitution *Ad Augendam*, by the words "Rimulis juris postpositis." The Summary Trial does not differ from the ordinary, in any thing that is essential to a perfect trial for the attainment of the ends of justice. It is only the accidentals and accessories that are dispensed with in the Summary Procedure. Whilst it secures the ends of justice equally with the ordinary trial, it does so more directly and with less circumlocution "Non procedit ad juris apices."

Although the reader, from a preceding chapter (xvii.,) in which are found many decisions and principles regulating canonical procedure, might deduce all that is necessary to be known concerning the Summary Trial, yet it will not be out of place, because of the importance of the matter, to give a special chapter to this subject.

The Summary Trial, or Processus Criminalis Summarius, was originally instituted for the benefit of religious only, but it can be, and often is employed towards the secular clergy; in fact, is the only one, which at present would be practicable, or desirable in the United States.

What I state in this chapter concerning this form of canonical procedure, I take principally from Bouix, *Trac. de. jur. reg., par.* 6, *sec.* 2, *c.* 2, *quæs.* 3. Any thing not applicable to seculars I note, and with the same learned author as my guide, correct accordingly, so that it forms a code of laws for Summary Procedure as used towards the secular clergy.

I. No criminal proceedings can be instituted even against Regulars, unless there has been a previous Accusation or Denunciation; or common Report and the indications of crime have given cause for an official inquiry; or unless an exception made in some other trial has given occasion to the process.

To Accuse, in the canonical sense of the word, is to affirm before the judge that one has done wrong, to the end that he may be publicly punished, assuming at the same time the *onus probandi*.

To Denounce, is to make known to the Superior as

Judge some crime, to the end it may be publicly punished, but without assuming the *onus probandi.*

Judicial Examination or Inquiry, is the act of the judge, to discover whether one has committed some crime, to the end of inflicting public punishment.

This Judicial Examination is made either *ex officio*, or at the instance of some denunciator. The ecclesiastical judge is not allowed to make a judicial inquiry against any one on suspicion, or slight rumor, or even on denunciation; it is absolutely necessary that the one about whom an inquiry is instituted should have been defamed, *i. e.*, that the report should have been spread abroad among the people that the crime was committed by him.

II. It is necessary that the judge be competent. This competency must extend to all causes for which he receives jurisdiction. He cannot, however, act as judge in a cause in which he before pleaded as an advocate; nor if he has a similar case, in which he is either the accused or the prosecutor; nor if an exception is taken against him "tanquam suspectus," unless it rests on frivolous grounds; nor if he is excommunicated or infamous.

The following, taken from Ferraris, and quoted by Bouix, *trac. de jud. eccl., p.* 1, *sec.* 4, *c.* 1, will explain still further the qualifications required in a judge.

"A judge wanting the proper knowledge required by his office (carens debita scientia), and judging wrongfully through culpable ignorance, sins mortally, and is bound to restitution, for the entire damage caused the injured party, either in the substance of the trial, or in superfluous expenses."

Even, says Bouix, should a judge make a mistake, "absque gravi culpa," he must try to remedy it by privately telling the injured party to appeal.

Ferraris says further : "A judge deficient in the knowledge necessary for the discharge of his office, cannot be absolved, unless he renounces his office, or firmly purposes to do so; for the simple reason that no one can conscientiously retain a position, whose duties he cannot fulfil without inflicting damage, or exposing himself to the danger of inflicting damage on his neighbor.

"A judge sins mortally in the exercise of his office, who without cause, notably delays the expedition of trials; and is bound to restore to the injured party the losses and expenses which ensue from the unjust delay, because he is the unjust cause of these losses and expenses."

A judge sins mortally who accepts notable gifts or presents contrary to the Decrees of the Church cited by Ferraris.

III. In the document (libello) of accusation or denunciation, it is necessary to give the name of the judge before whom the accusation is lodged; the names of the accuser and of the accused; the crime of which he is accused, or for which he is denounced; and the time, at least the year in which it is alleged to have been committed.

In Summary Procedure, and in all brief and light causes (and this is *de jure communi*), it is not necessary that the accusation or denunciation be made in writing, but it suffices that it be made before the judge by word of mouth, and that it be immediately inserted in the acts so that afterwards, if necessary, a copy can be had.

IV. Persons *de jure* disqualified, ought not to be allowed to make an accusation or denunciation.

V. The clerk or chancellor to be employed, ought to be a Public Notary (notarius publicus). If, therefore, such had not been appointed in the diocese (or religious order), the judge should select and depute some one for this office.

VI. An oath *de non calumniando* ought to be administered to the accuser, or denunciator, and to the witnesses.

Juramentum calumniæ is that by which the parties to the trial swear that in their actions, and exceptions and defence, they are not actuated by fraud and calumny, and that they wish to do all in good faith. *Juramentum veritatis et malitiæ* is implied in this definition.

VII. The accused must be cited to appear. *He cannot be condemned unheard, unless he is contumacious.*

Citation is a legal action, by which one is called to trial by the mandate of the judge, for the purpose of discovering the truth, or what is right and just in the case (juris experiundi causa).

Contumacy is a wilful disobedience to a lawful summons.

VIII. A sufficient time should be allowed the accused to gather his evidence and prepare for his defence.

IX. To the accused must be communicated the article

or heads of accusation for which the trial was instituted against him, as well as the depositions of the witnesses.

I will here add a quotation from the same chapter in Bouix, *quæs. 2, n.* 3, confirmatory of what has already been said, viz.: that the names of the witnesses must be communicated to the accused, to enable him to defend himself: "According to the more common opinion of canonists, the names of the witnesses are not to be communicated to religious, but only their depositions. But outside of religious orders, even in Summary Trials, to furnish the accused with the names of the witnesses is *de jure communi.*"

X. A patron, or skilled counsellor, must be given to the accused asking one to help him in his defence.

The same concession must be made to a poor priest, as we have already seen.

XI. The just exceptions of the accused must be admitted.

An exception in the strict sense of the law, is the exclusion of an action, by which the accused either retards the trial, or quashes it altogether.

Exceptions are divided chiefly into dilatory and peremptory.

Peremptory exceptions are those, which, if proved, put an end at once to the action; if, for example, the defendant objects, and proves that he never entered into the contract which the plaintiff claims he did.

Dilatory exceptions have reference to the person of the judge, or of the prosecutor, or are made against the witnesses. Exceptions against the latter may be taken after the *contestatio litis.*

Regularly all exceptions ought to be proposed before the *contestatio litis.*

Exceptions may be taken *viva voce,* but the accused must prove that they are just.

We will now inquire into the legitimate reasons for taking exception to the judge.

That reason is considered just and indubitable, which the law looks upon as such. The reasons for excepting to the judge are various, but they can be classed under three heads:

a. When the judge to whom exception is taken is an enemy of the accused. This can be presumed to be the case: 1. If he has a lawsuit, or judicial controversy with the judge. 2. If the judge had made threats against him, to the effect that when the opportunity offered he would do him an injury. 3. If he denies him marks of friendship which he is accustomed to exhibit to others in the same condition and state of life.

b. When the judge to whom exception is taken has a special affection for, or is on intimate terms of friendship with the adversary of the accused. It is concluded that such is the case: 1. If he is related to him by consanguinity, or affinity: 2. If he is his Master (Dominus). 3. If he is his companion, or colleague. 4. If he is his warm friend, " familiaris magna scilicet, non modica familiaritate." 5. If he is his patron, or client.

c. When the judge to whom exception is taken is prejudiced in favor of the cause to be tried. This is considered to be so: 1. If in the same case he acted as advocate, or procurator. 2. If, as a private individual, he has a similar cause before another tribunal. 3. If from the cause to be tried some special emolument will accrue to the judge himself.

N. B. If the exceptor contends that the judge has not jurisdiction, or that from some defect, *v. g.*, want of knowledge, his jurisdiction is impeded, it belongs to the judge to pronounce on the value of the exception, and the exceptor cannot appeal unless from a definite sentence. If he objects only that the judge is prejudiced against him "sit sibi suspectus," which is the case in all the instances enumerated above, the judge cannot by this very fact proceed farther, but must submit the exception to the decision of arbitrators.

XII. The witnesses, whom the accused proposes for his defence, must be heard.

XIII. The accused cannot be condemned to the regular penalty attached to his fault, "pœnam ordinariam," unless upon conviction, or the confession of his guilt.

XIV. A sentence can be imposed, only in accordance with the evidence, "secundum allegata et probata."

XV. In grave causes, a religious can have not only recourse (recursus) to a higher tribunal, but he has the right of appeal in the strict sense of the word. In common convictions which do not imply infamy, or a severe punishment, there is no appeal allowed to Regulars: "vox appellationis audienda non est."

With regard to seculars, the right of exception and appeal is the same in the Summary, as in the Ordinary Trial.

Bouix, *Trac. de jud. eccl., par.* 2, *Sec.* 4, *S. Sec.* 2, *C.* 3, *N.* 2 and 7.

XVI. When there is question of Religious, besides the above regulations, the rules of the religious Order to which they belong, are to be observed in criminal trials of this kind.

CHAPTER XX.

SENTENCES EX INFORMATA CONSCIENTIA.

The sentence *ex informata conscientia* is restricted to two cases : 1. The prohibiting of the reception of higher orders. 2. The suspending from orders already received "ab ordinibus, officiis, dignitatibus ecclesiasticis," but not from benefices. The Decree conferring this power is found in Sess. xiv. *de Reform.* of the Council of Trent, chapter 1, and is as follows:

" Cum honestius, ac tutius sit subjecto, debitam Præpositis obedientiam impendendo, in inferiori ministerio deservire, quam cum Præpositorum scandalo, graduum altiorum appetere dignitatem ; ei, cui ascensus ad Sacros Ordines a suo Prælato, ex quacumque causa, etiam ob occultum crimen quomodolibet, etiam extrajudicialiter, fuerit interdictus; aut qui a suis Ordinibus, seu gradibus, vel dignitatibus ecclesiasticis fuerit suspensus, nulla contra ipsius Prælati voluntatem concessa licentia de se promoveri faciendo, aut ad priores Ordines, gradus, et dignitates, sive honores restitutio, suffragetur."

In this chapter, I will show that the sentence of suspension *ex informata conscientia* can be inflicted : 1. For occult crime only. 2. When a canonical trial, or in this country, a Quasi Judicial Investigation cannot be had. 3. When the evidence of the crime is such as is sufficient to prove it before the Sacred Congregation of the Council.

I. Suspension *ex informata conscientia* can be inflicted for occult crime only.

Some canonists have held, and still teach, that under certain circumstances, suspension *ex informata conscientia* can be inflicted, though very rarely, for public crimes. But, in view of the positive and unequivocal Decisions of Rome, which I will cite to the contrary, such doctrine is now untenable. Any canonist of note who holds this opinion either wrote before these Decisions were given, or was not cognizant of them at the time of writing.

The ANALECTA JURIS PONTIFICII, 7th series, published at ROME, 1864, to which I refer my clerical readers for proofs *in extenso* of the above proposition, viz.: that suspension *ex informata conscientia* can be inflicted for occult crime only, reviews a work published at Vienna, entitled, "Pugna Juris Pontificii statuentis suspensiones extrajudicialiter, seu ex informata conscientia, et imperii easdem abrogare molientis," written by a Roman ecclesiastic, M. Salvatore Pallottini. From the ANALECTA itself, and the teaching of this author, therein quoted, who supports his teaching by many positive Decisions of Rome, I extract the following brief demonstration of the proposition that suspension *ex informata conscientia* can be lawfully employed for occult crimes only.

To understand well this question of suspension extrajudicially, or *ex informata conscientia*, we must keep in mind an historical fact which bears directly upon it, and which was even the efficient motive of the legislation of the Council of Trent in the matter. That historical fact is, that before the Council of Trent promulgated the law permitting bishops to suspend *ex informata conscientia*, they had no power to take action against, or inflict punishment on any clergyman, except for crimes that were not occult, and then only after conviction by an ecclesiastical court. Before the promulgation of the law of suspension *ex informata conscientia* by the Council of Trent, a bishop was perfectly powerless to punish occult crimes. He could only admonish, exhort, rebuke, threaten the culprit with the Divine anger, and with the judgment of God: in a word, before the Council of Trent, a bishop was restricted to moral persuasion only, to induce delinquents guilty of occult crimes to mend their ways. This is an historical fact. It goes very far to throw light upon the true meaning and extent of the legislation of the Council of Trent, giving bishops the power to suspend extra-judicially, "etiam ob occultum crimen."

The Decretals of the Church had already given to bishops all the means necessary for the punishment of crimes which were notorious, *jure, vel de facto*. The Council of Trent gave them, besides, the power of punishing crimes that were not notorious *jure, vel de facto;* or, in other words, it gave bishops the power of punishing occult crimes which, before the time of the Council of Trent, they were powerless to correct by any *official* action. This is evidently insinuated by the wording of the Decree of the venerable Fathers of Trent: " Ex quacumque causa, etiam ob occultum crimen, quomodolibet etiam extrajudicialiter."

To show how utterly at variance with the teaching of Rome is the doctrine which advances that suspension *ex informata conscientia* can be inflicted for public crimes, I will quote a few paragraphs from the work of M. Salvatore Pallottini, mentioned above, and which are found in the ANALECTA JURIS PONTIFICII:

" Manifestum fit, suspensiones extrajudicialiter, seu ex informata conscientia, iis duntaxat casibus ferri posse, ubi de crimine occulto, non vero publico res esset.

" Quoties proinde, episcopi extrajudicialiter, seu ex informata conscientia pro delictis publicis, non servata juris forma, pœnas irrogaverint, vel censuras tulerint, toties prælaudata Sacra Congregatio, Concilii Tridentini interpretum, nullas atque irritas, easdem declaravit.....

" Immo expresse declaravit Concilium Tridentinum aliam formam pro criminibus publicis coercendis præstituisse.

"Quin immo Sacra Congregatio NULLAS ATQUE IRRITAS SUSPENSIONES EXTRAJUDICIALITER, SEU EX INFORMATA CONSCIENTIA, OB PUBLICA CRIMINA LATAS DECLARARE SUEVIT, UBI SUSPENSI, SPRETIS OMNINO SUSPENSIONIBUS, MISSAS CELEBRAVERINT, CONFESSIONES AUDIERINT, NEC NON CETERA SACRI ORDINIS, IN EPISCOPORUM CONTEMPTUM, PERAGERE VISI FUERINT. Luculentum de quo exemplum exhibetur in S. Agathæ Gothorum suspensionis, irregularitatis et privationis beneficii: nam, proposito dubio; an constet de validitate suspensionis in casu, Sacra Congregatio die 26 Feb., 1853, responsum dedit: NEGATUR, salvo jure episcopi procedendi prout *de jure*. Qua inde reproposita quæstione, et acriter formiterque discusso articulo, num crimen occultum fuisset quo tempore saltem lata fuit suspensio, sub consueta formula: an sit standum vel recedendum a decisis in primo dubio in casu, eadem Sacra Congregatio, die 28 Maii, ejusdem anni 1853, respondit: IN DECISIS ET AMPLIUS.

"QUIS INDE AMBIGET ADHUC," continues this author, "QUOD SANCTIO TRIDENTINORUM PATRUM, LOCUM TANTUMMODO IN CASIBUS HABEAT, QUIBUS DE CRIMINIBUS OCCULTIS AGITUR? Adeo quippe verum est, ut in cap. 1, Sess. xiv., Con. Trid. de Refor., de criminibus duntaxat occultis res sit, ut nequeant episcopi decretum suspensionis clericis intimare, modo et forma processus ordinarii. Nam, si ex charitate Christiana nemo alterius diffamationem procurare debet, id eo vel magis in casu quo de clericis agitur retinendum. Ea idcirco mente Tridentini Patres pœnitentias præceptivas, vel suspensiones ferre posse episcopos pro criminibus occultis sanxerunt, ne tamen intimatione decreti clericorum famæ ac honestati quid minimi detraheretur. Qua de re pœnitentiæ, vel suspensiones hujusmodi, modo ac forma ordinaria penitus prætermissa, notificari debent privatim, et per subscriptionem ipsius suspensi acceptando decretum in manu judicis."

In support of the above quotations from M. Salvatore Pallottini, showing most clearly the teaching of Rome in the matter under discussion, I am enabled to adduce other positive decisions, which I find in the ANALECTA JURIS PONTIFICII, 13th series, 1874, in an article entitled "A practical Treatise on Diocesan Officialties."

The ANALECTA says: "The procedure *ex informata conscientia* cannot be used for a public suspension and for reasons ('motives') which are not occult. In such cases it is necessary to have recourse to public canonical proceedings." Decision Mar., 1858.

If there was any room for doubt as to the meaning of this decision of the Sacred Congregation, which there is not, it being too clear and unequivocal, that doubt would be set at rest by the letter of the Sacred Congregation written to the bishop of Aquino, in connection with the decision itself, which I here transcribe in English:

"According to the information which your lordship has sent, concerning Rev. Camillus M., priest, I must notify your lordship in the name of this Sacred Congregation, that as there is question of public and defamatory acts (di tituli publici et infamanti), YOUR LORSDHIP IS OBLIGED TO PROCEED ACCORDING TO CANONICAL PRESCRIPTIONS; CONSEQUENTLY, YOU CANNOT AVOID THE OBLIGATION YOU ARE UNDER, OF INSTITUTING A REGULAR TRIAL. The priest appealing to us HAS FULLY THE RIGHT TO REQUIRE SUCH TRIAL, and your lordship CANNOT IN CONSCIENCE REFUSE IT. You should see that the trial is instituted immediately and regularly, according to the orders given before by this Sacred Congregation." Rome, March, 1858.

In speaking of the decision quoted above, and to which this letter alludes, the ANALECTA JURIS PONTIFICII says: "Secret penalties, by which occult crimes are repressed, may be inflicted *ex informata conscientia*. Public and disgraceful crimes, on the contrary, require judicial proceedings."

Again, the ANALECTA JURIS PONTIFICII has the

following clear and explicit teaching on the subject under consideration:

"Ordinaries have the power of proceeding extra-judicially only when there is question of inflicting a paternal punishment, or a slight correctional penalty; but a canonical trial is rigorously required for grave corrections, and for any public spiritual penalty. THIS PRINCIPLE OF CANONICAL LEGISLATION IS ABSOLUTE. SUSPENSION EX INFORMATA CONSCIENTIA DOES NOT DEROGATE FROM IT, AND IS NO EXCEPTION TO IT. For, if suspension is a spiritual penalty, of which there can be no doubt, it is, on the other hand, no less certain that this penalty must remain secret and occult as well as the offence in punishment of which it is decreed, since it is inflicted *ex informata conscientia*, or without the formalities of a canonical trial. If the suspension be divulged and becomes public, IT IS BY THIS VERY FACT TAINTED WITH NULLITY, FOR PUBLIC SUSPENSION CANNOT BE INFLICTED EXCEPT AFTER A CANONICAL TRIAL. SUCH IN OUR DAY IS THE IGNORANCE OF CANONICAL PRESCRIPTIONS, THAT IT MAY BE AFFIRMED WITHOUT TEMERITY, OF ONE HUNDRED SUSPENSIONS AND INTERDICTS (against receiving orders) *ex informata conscientia*, INFLICTED IN A GIVEN TIME, NINETY-FIVE ARE NULL *ipso jure*, BECAUSE THEY GIVE PUBLICITY TO THIS EXTRA-JUDICIAL PUNISHMENT."

I might produce other authorities and decisions to prove that suspension *ex informata conscientia* can be inflicted for occult crime only, but the proofs I have given I consider most satisfactory, and are amply sufficient. I will content myself with remarking that the

Pope alone has the power to depose a priest *ex informata conscientia*. A bishop can only suspend, and that only for a short time, hardly ever over six months. This suspension must be kept secret. To make it known is to transgress an obligation of strict justice.

The canonical method of passing sentence *ex informata conscientia* is this: The bishop sends for the guilty clergyman, presents to him the decree of suspension, and demands his signature to it. LIKE THE OFFENCE ITSELF FOR WHICH IT IS INFLICTED, ALL THE PROCEEDINGS MUST BE KEPT SECRET.

D. Bouix, a canonist of note, advances the opinion that a clergyman may sometimes be suspended *ex informata conscientia* for public crimes. I am confident when he wrote, that he was not aware of the positive decisions of Rome to the contrary. The ANALECTA JURIS PONTIFICII alludes to his teaching on this point, when it accuses him of "extravagant opinions" in his treatise *De Judiciis*, when speaking of sentences *ex informata conscientia*. How well founded and just is the criticism is evident from the teaching of Rome as given above. The very words of Bouix himself confirm the correctness of the teaching *de suspensione ex informata conscientia*, as delivered by the ANALECTA JURIS PONTIFICII, and evince how uncertain is this distinguished author himself of the position he advances, viz.: that suspension *ex informata conscientia* may, in some rare cases, be inflicted for public crimes. The following from *Trac. de jud., par.* 2, *p.* 325, are Bouix's own words:

" Positæ conclusioni (nempe potestatem episcopalem

suspendendi *ex informata conscientia* locum habere etiam quando crimen est publicum) ADVERSARI VIGENTEM HODIE APUD ROMANOS CANONISTAS PERSUASIONEM, MIHI ROMÆ DEGENTI APERTE INNOTUIT. Ipsi namque existimant, NON POSSE EPISCOPUM *ex informata conscientia* PROCEDERE QUANDO DELICTUM EST FAMA VULGATUM; sed NECESSARIO TUNC ADHIBENDAM ORDINARI JUDICII FORMAM. Cumque nonnullis eorum patefecerim mihi esse in proposito, contrariam sententiam tueri, ACRITER OBSISTERE, et NE, UT PROBABILEM QUIDEM, HANC MEAM OPINIONEM ADMISERUNT: UTPOTE QUÆ IPSIS A SENSU ET MENTE TRIDENTINORUM APERTE ABERRARE VIDERETUR."

In another place Bouix says: " Nolim tamen, quoad suspensiones in perpetuum, lectorem *fidere conclusioni meæ*, posse silicet (episcopos) eas *ex informata conscientia* pronunciare, NAM CONTRARIUM TANQUAM CERTUM, ROMÆ, A JURIS SACRI PERITIS HABERI MIHI DIXERUNT NONNULLI. UT ADEO SUSPICOR, ME VERITATEM IN HAC RE, IGNORATIS DOCUMENTIS, NON FUISSE SATIS ASSECUTUM."

II. Having conclusively and satisfactorily proved that suspension *ex informata conscientia* can never be inflicted for public crimes, but for occult crimes only, I will now proceed to show, that it cannot be employed against ALL OCCULT crimes, but against SUCH ONLY AS CANNOT BE REACHED BY A CANONICAL TRIAL, or, in the United States, by A QUASI-JUDICIAL INVESTIGATION.

This opinion, it seems to my humble judgment, is conformable to the legislation of the Council of Trent itself, and even implied therein.

In Sess. xiv., c. 1 *de Refor.*, the Fathers of the Council

of Trent gave bishops the power of suspending extra-judicially, or *ex informata conscientia*. In Sess. xxiv., c. 5, they most unequivocally and most explicitly confirm, as the common and general law of the Church, the Constitution of Innocent III. given above, instituting canonical trials. Their words are: " Constitutio sub Innocentio III., in Concilio Generali, quæ incipit *Qualiter et quando*, quam sancta synodus in præsenti innovat, AB OMNIBUS OBSERVETUR." In the one session (xiv.), the Council dispenses bishops from proceeding against delinquent clergymen juridically, and allows suspension extra-judicially, or *ex informata conscientia*; in the other (Sess. xxiv.), they COMMAND the Constitution of Innocent III., requiring canonical proceedings, "to be observed by all."

This apparent contradiction is a very proof of what I advance, that extra-judicial suspension, or suspension *ex informata conscientia*, can be lawfully used for occult crime only, when a judicial, or, in this country, quasi-judicial investigation cannot be had. For, it cannot be called in question that the Council of Trent, in Sess. xxiv., formally, and specifically, and in its fullest extent, sanctioned and confirmed and promulgated anew the Constitution *Qualiter et quando* of Innocent III. It is evident, therefore, that the general law of the Church gives peremptorily and explicitly to every clergyman charged with any crime, the right to a canonical investigation of his case, when such investigation is possible.

A canonical trial, therefore, or in the United States, for the present, a quasi-judicial investigation, must be employed according to the general and common law of the

Church, towards all clergymen charged with crime, if such investigation is at all possible. Justice does not brook any curtailment of her rights. No secondary consideration on earth can or ought to come between her and the individual who appeals to her for aid. Therefore, and my conclusion is drawn from the teaching of the Council of Trent itself, which approves explicitly, and reiterates the binding obligation of the Decree of Innocent III., *Qualiter et quando*, every clergyman must be given a trial for even occult crime, when such trial can be had.

On the other hand, the Council of Trent, Sess. xiv., allowed suspension extra-judicially, or *ex informata conscientia*. This evidently and beyond the shadow of a doubt was intended by the venerable Fathers of Trent as an exception to the general law of the Church instituted by Innocent III., and promulgated anew by them. Who, I ask, ever heard of an exception taking the place of the rule, when the latter could be applied? It would for this very reason become irregular and unlawful. It is clear therefore to my mind, and it seems incontrovertible, that the Fathers of the Council of Trent wished the exception of Sess. xiv., ch. 1 to the general law laid down in Sess. xxiv., ch. 5; *i. e.*, the power of suspending extra-judicially to be used like all other exceptional laws, only when the general law could not be enforced, or in other words, when a canonical investigation could not be employed. Is not this reasoning sound and logical? It seems to me that it settles satisfactorily, and in conformity with common-sense, with the legislation itself of the Council of Trent, and with the principles of right and justice, the vexed question as to the extent to which the power of suspending extra-judicially, or *ex informata conscientia*, can be extended.

This view of the question is confirmed in my mind by the late "Instructio" *Quamvis*, 20 July, 1878, of the Sacred Congregation of the Propaganda. It is there stated (N. 4) that a missionary rector of whose removal there is question, must be informed "per extensum," by letter, of the cause of his removal. There is one case mentioned, in which prudence may forbid to state "per extensum" the cause prompting his removal, viz.: "in casu criminis occulti." This shows that occult crimes must sometimes be brought before the quasi-judicial Council for investigation. The obvious and natural inference from this is, that all occult crimes which can be investigated by the Council, should be brought before it, leaving only those to be dealt with by the procedure *ex informata conscientia* which the quasi-judicial Council or Commission of Investigation appointed by the bishop cannot reach.

Smith, in his *Notes*, etc., says, that suspension *ex informata conscientia* for occult crimes, "should be adopted only when scandal to the faithful, or matter of triumph to heretics, and serious injury to the Church, would be the result of an ordinary trial." I certainly cannot, in view of the principle I have just enunciated, agree with him.

In the Church, and the same may be said of the enactments of Canon Law, every principle is fixed and determined, and no principle is tenable that cannot be carried out to its ultimate consequences. The Church is "the pillar and ground of the truth." She is pre-eminently just. Justice inspired every line of her sacred canons; and, blended with mercy, is found vivifying every one of them. Let men be scandalized at the action of the Church, as were their prototypes of old at the conduct of the Son of God, let heretics triumph in their own way, the Church can never be injured by adhering to the principles of justice; and to these principles in all the enactments and enforcements of her canons, she will inflexibly adhere till "time shall be no more." These principles, like God Himself, their author, are immutable and unyielding. They have ever been, and ever will be, the unchanging and unchangeable polar star, guiding the Church in all her canonical legislation, amidst the sea of passions and prejudices, and misconceptions and errors, in which men here below are continually tossed. When truth and justice require her to act, the faithful will not be scandalized: heretics may rave, but the Church herself will shine forth as she has ever done from the beginning, the fearless champion of truth, right and justice, regardless of the consequences. "Fiat justitia, ruat cœlum," is a proverb which well expresses the attitude of the Catholic Church, when there is question of the rights of God or man.

Besides, how can any intelligent, or even ordinarily well-instructed Catholic, be scandalized at canonical trials for even grievous crime which is not public? They should rather, it seems to me, be edified, to see and know how carefully the Church guards the purity and sanctity of the Priesthood, and the honor of the Catholic Church. They may have human pity for the culprit who has disgraced his dignity, and brought merited punishment on himself, but they cannot but rejoice in their Catholic hearts, to see the honor of religion vindicated. Should they even be scandalized, it can, at most, be but a pharisaical scandal, which no one is bound to regard, much less bishops and priests.

Again, what triumph can it be to heretics to know that an unworthy priest is arraigned before the bar of an ecclesiastical court to answer for his misdeeds? Should the fact of a priest's delinquency be known to them, is it not a vindication, even in their eyes, of the Church's honor and sanctity, to know likewise that he was arraigned for his crime and suffered the just punishment thereof? Do not they themselves, having preserved, amongst others, this principle of Catholicity, summon their ministers before their church tribunals, to answer any serious charge made against them? In fact we recognize in their conduct on these occasions another verification of the words of the Gospel: " The children of this world are wiser in their generation than the children of light." For Protestant sects never condemn their ministers without a formal investigation.

The learned author to whom I allude, might as well, it seems to me, have said at once, that suspension *ex informata conscientia* can be inflicted for all occult crimes, as to have made the restriction he has. For, in every case, without any exception, when there is question of occult crime, the inconveniencies he mentions will to a greater or less degree result from a canonical or quasi-judicial investigation, or at least the bishop may judge that such inconveniencies will result, and then farewell to all canonical proceedings for any and every occult, and even, for that matter, public crime, for the same inconveniencies more or less attend both. This in fact is the plea which must answer for the terrible abuse that has been made in the United States of the suspension *ex informata conscientia.*

With the Council of Trent before me, the only inquiry, it seems to me, to be made, when there is question of proceeding extra-judicially, or *ex informata conscientia*, is: Can the general law of the Church requiring a canonical investigation be enforced? If it can, let a canonical investigation take place. No one can do wrong by obeying the Church, no matter what the consequences may be. If the general law of the Church, or for these United States now, the special law of a quasi-judicial investigation cannot be employed, then let the *exception,* or the procedure *ex informata conscientia*, come forward to perform its legitimate function, and put an end to evil.

In the view I have taken of this question, conformable, it seems to me, to the minds of the Fathers of Trent, to the dictates of right reason and impartial justice, I am strengthened and confirmed by the consideration of the nature of the power of proceeding extra-judicially, or *ex informata conscientia.* What, in fact, is this power? It is the power of inflicting on an individual a punishment sometimes worse than death itself, for many a priest, if he had the choice, would prefer death. There is question in suspension *ex informata conscientia* of inflicting *such a punishment, without giving any reason whatever for it, and without giving the culprit any opportunity of defending himself.* In this dread and terrible punishment, there is but one single ray of light to illumine the gloom of grief and agony that shrouds the soul in consequence, and to mitigate the severity of the chastisement, and that is the privilege which the Church herself confers, of having recourse to the mercy and clemency of the Holy Roman See.

Who, therefore, does not see at a glance, that this power of suspending *ex informata conscientia*, is one which the Church, so just, so merciful, so considerate in all her dealings with her children, so uncompromisingly opposed to the very appearance of injustice, wishes to be employed for occult crime, only when there is no other possible means of reaching the disorder, or when a canonical or quasi-judicial investigation cannot possibly be had? It is opposed to all our feelings and instincts of justice, and to all we know of the Church's mercy and clemency, to suppose that this power could be any thing else but an *exceptional* power, to be used for occult crime only when the general and common law of the Church is unable to take cognizance of it. For such an emergency alone, was it granted by the Church, as the Council of Trent seems to insinuate, or rather imply.

Even military tribunals in time of war, which administer justice most expeditiously, do not dare to exercise a power equal to that of passing sentence extra-judicially, or *ex informata conscientia,* possessed by all the bishops of the Church. Does not this alone prove, that a power which exceeds in rigor that of any tribunal on earth was intended by the Church to be employed only when all other means are unable to remedy the evil?

The exercise of this power of suspending *ex informata conscientia*, otherwise than in cases in which the ordinary and general laws of the Church cannot reach the evil, is, in fine, diametrically opposed to the instructions and admonitions of the venerable Fathers themselves of the Council of Trent. In Sess. xiii., c. 1 *de Refor.*, they admonish bishops to be pastors over their clergy, not persecutors, "percussores;" to love them as children and brethren, "tanquam filios et fratres;" to leave no means untried, before unsheathing the sword of justice, to lead back the erring into the path of rectitude; and finally, when punishment does become necessary, to blend in the infliction thereof, "mildness with rigor, mercy with judgment, and lenity with severity."

III. What proofs, or evidence of occult crime is required, that a bishop may act extra-judicially, or *ex informata conscientia?* A few words will suffice to explain this point.

Smith, in his *Notes*, etc., says, the private information on which the bishop acts in suspending *ex informata conscientia*, must be "incontrovertible." And again: "It must not be founded upon mere conjecture, but upon moral certainty.... An indubitable and certain information is essential."

Even when the information is "incontrovertible," and sufficient to produce "moral certainty," even when it is "indubitable and certain," it may not always justify an ecclesiastical superior in suspending *ex informata consci-entia*. For this, the information must not only be "incontrovertible," " morally certain," " indubitable and certain" in itself, but moreover available, as Bouix teaches, *Trac. de. jud.*, to prove the crime satisfactorily to the Sacred Congregation of the Council.

From private information, marked by all the qualities enumerated by Smith, "incontrovertible," "indubitable and certain," and " morally certain," a bishop may be sure of the commission of a crime; yet with all this, if his private information is of such a nature that it could not be brought in evidence before the Sacred Congregation, he would not be justified in using this knowledge to suspend extra-judicially, or *ex informata conscientia*. For this Bouix gives two reasons. 1. The *natural law forbids any judge to use his own private knowledge to pass sentence of condemnation on the guilty*. On this point *all doctors agree unanimously*. 2. He who has been suspended *ex informata conscientia*, has the right of recourse to the Holy See. Now, if the private knowledge, upon which the bishop bases his suspension, though more than sufficient in his own mind to convict of crime him whom he thus suspends, but would not be sufficient to prove it before the Sacred Congregation of the Council, this latter will most undoubtedly reverse his decision, and perhaps reprove the bishop for his imprudence. For, no matter how sure he may be that the crime was committed, as long as he cannot prove it satisfactorily to Rome, he will appear in the awkward and unenviable light of being unjust to his subject, and of persecuting an unoffending and innocent priest.

In conclusion, to sum up all in one sentence, the entire question of suspension extra-judicially, or *ex informata conscientia*, is a power which can be employed against occult crimes solely, and then only when there is no possibility of a canonical investigation, and when, moreover, the evidence of the crime is sufficient to prove it satisfactorily before the Sacred Congregation of the Council.

CHAPTER XXI.

THE "INSTRUCTIO" OF THE SACRED CONGREGATION OF THE PROPAGANDA, AS TO THE METHOD TO BE OBSERVED BY THE BISHOPS OF THE UNITED STATES, IN TAKING COGNIZANCE OF, AND ADJUSTING THE CRIMINAL AND DISCIPLINARY CAUSES OF CLERGYMEN. INSTRUCTIO S. CONGREGATIONIS DE PROPAGANDA FIDE DE MODO SERVANDO AB EPISCOPIS FEDERATORUM SEPTENTRIONALIS AMERICÆ STATUUM IN COGNOSCENDIS ET DEFINIENDIS CAUSIS (a) CRIMINALIBUS ET DISCIPLINARIBUS CLERICORUM.

Quamvis Concilium Plenarium Baltimorense II., ab Apostolica Sede recognitum, certam quamdam judicii formam, jam antea a Concilio Provinciali S. Ludovici sancitam in criminalibus clericorum causis ab ecclesiasticis curiis diœcesium Fœderatorum Septentrionalis Americæ Statuum pertractandis servandam esse decreverit, experientia tamen compertum est, statutum judicii ordinem haud (b) undequaque parem esse ad querelas eorum præcavendas, quos pœna aliqua mulctari contigerit. Sæpe enim postremis hisce temporibus accidit, ut presbyteri judiciis ea ratione initis latisque sententiis damnati, remoti præsertim ab officio rectoris missionarii, huc illuc de suis Prælatis conquesti fuerint, et frequenter etiam ad Apostolicam Sedem recursus detulerint. Dolendum autem est (c) non raro evenire, ut in transmissis actis, plura eaque necessaria desiderentur, atque, perpensis omnibus gravia sæpe dubia oriantur, circa fidem documentis hisce, in causis allatis, habendam, vel denegandam.

Quæ omnia Sancta Congregatio Fidei Propagandæ præposita serio perpendens, aliquod remedium hisce incommodis parandum, ac ita (d) justitiæ consulendum esse censuit, ut neque insontes clerici per injuriam pœna afficiantur, neque alicujus criminis rei ob minus rectam judiciorum formam a promerita pœna immunes evadant. Quod quidem facili pacto obtineret, si omnes præscriptiones a Sacris Canonibus sapienter editas (e) pro ecclesiasticis judiciis, præsertim criminalibus, ineundis et absolvendis servandas omnino esse præciperet. Verum animo reputans, in prædictis Fœderatorum Statuum regionibus id facile servari non posse, ea ratione providendum esse duxit, ut saltem illæ de admisso crimine accurate (f) peragantur investigationes, quæ omnino necessariæ existimantur, antequam ad pœnam irrogandam deveniatur.

Itaque SSmo. Domino Nostro Divina Providentia PP. Leone XIII. approbante, in generalibus comitiis habitis die 25 Junii 1878, S. Congregatio decrevit, ac districte (g) mandavit, ut singuli memoratæ regionis sacrorum Antistites, in Diœcesana Synodo quamprimum convocanda, quinque, aut, ubi ob peculiaria rerum adjuncta, tot haberi nequeant, tres saltem presbyteros, ex probatissimis, (h) et quantum fieri poterit in jure canonico peritis seligant, quibus, consilium quoddam judiciale, seu, ut appellant, Commissio Investigationis constituatur, eidemque unum ex electis præficiant. Quod si ob aliquam gravem (i) causam Synodus Diœcesana statim haberi nequeat, quinque, vel tres, prouti supra, per Episcopum interim ecclesiastici viri ad munus de quo agitur deputentur.

Commissionis ita constitutæ (j) princeps erit officium criminales atque disciplinares presbyterorum aliorumque clericorum causas, juxta normam mox proponendam, ad examen revocare, rite cognoscere, et ita episcopo, in ipsis definiendis, auxilium præbere. Satagant propterea oportet ad hoc munus electi, ut accurate (k) fiant investigationes, ea proferantur testimonia, atque a præsumpto reo omnia exquirantur, quæ ad veritatem eruendam necessaria censentur, ac ad justam sententiam tuto prudenterque ferendam certa vel satis firma argumenta suppeditent.

Quod si de alicujus (l) Rectoris Missionis remotione agatur, nequeat ipse a credito sibi munere dejici, nisi tribus saltem prædictæ Commissionis membris per Episcopum ad causam cognoscendam adhibitis, eorumque consilio audito.

Electi Consiliarii in suscepto (m) munere permanebunt ad proximam usque Diœcesanæ Synodi celebrationem, in qua, vel ipsi confirmentur in officio vel alii designentur. Quod si interim, morte, (n) vel renunciatione, vel alia de causa, præscriptus Consiliorum numerus minuatur, Episcopus, extra Synodum, alios in deficientium locum, prout superius statutum est, sufficiat.

In causis cognoscendis, iis præsertim in quibus (o) de Rectore Missionario definitive a suo officio amovendo agatur, judicialis Commissio hanc sequetur agendi rationem.

1. Ad Commissionem Investigationis non recurratur, nisi prius clare et præcise exposita ab Episcopo causa ad dejectionem finalem movente, et ipse Rector Missionarius malit rem ad Consilium deferri, quam se a munere et officio sponte dimittere.

2. Re ad Consilium delata, Episcopus, vicario suo generali vel alii sacerdoti ad hoc ab ipso deputato, committat, ut relationem causæ in scriptis conficiat, cum expositione investigationis eo usque peractæ, et circumstantiarum, quæ causam vel ejusdem demonstrationem specialiter afficiant.

3. Locum, diem, et horam opportunam ad conveniendum indicet, idque per litteras ad singulos Consiliarios.

4. Per litteras etiam Rectorem Missionarium de quo agitur, ad locum et diem constitutum ad Consilium habendum advocet, exponens nisi prudentia vetat, uti in casu criminis occulti, causam ad dejectionem moventem, per extensum, monensque ipsum Rectorem, ut responsum suis rationibus suffultum ad ea præparet in scriptis, quæ in causæ expositione, vel jam antea oretenus, vel tunc in scriptis relata fuerint.

5. Convenientibus Consiliariis tempore et loco præfinitis, præcipiat Episcopus silentium servandum de iis quæ in Consilio audiantur; moneat Investigationem non esse Processum Judicialem, sed eo fine habitam, et eo modo faciendam, ut ad cognitionem veritatis diligentiori qua poterit ratione perveniatur, adeo ut unusquisque Consiliarius, perpensis omnibus, opinionem de veritate factorum, quibus causa innititur, efformare quam accurate possit. Moneat etiam, ne quid in Investigatione fiat,

quod aut ipsos, aut alios periculo damni vel gravaminis exponat, præsertim ne locus detur actioni libelli famosi, vel alii cuicumque processui coram tribunali civili.

6. Relatio causæ legatur coram Consilio ab Episcopi officiali, qui etiam ad interpellationes respondebit, a præside, vel ab aliis Consiliariis per præsidem faciendas ad uberiorem rei notitiam assequendam.

7. Deinde in Consilium introducatur Rector Missionarius, qui responsum a se confectum leget, et ad interpellationes similiter respondebit, facta ipsi plena facultate ea omnia in medium afferendi, intra tempus tamen a Consilio determinandum, quæ ad propriam defensionem conferre possunt.

8. Si contingat Rectorem Missionarium de cujus causa agitur, nolle ad Consilium accedere, iterum datis litteris vocetur, eique congruum temporis spatium ad comparendum præfiniatur, et si ad constitutum diem non comparuerit, dummodo legitime præpeditus non fuerit, uti contumax habeatur.

9. Quibus omnibus rite expletis, Consiliarii simul consilia conferant, et si major pars Consiliariorum satis constare de factis arbitretur, sententiam suam unusquisque Consiliarius in scriptis exponat, rationibus quibus nititur expressis; conferantur sententiæ; acta in Consilio ab Episcopi officiali redigantur, a præside nomine Consilii subscribantur, et simul cum sententiis singulorum in extenso, ad episcopum deferantur.

10. Quod si ulterior investigatio necessaria vel congrua videatur, eo ipso die vel alio ad conveniendum a Consilio constituto, testes vocentur, quos opportunos Consilium

judicaverit, audito etiam Rectore Missionario de iis quos ipse advocandos esse voluerit.

11. Singuli testes *pro causa* seorsim et accurate examinentur a præside, et ab aliis per præsidem, absente primum Rectore Missionario. Non requiratur juramentum, sed si testes ipsi non renuant, et se paratos esse declarent ad ea quæ detulerint juramento, data occasione, confirmanda, fiat adnotatio hujusmodi dispositionis, seu declarationis in actis.

12. Consentientibus testibus, et dirigente prudentia Consilii, repetatur testimonium coram Rectore Missionario, qui et ipse testes si voluerit, interroget per præsidem.

13. Eadem ratione qua testes *pro causa*, examinentur testes *contra causam*.

14. Collatis tunc Consiliis, fiat ut supra, No. 9.

15. Quod si testes nolint aut nequeant Consilio assistere, vel eorum testimonium nondum satis luculentum negotium reddat, duo saltem ex Consilio deputentur, qui testes adeuntes, loca invisentes, vel alio quocumque modo poterunt, lumen ad dubia solvenda requirentes, relationem suæ investigationis ad Consilium deferant, ut ita nulla via intentata relinquatur ad verum moraliter certo cognoscendum, antequam ad sententiæ prolationem deveniatur.

16. Omnia acta occasione judicii in medium allata, accurate in Curia Episcopali custodiantur, ut in casu appellationis commode exhiberi valeant.

17. Si vero contingat, ut a sententia in Curia Episcopali prolata ad Archiepiscopalem provocetur, Metropolita-

nus, eadem methodo, in causæ cognitione et decisione procedat.

Datum Romæ, ex ædibus præfatæ S. Congregationis, die 20 July, anni 1878.

      Joannes, Cardinal Simeoni, *Præfectus*.
Joannes Baptista Agnozzi, *Secretarius*.

CHAPTER XXII.

A BRIEF COMMENTARY ON THE PRECEDING "INSTRUCTIO."

NOTE.—The letters *a, b, c, d,* etc., in the following commentary, are references to the first part, or introduction of the "Instructio", given in the preceding chapter, and are marked therein in the same manner. The references in the commentary marked 1, 2, 3, 4, etc., indicate the paragraphs marked thus in the "Instructio."

Fully aware of the importance of the Document given in the preceding chapter upon which I purpose now to make a few comments, and impressed with a profound veneration and love for the august authority whence it emanates, our Holy Father, Leo XIII., "quem Deus nobis diu sospitem servet," I declare beforehand my full and entire submission to any interpretation that may be given to it, by its only authorized interpreter, the Sacred Congregation of the Propagation of the Faith.

Although this important document must be interpreted *au pied de la lettre*, nevertheless, the principles of canon law, of judicial informations, and of canonical trials, given in the foregoing chapters, will be an immense help to understand it well. The principles contained in the authentic documents pertaining to canonical procedure, and the Decisions of Sacred Congregations found in these chapters, as well as the eminent canonist Bouix, will be my guides in the following brief commentary.

The motives determining the promulgation of the above "Instructio" by the Sacred Congregation of the Propaganda, are mentioned in the first paragraph, viz.: 1. Because the form of trial instituted by a Provincial Council of St. Louis, and adopted by the II. Plenary Council of Baltimore, had not proved (b) adequate, "haud undequaque parem esse," for the purpose for which it was enacted, and in consequence, priests who had been punished, especially such as had been removed from their office of Missionary Rectors, complained of their prelates, and frequently even had recourse. to the Holy See. 2. Because it not unfrequently (c) happened, that in the acts of ecclesiastical proceedings transmitted to Rome, many and essential things were wanting; and all things duly considered, grave doubts often arose as to the amount of faith to be granted or denied the documents in these cases.

These facts, whilst they show to the bishops and clergy of the United States the necessity of a more thorough knowledge of Canon Law, proved to Rome, that the form of judicial trial promulgated for this country by the II. Plenary Council of Baltimore was not adequate to insure the punishment of those only who deserved punishment. We are left to conjecture what the Sacred Congregation would have said, had they been aware that the Decree marked 77 of the II. Plenary Council of Baltimore was very rarely if ever observed in the United States, even "in causis criminalibus." At least it does not appear that they were cognizant of this fact, unless we suppose it was the reason of the positive (g) injunction, "decrevit ac districte mandavit," that this "Instructio" should be conscientiously and rigorously observed.

If we now inquire into the nature and end of the "Instructio," we will find that it does not enjoin a canonical trial, for N. 5 says: "Moneat (Episcopus) investigationem non esse processum judicialem;" nor can its prescriptions be called a *processus informatorius*, or an examination of witnesses and documents, to ascertain if it be lawful to summon an individual for trial, or even a simple examination of the case for the same purpose. The investigation of the "Instructio" presupposes that the cause (No. 2) has been already instituted. Hence it is, on the one hand, more than a *processus informatorius*, and on the other, it does not go as far as a *judicial trial*. FOR THE PRESENT, THE "Instructio" TAKES THE PLACE OF THE LATTER (e and f) IN THE UNITED STATES, AND IS A THOROUGH (f, j, k, and No. 15) QUASI JUDICIAL (h) INVESTIGATION, MADE IN VIEW OF A JUST (d, f, j, k) PUNISHMENT.

Most of the formalities and prescriptions laid down for canonical trials are required by the "Instructio." Thus, not only the verbal confrontation, or legitimation of the proceedings (Nos. 11, 12 and 13), but even the personal confrontation (No. 12) is sometimes allowed, whilst in regular canonical proceedings, as we have seen, it is only in capital causes· that the ecclesiastical tribunal has power to grant the latter (ch. xvii., Tit. xiv.)

As to the "Consiliarii," they are more than examining officials, (juges d'instruction, ch. xvii., Tit. viii.) Yet they are not judges in the strict sense of the word. They are indeed called (h) " consilium quoddam *judiciale*," and give a decision, "*sententiam suam* unusquisque Consiliarius in scriptis exponat" (No. 9), but it is certain that this decision is not a definite sentence, for No. 5 says: "Investigationem *non esse processum judicialem*," and again " Unusquisque Consiliarius. ... *opinionem* (No. 5) de veritate factorum. ... efformare possit."

Many duties, however, devolving on judges in canonical trials, must be performed by the " Consiliarii," and they are granted by the " Instructio " many of the rights pertaining to the same, ex. gr. *contestatio litis, examen rei,* (Nos. 6 and 7,) *repetitio testium,* (Nos. 10, 11, 13 and 15), and *confrontatio testium* (No. 12).

These few observations are sufficient to show how the Counsel, or Commission of Investigation instituted by the " Instructio," takes the place in the United States, for the present at least, of a regular canonical trial, and is a thorough and searching quasi-judicial investigation made in view of a just punishment. Consequently, as I have already remarked, the principles contained in the authentic canonical documents found in the preceding chapters, and the Decisions of Sacred Congregations therein contained, are a great help in the proper understanding of the prescriptions of the " Instructio."

Having premised these general remarks, I will now come to particulars. And first, it is of the utmost importance to understand the nature of the "Consilium quoddam judiciale," the manner of instituting it, etc.

The Counsel, or Commission of Investigation, should consist of five, or at least of three priests. " Each bishop (g) of the United States, in a Diocesan Synod, to be convoked as soon as possible, will select with care, five, or where on account of peculiar circumstances this number cannot be had, at least three priests; of those most acceptable to the clergy, and as far as possible well versed in Canon Law, who will form a quasi-judicial Counsel or Commission of Investigation over which one will be appointed to act as president."

As I have already remarked, the "Consiliarii" thus selected are more than examining officials, or judges of information (juges d'instruction, ch. xvii., Tit. viii.), and yet they can pass no definite sentence, for they are not judges. They are called "Consiliarii" throughout (m, and Nos. 3, 5 and 9) the "Instructio," and together, form a Counsel, or Commission of Investigation, to aid the bishop in passing a just sentence.

A most important point to ascertain with regard to the "Consiliarii" is, whether the term is to be taken in the canonical sense of the word. Bouix, *trac. de jud. eccl., par.* 2, *sec.* 2, *c.* xii., will help us much in this research.

"Quid sint assessores? Hi (ait Schmalzgrueber) ab *assidendo* sic dicti sunt, quod eum in finem assumantur, ut judici assideant, eumque *suo consilio in judicando* adjuvent: unde etiam CONSILIARII vocantur. Assessor is est, quem ille qui judicandi potestatem habet, sibi associat, ut ei assideat et assistat, et ad recte causam dicendam eum instruat. Ex qua descriptione, desumi potest, quod assessoris officium versatur. . . . *ut invigilet ad veritatem indagandam, et qui juris sit judicem instruat.*" Pellegrini, praxis vicariorum, *par.* 4, *sec.* 16, *n.* 20.

Now, the office and duties of "assessors," as laid down by these three eminent canonists, Bouix, Schmalzgrueber and Pellegrini, perfectly agree with the office and duties of the "Consiliarii," as put forth in the "Instructio." For, the duties expressed by these words, "ut invigilet ad veritatem indagandam," is clearly expressed in f, j, k, and Nos. 5 and 15, and those conveyed by these words: "Et qui juris est judicem instruat," is explicitly affirmed in j, and No. 9 of the "Instructio."

It may be objected that the "Consiliarii" of the "Instructio" do not sit in judgment with the bishop, or judge, as the latter is not supposed to be present at their deliberations, constituting as they do simply a Commission of Investigation (h), and not a judicial (No. 5) tribunal properly so called. To this I answer, that the officialty of "assessores," which, as we have seen, has the same meaning precisely as Consiliarii, is not at all essential to a trial, as may be seen in any work on Canon Law; but has simply for object to subject the case to a careful examination and strict investigation for the ascertaining of the whole truth in the matter, so that from the information thus acquired they may be enabled to instruct the judge in what is right in the premises, and thus help him to pass a just and impartial sentence.

The next question that suggests itself is: Who are eligible to this important office of "Consiliarius?" The "Instructio" does not require too many qualifications, and this purposely no doubt, to render the selection less difficult, and to obviate beforehand the objection that suitable persons could not be found.

It prescribes, however, that five, or when that number cannot be had, three priests at least, be chosen, who will form a quasi-judicial Counsel, or Commission of Investigation ; that these be *selected in Synod with the utmost care,* " seligant;" that they be *most acceptable to the clergy,* " ex probatissimis," and that, if possible,they be *well versed in Canon Law,* "quantum fieri poterit in jure canonico peritis." These are the general rules laid down by the " Instructio " for the selection of the " Consiliarii."

It is clear from the text (g) of the " Instructio," that as a rule, the " Consiliarii" must be chosen *in Synodo.* It is only when for some grave reason (i) a Synod cannot be called immediately, or some unforeseen cause (n) " morte, aut renunciatione, vel alia de causa," demands it, that the bishop can appoint them *extra Synodum.*

The next point of importance is to ascertain how the " Consiliarii" are created. Is it by a vote of the clergy in Synod assembled, or by the appointment of the bishop? The " Instructio " evidently confers on the bishop (g and n) the appointment, or power of selecting the " Consiliarii."

It may be objected, that if the selection of the " Consiliarii" is not made by a vote of the clergy, but by the bishop himself, there is no reason why a Synod should be called, a point upon which the " Instructio" rigorously insists, unless some grave motive interferes with its convocation.

To this I answer, that a very good and substantial reason for selecting the " Consiliarii" in Synod is, that it has been *prescribed by Rome,* and this most rigorously, *sub pœna obedientiæ,* " DECREVIT (S. C.) AC DISTRICTE MANDAVIT." Besides, there are very good reasons why the bishop should select them in Synod. For, the "Consiliarii" must be chosen with the greatest care, "seligant;" they must be priests most acceptable to the clergy, "ex probatissimis;" and finally, they must be men, as far as such can be found, well versed, "peritis," in Canon Law. Now, how will the bishop know who are the clergymen of the diocese, possessed of the above qualifications, especially that which requires that they be most acceptable to the clergy? It is evident that a Synod, or assemblage of the clergy, is the most proper, the surest, and the easiest means of ascertaining this. None know better each other's qualifications than the clergy themselves. The bishop surrounded with his clergy in Synod can discuss the matter with them, consult them, hear their suggestions and opinions as to the fittest men for the office, and be thus enabled to appoint men who will not only perform creditably to themselves and to the bishop the duties of their office, but will also be most acceptable, "ex probatissimis," to the clergy. Hence the importance Rome attaches to having the "Consiliarii" appointed *in Synodo.*

Thus far we have seen the nature and duties of the "Consiliarii;" who amongst the clergy are to be chosen for this office, viz.: those most acceptable to them and best versed in Canon Law; and how and when they are to be appointed. I need scarcely add that the "Conciliarii" ought to be honest, upright, sterling, conscientious men, unbiassed, impartial and unprejudiced, profoundly impressed with their responsibility, and the consequences of their acts. Relatives of the bishop ought not to be selected, as we may infer *a pari* from a Provincial Roman Council of 1725, nor should brothers act in the same

Council, as we may also infer *a pari* from the Decision given, ch. xvii. Tit. xvii.

The "Instructio" says (n): "Quod si interim, morte, aut renunciatione, vel alia de causa, præscriptus Consiliariorum numerus minuatur." The first two causes mentioned, death or resignation, offer no difficulty. But what causes are included in the "alia de causa"? It might be answered, sickness, or the unavoidable absence of one or more of the "Consiliarii." May not, however, be included in this expression "alia de causa," cases in which the duly appointed "Consiliarii" cannot justly take part in the "Counsel," without frustrating, to a certain or even great extent, the aim of the law, because they become unacceptable, or are no longer "ex probatissimis"? Such cases may easily arise. For example, if one of the "Consiliarii" has himself to undergo a quasi-judicial examination, it is evident that he cannot be the subject of investigation, and at the same time remain a member of the Commission of Investigation. Again, a "Consiliarius" could not with propriety be a member of the quasi-judicial counsel, though duly appointed, if he had a' similar case before the members thereof, in which he was interested; or if he himself had been recently punished for an offence similar to that before the Counsel of which he is a legitimate member.

There are many other cases in which the impropriety and injustice of a "Consiliarius" acting as a member of the Commission of Investigation, are apparent at first sight. I need not particularize them all. They will be found included in the answer of three eminent canonists to the question presented below. I would call the attention of my clerical readers to the fact, that I state nothing here or elsewhere in these pages on my own unauthoritative opinion. It would, indeed, be great presumption and folly for me to do so, in such important and delicate matters.

Bouix, *trac. de jud. eccl., par.* 2, *sec.* 2, c. xii., *quæs.* 6, asks the question: "An assessor (another name, as we have already seen, for Consiliarius) recusari possit tanquam suspectus?" In the application of this question to the "Instructio," the exception may be taken by the bishop, or by the accused. Bouix answers the above question thus: "Potest allegari suspectus ex causa, licet non habeat jurisdictionem: et si judex (in the 'Instructio' the bishop) non admittit suspicionem, *fit ipse suspectus.*" This answer is quoted from Pellegrini, *p.* 2, *præmisso* 3, *n* 26, citans Abbatem Panormitanum. Bouix adds: "Ratio est, quia dando consilium judici, potest in ejus sententiam influere, et sic gravamen alteri ex partibus inferre. Unde parti, quæ gravamen timet, merito conceditur, ut possit arcere assessorem, qui ipsi ex causa suspectus est."

Exceptions, therefore, against the "Consiliarii," founded on good grounds, are in order. The just causes of exception to them may be seen in Chap. xix., where I spoke of the reasons justifying an exception taken against the judge. Evidently the reason adduced by Bouix, for taking exception to "assessores," applies with equal, if not more force, to the "Consiliarii" of the "Instructio." For the latter have the same, if not greater influence over the judge, than even the "assessores" in a canonical trial, as in the latter case the judge is present, whereas he does not preside or take part in the Counsel of the " Instructio," but simply receives the *Acta* of the same, and bases (no. 9) his sentence thereon.

I can, therefore, see no reason why the just exceptions taken against one or more of the " Consiliarii " must not be accepted. In fact, were not these just exceptions admitted, all the evils and inconveniencies of which the " Instructio " speaks in the first paragraph, and which it was intended to remedy, would still continue to exist, and the end of its promulgation would be frustrated. For, were the just exceptions of the accused to be disregarded, it could scarcely be said of that " Consiliarius," against whom the exception was taken, that he is "ex probatissimis." Were just exceptions against the " Consiliarii " to be ignored, it is *per se* evident that the Counsel would be powerless to suppress complaints, for the just exceptions of the accused being denied, there would be *valid and serious reasons for complaint.* A necessary consequence of this, *recourse to the Holy See for justice,* would be of as frequent occurrence as ever. The very documents of the Counsel sent to the Metropolitan, in cases of appeal, or to the senior bishop, or to Rome, would be tainted with suspicion, as having been gotten up by one or more objectionable members of the Counsel. Finally, according to Bouix, Pellegrini and the " Lucerna Juris," the judge himself, or the bishop, becomes *justly suspected,* gives ample reason to the accused for appealing to a higher tribunal, or to Rome, and runs the risk of passing an unjust sentence.

Is the "Instructio" a law for *all* the dioceses and vicariates apostolic of the United States, and binding upon all the prelates thereof? It is, most undoubtedly. This is evident from the words (g) of the "Instructio" itself: "SSmo. D. N. Divina Providentia PP. Leone XIII. approbante, in generalibus comitiis, habitis die 25 Junii, 1878, S. Congregatio DECREVIT AC DISTRICTE MANDAVIT, ut SINGULI..... ANTISTITES," etc. We cannot, therefore, doubt that the "Instructio" has the force of LAW FOR ALL ARCHBISHOPS, BISHOPS AND VICARS APOSTOLIC THROUGHOUT THE WHOLE UNITED STATES OF AMERICA.

What causes must be brought before the quasi-judicial Counsel, or Commission of Investigation? The "Instructio" explicitly answers (a and j): "Causæ criminales et disciplinares;" and again, "Criminales atque disciplinares causæ."

Does the "Instructio" take from the bishops the power of suspending *ex informata conscientia*, as the words, "in casu criminis occulti" (no. 4) would seem to insinuate? Most assuredly not. For, as I said in Chap. xx., when treating of suspension extrajudicially, or suspension *ex informata conscientia*, the latter cannot be inflicted for all occult crimes, but in such cases only where a canonical trial, or with us now, a quasi-judicial investigation is impossible. Not often, in fact, is this the case. Occult crimes can almost always be reached and punished by a regular canonical investigation. Hence the words of the "Instructio:" "In casu criminis occulti." This fact, acknowledged by these words of the Sacred Congregation, that occult crimes can be the subject of the quasi-judicial investigation, is a proof of the views I advocated on this point, when treating above on suspension *ex informata conscientia*.

Another reason why the expression, "in casu criminis occulti," does not infringe on the just exercise of the power of suspending *ex informata conscientia*, is one taken *à pari*. According to the decree of Gregory XVI., instituting ecclesiastical tribunals of justice for all the Pontifical States, all sentences are null and void, unless passed by an ecclesiastical court composed of the ordinary, or vicar-general, and four judges; yet this law does not derogate from the sentence *ex informata conscientia*. In like manner *à pari*, the "Instructio" does not interfere with the just exercise of this power. The quasi-judicial investigation of the "Instructio," therefore, is prescribed for all causes disciplinary, as well as criminal, as also for all cases of occult crime, when such investigation is possible.

Was the "Instructio" intended only, or chiefly, to settle the difficulties of Missionary Rectors?

All clergymen, from the tonsured clerk to the ordained priest, charged with any serious fault *contra mores, vel disciplinam*, have now the right to a quasi-judicial investigation of their case, according to the method laid down by the "Instructio." It is said in the "Instructio" (o): " Iis præsertim (causis) in quibus de Rectore Missionario. . . . agatur." This sentence, whilst it indicates that the "Instructio" was primarily and chiefly intended to settle all causes having reference to Missionary Rectors, intimates at the same time that it can be applied also to others besides Rectors. This is evident from the qualifying adverb *præsertim*.

From N. 1, indeed, until the end, "Rectores Missionarii" alone are mentioned, yet there can be no doubt that the prescriptions of the "Instructio" must be applied to all clergymen, "in causis criminalibus et disciplinaribus." For the "Instructio" speaks (o) of causes in general, "*in causis* cognoscendis," which implies, of necessity, not those alone of Missionary Rectors, but of all others, and again (j) it is said: "criminales atque disciplinares presbyterorum aliorumque clericorum causas."

As to the paragraph marked *l*, beginning *Quod si*, it does not mean, that the *norma agendi* mentioned therein, must be employed whenever there is question of changing a Missionary Rector. The intent of this paragraph is, simply to require the bishop to lay the matter before three at least of the "Consiliarii," and consult them, and advise with them, before removing a Missionary Rector *against his will*. For all other cases, Missionary Rectors, as well as assistants, can be removed as heretofore, "ad nutum episcopi." Yet, there must be always a good and sufficient reason for each removal, otherwise the bishop may be obliged to reinstate him in his former position, as has several times happened in this country.

Nos. 1, 2, 3 and 4 of the "Instructio," suppose a preliminary information to have been taken, to ascertain if it be lawful to summon the accused before the Commission of Investigation. This is done by an examination of witnesses, documents, etc. I have already spoken, in Chap.

xix. (Processus Summarius) of the different ways of procedure in canonical trials.

If the accused is brought to trial *per viam accusationis*, which is now of rare occurrence, a preliminary information is not required, for the simple reason that the accuser takes upon himself the *onus probandi*. Should he fail to prove the crime against the one whom he accused, and the accusation is shown to have been instigated by malice, he is liable to be punished as a calumniator.

When the accused is brought to trial *per viam denunciationis*, a preliminary examination is necessary, as a *semi-plena probatio* of the crime is required before proceedings are taken against the accused.

But the way now ordinarily followed to bring the accused to a canonical trial is *per viam inquisitionis*. The procedure prescribed by the " Instructio," is *per viam inquisitionis specialis quoad personam et delictum*. In the preliminary examination of the case, which must be made before the investigation prescribed by the "Instructio" can be instituted, there ought to exist a *semi-plena probatio*, at least, of the guilt of the accused. *Semi-plena probatio* "illa est ex qua judex, valde probabiliter, veritatem de re controversa introspicit, non tamen certam habet." Bouix. *Plena probatio* "illa dicitur quæ plenam fidem facit judici, de re in judicium deducta, seu quæ eum in causam instruit, ut nullo alio ulterius requisito, sententiam ferre, et controversiam definire possit." Ib. The different kinds of *plena* and *semi-plena probatio* may be found in any treatise *de jud. eccl.*

Although *prævia infamia* may be called a *semi-plena*

probatio, yet it is more prudent and more conformable to justice, to have secured at least a *semi-plena probatio* in the ordinary acceptation of the word, by the preliminary information, before the formal quasi-judicial investigation by the Counsel is made. *Prævia infamia*, in the Constitution of Innocent III., *Qualiter et quando*, which I have given at length in Chap. xvi., is authoritatively defined as follows: " Si per clamorem et famam ad aures Superioris pervenerit, non quidem a malevolis et a maledicis, sed a providis et honestis; nec semel tantum, sed sæpe, quod clamor innuit et diffamatio manifestat."

Let us now make the application of these canonical prescriptions to the " Instructio." No. 1 supposes that the accused knows of the preliminary information before his citation. He is of course free to approach the judge, or his bishop, and adjust matters with him, rather than undergo a quasi-judicial investigation.

It is certain that a preliminary examination of the case to be investigated by the Counsel is prescribed by the " Instructio," for in No. 2 we find these words: " Cum expositione investigationis *eo usque peractæ*." Besides, without such preliminary examination, it would be impossible to comply with the prescriptions Nos. 1, 2, and 4 of the " Instructio."

The question arises, Is it necessary that a *semi-plena probatio* of the crime be obtained in this preliminary examination, before the accused is cited to appear before the Counsel? This is not formally and specifically required, but it is certain, that the " Instructio" insinuates and implies that such proof ought to exist, for No. 2

says: "Ut relationem causæ in scriptis conficiat, cum expositione investigationis eo usque peractæ, et circumstantiarum quæ causam, vel ejusdem *demonstrationem* specialiter afficiant." Hence I think it safe to assert, that no one should be cited before the Commission of Investigation, unless a *semi-plena probatio* at least of his guilt exists. Both prudence and justice seem to demand this. The very act of a clergyman being summoned to answer for crime is more or less detrimental to his good name, and he and religion are more or less injured thereby. It is clear, therefore, it seems to me, that nothing less than a *semi-plena probatio* of guilt, can justify the authorities in exposing an individual and religion to such inconveniencies and evils.

I have already proved that the accused can take just exception to one or more members of the Counsel. But how should such exception be taken? The proper course for the accused is to write out his exceptions immediately upon being summoned, and the proofs upon which they rest, and send them to the bishop, or better still, present them to him in person. If this is not done before the day appointed for the investigation, the "Consiliarii" are tacitly acknowledged by him to be acceptable, and besides the bishop might be unable to replace them by others.

The manner of Citation indicating the place and day is explicit, and needs no comment. Nothing is said, however, about the interval of time between the citation and the investigation, which should be allowed the accused to prepare for his defence. This was not necessary, as the natural law supplies this. The *jus naturale* peremptorily requires that the accused, according to his circumstances, should be given a sufficient length of time to appear, and get ready his defence. The "*Instructio*," moreover, intimates this much. For, according to No. 4, he is cited by letter, which explains *per extensum* the nature and proofs of his offence to which he is invited to reply. Ample time, therefore, should be given him to prepare an answer which may be a matter of momentous importance to himself.

There may be varied interpretations given of the expression, "*per extensum*," but in its natural, obvious sense, it signifies the offence, with all its notable circumstances and particulars, the proofs of the same, the names and depositions of witnesses, etc.; for the right of lawful defence rigorously requires (Chap. xvii., Tit. xv.) that the accused should be informed of all important points bearing on the accusation, and which, moreover, are necessary to enable him (Chap. xvii., Tit. xv.) to prepare (No. 4) his written answer.

It may be objected, that this looks more like a defence proper, than a simple answer, "responsum," of which the "Instructio" speaks. I reply, that the expression "responsum" there used, does not by any means exclude the meaning of defence, but rather implies it. If the answer is an acknowledgment of guilt, it is of course no defence, except in so far as an humble confession will ever favorably impress a just and compassionate judge, and move him the more to mercy. But if the answer is a complete or partial denial of guilt, or offers evidence of circumstances mitigating, or extenuating the gravity of the offence, although it is only read (No. 7) before the Counsel, and although the latter has not the power to pronounce a definite sentence, nevertheless, the investigation being made in view of a just punishment (d. j. k.), and the written, as well as the oral answers of the accused making without doubt a part of the *Acta Consilii*, which must be written in the vulgar tongue (Chap. xvii., Tit. ix.), and sent to the bishop (Nos. 9 and 16, Chap xvii., Tit. xviii.), the answer of the accused, if not an acknowledgment of guilt, is most assuredly, in its final destination, a defence in the most rigorous acceptation of the word.

Not unfrequently, in this country, clergymen are met with, who do not understand the English language, or have but an imperfect knowledge of it. Natural justice suggests, in such cases, that they be allowed to answer orally, or in writing, in their own language. This circumstance of priests in a diocese being of different nationalities, and speaking different languages, should be taken into consideration by the bishop, in the selection of the "Consiliarii."

From the importance of the answer of the accused, which, I have just shown, is a true defence, it follows that great care should be taken in its preparation. It suggests, as well as the "Instructio" itself (c), the necessity and importance of a knowledge of Canon Law. If the accused therefore is ignorant of the principles of the latter, it would be advisable for him to ask, in the preparation of his reply, the assistance of a fellow-clergyman better informed in such matters.

In canonical trials, as we have seen, Chap. xvii., Tit. xvi., poor clergymen have a right to an advocate for their defence, appointed by the episcopal court. The reason for this just provision exists equally in the quasi-judicial investigation, and therefore, *a pari*, a clergyman, if he wishes it, ought to be allowed the assistance of a *confrère* to help him in his defence, although the accused must himself (No. 7) read his answer to the members of the Commission of Investigation.

As the official appointed by the bishop (No. 6) performs some of the duties of the public prosecutor (Chap. xvii., Tit. vi.), and of those of the chancellor in a canonical trial (No. 9, and Chap. xvii., Tit. ix.), duties, I need scarcely add, that should be complied with most conscientiously and with the utmost impartiality, the "Consiliarii" can, and *it is their duty even, to assume, to a certain extent, towards the accused, the part of an advocate in a canonical trial*, especially when they enter into serious deliberation, and exchange views (No. 9) on the matters submitted to their judgments. In fact, without assuming the duties of an advocate for the accused to a certain extent, they cannot conscientiously comply with the letter of their duties, as marked out by the "Instructio." For, they are obliged to make an accurate investigation (f. k.), and to examine the case carefully, in all its bearings, and under all its aspects, which they cannot well do, without becoming, in one sense, the advocate of the accused. They must, at least, search out and advocate *the truth*, which will often be a real defence of the accused, and bring to light all mitigating and extenuating circumstances in his favor,

The object of the "Consiliarii," from the moment they meet to investigate a case, until they are relieved from its consideration, IS NOT SO MUCH TO TRY TO PROVE THE GUILT OF THE ACCUSED, AS TO ASCERTAIN THE WHOLE TRUTH, AND NOTHING BUT THE TRUTH, IN HIS CASE (k, and Nos. 5 and 15). THEIR SOLE AND ONLY DUTY IS TO DISCOVER THE TRUTH, and to make known the same to the bishop, COUNSELLING HIM TO WHAT THEY BELIEVE IN THEIR CONSCIENCES TO BE JUST AND MERCIFUL IN THE PREMISES. Before they form their judgment, or record their opinion, they should seriously call to mind their own responsibility to God and to the bishop, to the priest and to the people ; and then weighing the evidence on both sides, evenly and impartially, in the balance of justice, and in the "scales of the sanctuary," and giving the accused the benefit of every doubt, pronounce their sentence, which should rather lean to the side of mercy, than judgment. "For judgment without mercy to him that hath not done mercy ; and mercy exalteth itself above judgment." St. James, ii., 13. If the " Consiliarii " act in this Christian, just, and merciful spirit, and the accused in his written defence and oral answers (an oath cannot be adminstered to him, Chap. xvii., Tit. xii.), keeps himself within due bounds for proving his innocence, or bringing forward the circumstances that mitigate or extenuate his guilt, without animadverting unnecessarily on those who, by false reports, have tried to injure him ; in a word, if he is content to offer to the Counsel a plain, earnest, Christian defence—if, I repeat, both the accused and "Consiliarii" act in the above Christian and sacerdotal spirit, there will be no occasion to fear the evil hinted at in the last sentence of No. 5, which I pass over without comment.

To the prescriptions laid down by the letter of citation, the "Instructio" mentions an exception. In cases of occult crime, "in casu criminis occulti," prudence may forbid to inform the accused "per extensum," of the charge against him. In this case, he cannot be reasonably expected to prepare a written answer for the day he is required to appear before the Counsel. The *examen rei*, however, can be made. But, as the natural, divine and positive ecclesiastical law (Chap. xvii., Tit. iv.) gives to the accused the right of defence, and as two days even are considered too short a time (Chap. xvii., Tit. xv.) to prepare the same, he must be granted sufficient time for this purpose, and another day appointed for him to be heard.

When the crime is notorious, the culprit should be cited immediately before the Counsel, and the "Consiliarii" will act with the prudence and discretion suggested in Chap. xviii.

Intimately connected with citation is contumacy, spoken of in No. 8. The citation is made by letter (No. 4). If the letter of citation is handed to the accused by one deputed for the purpose (Chap. xvii., Tit. vii.), there can be, of course, no difficulty. The same may be said if the citation is conveyed to him by means of a registered letter, the reception of which he acknowledges by his signature. In these two cases the judge can know whether the citation reached the accused. If he does not put in an appearance after a second legitimate citation, unless lawfully hindered, he may then be accounted contumacious, and treated as such. But the case would be otherwise, if the two citations, however lawfully issued, were sent by simple, non-registered letters, for no one can be considered contumacious, unless it be certain that he received both citations, and was not legitimately hindered from appearing.

He who is contumacious can, though absent, be tried (Chap. xvii., Tit. x.), and he forfeits, moreover, his right to an alimentary pension (Chap. xvii., Tit. x.) until he submits to authority.

As to the witnesses (Nos. 10, 11, 12, 13 and 15), No. 12 gives the power of granting a personal confrontation (Chap. xvii., Tit. iv.) of the accused and the witnesses, when these latter are not unwilling. It may be asked in what cases does prudence suggest the granting of this privilege, which is rarely granted in regular canonical trials. I answer, whenever it may help to arrive at a certainty of the innocence or guilt of the accused, or clear up any doubt which may arise in the course of the investigation, "alio quocumque modo poterunt lumen ad dubia solvenda requirentes (Consiliarii)." N. 15 of " Instructio." " Nulla via intentata relinquatur ad verum moraliter certo cognoscendum, antequam ad sententiæ prolationem deveniatur." Ib.

Having already spoken of the necessity of a verbal confrontation, or legitimation of the proceedings, there is but one important point to discuss with reference to the witnesses, viz.: Has the accused the right to take exception to them? It cannot be doubted that he possesses this right. For this is a right essential to a lawful defence, which itself is a right, according to all canonists, bestowed upon him, not only by the positive, but also by the natural law.

I need not speak of exceptions to their depositions, either oral or written, which offer no difficulty, but of those only against their persons. The principal objections, or exceptions *contra personas testium*, are those which exclude them *de jure* from being witnesses. In this category are those who had been bribed to testify, the infamous, perjurers, enemies of the accused, unless they depose in his favor, and others, as may be seen in any regular treatise on Canon Law.

The justice of any exception must always be proved by the exceptor. Exceptions may be taken against the witnesses for the defence, as well as against those of the prosecution.

It now only remains to say a word on the decisions of the " Consiliarii" (No. 9), and on the definite sentence, in the case (No. 17), given by the bishop. THE SENTENCE OF THE LATTER MUST BE CLEAR, CANONICAL, UNCONDITIONAL, GIVING THE GROUNDS OF LAW AND FACT FOR THE SAME. (Chap. xvii., Tit. xviii.)

The decision of the " Consiliarii," as well as the sentence of the bishop, must be JUXTA ALLEGATA ET PROBATA, OR, TO BE MORE DEFINITE, JUXTA PROBABILIOREM SENTENTIAM.

In criminal causes, the judge, or bishop, MUST ACQUIT THE ACCUSED, IF HIS INNOCENCE BE MORE PROBABLE THAN HIS GUILT, whilst he CANNOT CONDEMN HIM, EVEN

THOUGH HIS GUILT BE PROBABLE. There must be a PLENA PROBATIO, or CERTAIN AND INDISPUTABLE EVIDENCE OF GUILT TO JUSTIFY A SENTENCE OF CONDEMNATION. This is not only the unanimous teaching of all theologians and canonists, but is dictated by the natural law, and prescribed by positive law. It is, therefore, according to these principles, which are beyond controversy, that the " Consiliarii," (Nos. 9 and 14) as well as the judge or bishop (No. 17), must form their judgments and pronounce sentence.

Although the expression in No. 17: " Sententia in Curia Episcopali prolata," might suggest a doubt, as to whether any other officials, besides those mentioned in the " Instructio ;" as, for instance, the members of the bishop's Council, spoken of in the II. Plenary Council of Baltimore, are to be understood by it, and thus insinuate, that the bishop would not be the only judge in criminal and disciplinary causes, yet I think the words of the " Instructio " : (j) " Ita episcopo in ipsis (causis) definiendis auxilium præbere," and again, the words " ad episcopum (No. 9) deferantur," are sufficient to show, that after the quasi-judicial investigation, and the opinion or decision of the " Consiliarii " is made known to him, the bishop can, without any further consultation, pronounce sentence, although even then, in view of the importance of the matter, it might be better and more prudent to take the advice of his Episcopal Council in the matter.

Of appeals, which are allowed by the " Instructio," (No. 16), I have, in Chap. xvii., Tit. xx., spoken at length.

In conclusion, I will answer an objection that may be

made by some to the above commentary, viz.: that it makes the quasi-judicial investigation too canonical. Well, I have only to say, that it has no authority whatever, except in as far as it is conformable to the spirit and letter of the "Instructio" itself, and in accordance with the authentic principles and Decisions of Sacred Congregations sustaining it. Of the justness of their application in the above brief commentary, every one is at liberty to judge for himself.

No doubt at this very moment, Rome would be well pleased, if in those dioceses where it is of easy observance, regular canonical procedure were instituted. The "Instructio" intimates this much, when, in the beginning, it asserts that canonical trials would be the most sure and efficacious means of administering justice, and that the only reason (f) for not prescribing them was, that these trials could not be well carried out in all the dioceses of the United States.

Besides, I don't think I am far astray, if at all, in interpreting the "Instructio" according to acknowledged canonical principles. As I view it, it is for us now a canonical document, or a rule of action, prescribed by the most venerable and august authority in the Church, our most Holy Father himself, for the observance of all our venerable prelates in all criminal and disciplinary causes that may arise among the clergy. And certainly, no one will deny, that some such *norma agendi* was not only much needed, but an imperative necessity. When we seriously reflect over the matter, when we examine the Canon Law of the Church, even as given in these scanty pages, we are amazed that such a loose condition of ecclesiastical discipline as has existed in the United States, should have been allowed to continue for so long a time.

Let us take only this matter of ecclesiastical trials, or canonical investigations, which we have been discussing in the preceding chapters. When a clergyman in this country has been charged with some offence, has any proper and serious investigation, as a rule, according to canonical principles, been made into the accusation? There has not. If it has been done, it was the exception. Many a time and oft has a delinquent been simply informed by his bishop that "he had no further use for him, and that he must seek employment elsewhere," putting him on the same footing with his maid-servant or his gardener. Is this according to the spirit or letter of the Canon Law of the Church, or in accordance with the above " Instructio" from Rome? I seriously doubt if Rome is even yet aware of how ecclesiastical matters have been and are managed by some of those whom she has elevated to the chair of authority, and to whom she has given jurisdiction over her clergy and faithful. Some of their acts have been such, that neither their venerable colleagues in authority, nor Rome, nor the Canon Law of the Church, nor justice, nor charity, nor humanity, can ever sanction; and of these I need only mention that crying evil of refusing delinquent clergymen a canonical investigation and a canonical punishment for their fault, and of sending them forth as wanderers and outcasts on the face of the earth, to beg their bread, or earn it by the sweat of their brows.

This is a grave disordination, a serious abuse, an unmitigated and an inexcusable evil condemned by the "Instructio" just given and explained, as well as by so many other venerable and weighty authorities found in the foregoing pages. The disturber of the public peace, the thief and the murderer, nay, the vilest criminal in Christian and civilized communities, is not condemned until the evidence before the bar of justice convicts him of crime. If he is unable to employ counsel, the court assigns a lawyer to defend him. In a word, he is given every opportunity to vindicate his innocence, or prove circumstances extenuating his guilt. Any reasonable doubt of the latter will be given in his favor, and restrain the tongues of judge and jury from uttering a sentence of condemnation. *And yet the civil law is but a reflex of the Canon Law of the Church.* It is perfectly astounding, then, how this latter has been so often disregarded in our midst, in its most solemn and strict injunctions in plain matters of right and justice. There will and must be an end to this. The honor and welfare of the venerable hierarchy of these States demand that they look into this matter, and correct this abnormal *modus agendi*, on the part of some of its members. It is too glaring an injustice, it is too hostile to the interests of religion and of the clergy, and to their own interests, for it to be allowed to continue. .

The faithful observance of the provisions of the "Instructio" *Quamvis* given above, is the first step towards the introduction of Canon Law into our land. It is the morning star of the sun of justice and equity in all ecclesiastical matters. As the morning star in the heavens is the har-

binger of day, which it ushers in, so the above admirable
" Instructio " of the Sacred Congregation is the precursor in the United States, sent by Rome, to prepare the
way for the introduction of the Canon Law of the Church
in all ecclesiastical matters, as far as it is useful and practicable, and which, when it does come, will wonderfully
promote the welfafe and happiness of our venerable hierarchy, devoted clergy and faithful laity, and give a new
impetus to the progress of the Catholic religion in our
midst.

CHAPTER XXIII.

ON CANONICAL PUNISHMENTS.

This chapter will be brief, as it treats on a subject familiar to all the clergy, being found in every text-book of Moral Theology. Yet it is necessary that I should say something on Canonical punishments, which are intimately connected with canonical procedure, whether this latter be in the form of a regular canonical trial, or of a quasi-judicial investigation only; for the end of a canonical trial, or quasi-judicial investigation, is to ascertain the whole truth in the matter charged against the accused, and thus form a judgment as to his guilt or innocence, and pass sentence accordingly. If found innocent, he is acquitted; if proved guilty, he is liable to be punished *juxta allegata et probata.*

What I state in this chapter on canonical punishments is chiefly taken from a work entitled: "Juris Canonici secundum Gregorii Papæ IX., libros v. Decretalium explanati Summa seu Compendium, Auctore R. P. Vitus Pichler, S. J."

A canonical punishment may be defined, "Justa delicti coercitio," or "a punishment proportioned to the fault, and inflicted by one having the power."

Canonical penalties may be divided into two classes: 1. *Pœnæ vindicativæ.* 2. *Pœnæ medicinales.*

The Pœnæ vindicativæ are Deposition and Degradation.

Konings defines Deposition: "Pœna ecclesiastica, qua clericus, non solum ab omni munere Ordinis ac Beneficii repellitur, sed etiam officio et Beneficio omnino privatur, ablato titulo, ita ut, ad illud sine nova collatione redire nequeat. Depositio irrogari potest ab episcopo, vel ejus vicario ad hoc deputato, at *in casibus in Jure expressis*, et *pro delictis atrocioribus*. Quamvis autem de se, pœna sit irremissibilis, tolli tamen per dispensationem Episcopi poterit, quoties crimen adulterio minus fuerit."

Degradation is the most grievous punishment that the Church can inflict on a clergyman. It is decreed only for the *most atrocious crimes*. By it a clergyman is solemnly and authentically deprived, not only of his Order, Benefice and Office, but even of the clerical state or profession, *i. e.*, of all clerical privileges, *Fori, Canonis*, etc. Once degraded, he can be punished by the secular power, according to the civil laws.

When the sentence of degradation is pronounced, it is called *degradatio verbalis;* when solemnly executed, *realis*. If one undergoing the punishment of *degradatio realis*, is not punished by the secular power with death, he is scarcely ever restored to his former state, which can be done by the Pope alone.

Konings defines Degradation: "Degradatio est solemnis privatio omnium titulorum, honorum, privilegiorum, et bonorum ecclesiasticorum, ita ut, degradatus, solo remanente ordinis caractere indelebili, ad conditionem laicalem reducatur."

"Degradatio non potest infligi nisi ab Episcopo, et *pro immanibus sceleribus*, cujusmodi sunt crimen hæresis manifestum, falsificatio Litterarum Apostolicarum, Sodomia frequentata, gravissima calumnia proprio Episcopo apposita, etc. Solus Papa in hac gravissima pœna dispensat."

I will be pardoned here for the expression of a thought which presents itself to my mind, and which is suggested by the words I have just written. It is, that it would not be amiss for even the most exemplary clergyman to read over in the *Pontificale Romanum* the ceremonial of the Degradation of a priest. It is impressive in the extreme, and calculated to inspire a horror for sin, which alone can bring so dread and terrible a punishment on a clergyman. One by one the sacred vestments are stripped from his person, and his anointed hands are scraped to erase from them as it were the Holy Oils of consecration. He stands after this terrible ceremony, a lone, pitiable object, bearing, it is true, the ineffaceable mark of the Priesthood on his soul, but for his humiliation and greater confusion, for whom there is no longer hope on earth, and none in heaven, except through the mercy of God and the tears and works of a penitential life. O God, how sad a spectacle is the degradation of a priest! How sad and humiliating and horrible to the unfortunate priest himself! How sad and painful and terrible to those who may witness it! And yet every sin degrades the sacerdotal character! Dearly beloved of Jesus Christ, His friends and the spiritual Fathers of His people, let us often think of the sanctity required by our high and sublime vocation, and endeavor by prayer and vigilance, and correspondence with divine grace, to become more and more holy. "Be ye holy, because I the Lord your God am holy."

Alas! that punishment should ever be necessary to keep clergymen in the path of duty! Considering the sanctity of the clerical state; its sublime and august dignity; the close and intimate contact into which it brings him with his God, that of consecrating bread and wine, and changing them into the Body and Blood of Jesus Christ, of which he partakes himself, and which he distributes to others; the saintly relations it establishes with his neighbor, for he stands between the porch and the altar to offer up sacrifice for the people; the immense helps it gives him of leading a holy life; the fearful accountability he has towards souls, and the terrible account he must one day render of his stewardship; all these, it seems, should make it impossible for him to sin, and thus bring upon himself punishment. And yet, alas! he sometimes does. Oh! sin, what a monster thou art! Thou didst once change a beautiful angel of paradise into a revolting demon, and thou dost, even now, sometimes enter into the paradise of the sanctuary, and transform an Angel of earth—a priest—into an enemy of God! We priests, above all men, should heed the solemn injunction of our dearest Saviour to His sorrow-stricken disciples in the garden of Gethsemane: "Vigilate et orate ut non intretis in tentationem."—"Neglect not the grace that is in thee, which was given thee by prophecy, with imposition of the hands of the priesthood. Meditate upon these things, be wholly in these things: that thy profiting may be manifest to all. Take heed to thyself and to doctrine:

be earnest in them. For in doing this thou shalt both save thyself and them that hear thee." 1. Tim. iv. 14-16.

Yet another thought suggests itself to my mind in connection with these terrible punishments of deposition and degradation, and with the main subject of my humble treatise, and to which I cannot refrain from giving expression.

We have just seen that deposition is inflicted for cases only which are determined by the law "in casibus in jure expressis," and "pro delictis atrocioribus," and that degradation is decreed only "pro immanibus sceleribus." And yet, alas! in the United States, under our hitherto miserable, abnormal and anomalous condition of ecclesiastical government, deposition and degradation have been inflicted on delinquent clergymen, not formally, it is true, but practically and to all intents and purposes, not indeed for the crimes which they were intended to punish, which, thank God, are unheard of amongst us, but for ordinary faults; aye, these terrible punishments have been more frequently employed against erring clergymen, than the paternal admonition, or the judicial precept, or the canonical investigation. For what else is it essentially, but the punishment of deposition and degradation, to dismiss helplessly from his diocese an erring priest, not contumacious? Is there not food here for reflection on the part of our venerable and beloved bishops?

I will now speak briefly on the medicinal, or correctional punishments inflicted by the Church on delinquent clergymen. They are called *pœnæ medicinales*, because they are administered to cure him who has proved himself morally infirm. Their object is his correction and reformation. These punishments are known under the name of Censures.

Censures are inflicted to the end that a delinquent and contumacious subject may be brought to a sense of duty, which milder means, as precepts, admonitions, etc., failed to effect, and that he may thus be induced to enter into himself to the correcting and amending of his life. Hence Deposition and Degradation of which I spoke above, though spiritual punishments are not censures.

Censures are divided into 1. Censuræ, *a jure, vel ab homine* latæ. 2. Censuræ, *latæ vel ferendæ sententiæ.* These terms explain their nature.

1. All Ecclesiastical Superiors, even Regulars, possessing ordinary jurisdiction *in foro externo et contensioso,* and they only, can inflict censures.

2. The subjects of censure are all Christians capable of guilt (doli capaces).

3. That censure may be justly inflicted, a sin mortal in its nature, committed with full knowledge and advertence, and joined to contumacy, formal or virtual, is required. Otherwise, the censure before God is not binding. Ex cap. 5; *de pæna in sexto.*—Council Trent, Sess. xxv. c. 3. *de Refor.* A censure is a grave penalty which can be inflicted for a grave fault only. The sin, moreover, must be external and complete in its kind as described by the letter of the law, or of the superior punishing, according to the fifteenth Rule *Juris in Sexto,* " Odia restringi, et favores convenit ampliari." This

condition Schmalzgrueber *l.* 5 *tit.* 39. *n.* 64. explains in these words : "Externum, ob quod censura concutienda est debet esse completum in suo genere secundum proprietatem verborum, quæ in præcepto seu lege infligente censuram, continentur." Besides these conditions, the fault for which the censure is inflicted must be joined with contempt of authority, either formal or virtual, or with contumacy. It is, therefore, necessary that *the fault in some measure continue, and be not merely of the past,* for the object of the censure is to correct the fault, and oblige the delinquent to purge himself of his contumacy and disobedient spirit. Thus Christ Himself (Matth. xviii.) did not wish a delinquent to be considered a heathen and excluded from the pale of the Church until he became *contumacious,* or *refused to hear the Church* after having been expostulated with, and *duly admonished.*

An *admonition,* therefore, ought to be given beforehand, and *disregarded,* before one can be considered *contumacious.* If the law itself imposes a censure for a certain fault, there is no need of a special admonition, because in this case the law itself sufficiently and always admonishes. Hence the following reasons excuse from censures. 1. Ignorance of the Law, or of the Fact, unless such ignorance should be gross, or affected, or mortally sinful. 2. Doubt of the Law or of the Fact, if, after diligent inquiry, the doubt remains. 3. Grave fear unjustly inspired, by reason of which the law is violated, for although it may not excuse from sin, yet he cannot be considered contumacious, who does a thing unwillingly. Such, however, would not be the case if the fear were directly inspired for the purpose of forcing one to do something in contempt of the law, or to communicate *in crimine criminoso* with one who is excommunicated. 4. A legitimate appeal, if interposed before the censure is inflicted. Finally, *innocence*, although the fact be proved *in foro externo, c. 2. 7. h. t. in sexto*.

4. That a censure may be lawfully inflicted *ab homine*, by a special sentence, it is necessary, 1. That a *triple admonition* precede it, with a sufficient interval of time between them, or *one peremptory admonition which is stated to be such, and in which the time allowed for three admonitions is given*. An admonition is also required, even when the judge wishes to denounce one who has incurred censure *ipso jure;* at least, this is necessary, that he may act licitly, unless the crime is notorious.

5. He who has incurred censure must be absolved therefrom, even though he has returned to a sense of duty, and, having put aside his contumacy, has given full satisfaction for his fault, as can be seen from the following proposition condemned by Alex. VII. " Quoad forum conscientiæ, reo correcto, ejusque contumacia cessante, cessant censuræ," unless the censure was inflicted with the clause of amendment expressly stated, as, " Donec se emendaverit, vel satisfecerit censuratus."

Who can absolve from censures?

If the censure was inflicted *ab homine* by a special sentence, he alone (at least *pro foro etiam externo*) who inflicted the censure, or his successor, or his superior having immediate jurisdiction, or their delegate, can absolve from it.

If the censure is incurred *ipso jure*, vel *lege*, or *ab homine*, but by a general decree, (which is equivalent to a law) and is not especially reserved, any approved confessor can absolve from it.

If the censure is reserved, then, he who reserves it, or his successor, or his superior having jurisdiction, or their delegate, can absolve *pro utroque foro*. This is *per se* evident. If the censure is reserved to the Pope, the Bishop has the power to absolve *pro foro interno* for occult censure not yet brought *ad forum contentiosum* —Council. of Trent, sess xxiv c. 6 *de refor.*, as well as the Religious of Mendicant Orders, except for the censures of the Bull *Cæna*, in case of necessity, or impossibility of going to Rome.

In articulo mortis all priests can absolve from any and every censure, only requiring of the penitent, that in case of restoration to health, he present himself to him who reserved the censure, and obey his injunctions.

How is absolution from censure given?

Although there is no prescribed form in Canon Law, or certain words for absolution from censure, and although the presence of the one to be absolved is not even required, as is the case in sacramental absolution from sin, yet *pro foro externo.* the rite used in the diocese ought to be observed, or that found in the *Pontificale Romanum*. *Pro foro interno* the following formula is used : " Ego te absolvo a vinculo excommunicationis (suspensionis, etc.,) quam incurristi propter causam N. et restituo te sacramentis Ecclesiæ et communioni fidelium (executioni tuorum ordinum, officiorum, beneficiorum etc., si absolvendus fuit in suspensione), in nomine Patris et Filii et Spiritus Sancti. Amen." But if the absolution is given in virtue of delegated power, the following words are used : " Auctoritate Omnipotentis Dei, SS. Apostolorum Petri et Pauli, et SSmi Domini nostri N... PP. (si absolvens delegationem habeat a Papa) in hac parte mihi concessa, absolvo et etc.," Monacelli in Formulario, *p.* 3. *in prælud. n. 75.*

In concluding this Chapter on punishments, which is the natural complement of those on canonical trials, and that on the Quasi Judicial Investigation, I may be allowed a remark which suggests itself to my thoughts in connection with the main topic of this humble work, and which may have been embodied in the ideas that occurred to the minds of my readers, whilst perusing these pages, and that is, how uncanonical is the terrible punishment that has so often been inflicted in the United States on delinquent clergymen, not contumacious, and often penitent, that of casting them forth on the world helpless, and frequently penniless, to beg their bread, or earn it in some secular pursuit, instead of giving them a home, or a refuge of some kind, where they could live as becomes their sacred character. In the whole *Corpus Juris Canonici*, in the multitudinous regulations of Œcumenical, General, and Provincial Councils, in all the Decisions of Sacred Congregations, there cannot be found one line justifying such a cruel and unjust punishment. Whenever there is question of erring clergymen, the church speaks of their correction and amendment, and of just punishment inflicted for that purpose, " Eadem sacrosancta tridentina

Synodus, in Spiritu Sancto legitime congregata... eos (episcopos) admonendos censet, ut... elaborent ut hortando, et monendo, ab illicitis deterreant, ne, ubi deliquerint *debitis eos pœnis coercere cogantur.* Sin autem ob delicti gravitatem virga opus fuerit, tunc cum mansuetudine rigor, cum misericordia judicium, cum lenitate severitas adhibenda est ut *sine asperitate* disciplina populis salutaris ac necessaria conservetur : et qui correcti fuerint, EMENDENTUR." The admirable spirit of charity, mercy and justice in dealing with the weak and the erring, conveyed in these words is expressed in every page *de Refor.* of the holy and Œcumenical Council of Trent, as any one can verify, who will take the trouble to glance over it; and besides, whilst undergoing this just punishment, the Church prescribes that they receive an alimentary pension, or the means of subsistence, as I have proved by so many venerable authorities, which is a far different thing from casting them forth into the streets to beg or starve. —" The ecclesiastical judge" (in this country, and according to the late " Instructio," *the bishop*) " IS BOUND IN CONSCIENCE TO PROVIDE FOR THE SUBSISTENCE OF THE CONDEMNED ; AND IF HE SHIRKS THIS DUTY OF JUSTICE HE CAN BE OBLIGED TO COMPLY WITH IT BY HIS SUPERIOR." Ita Stremler *des peines eccles. p.* 33, cited by Craisson in his *Manuale.*

It is from the ignoring altogether of the plain and fundamental principles of Canon Law, which hold as strictly and conscientiously in the United States as in any part of the world, that this terrible evil of homeless, helpless and wandering priests arises. Bishops are the spiritual Fathers of the clergy, "illos tanquam fratres et filios diligant," the protectors whom the Church has appointed over them. To this sacred and important trust they should be faithful under all circumstances, and never abandon any of them, however frail or unfortunate, unless he cuts himself loose from their protection by contumacy. Even then his true Pastor's heart will follow him with his prayers to the Throne of Grace, and when those prayers are heard, and his erring child returns to him as the humble and penitent prodigal, he will receive him with open arms and paternal kindness.

Let only the wise and merciful instructions and admonitions of the Church to her bishops be observed, and the legislation she has enacted for the correction of delinquent clergymen be faithfully and conscientiously carried out, *which inflicts canonical punishments in a canonical manner for canonical faults*, and there will not be found one priest in the United States without a fixed abode, wandering hither and thither "quasi ovis perdita aut errans."

CHAPTER XXIV.

WISDOM OF THE CHURCH IN HER JUDICIAL LEGISLATION.

As a consequence of the judicial legislation of the Church, a clergyman accused of any serious delinquency ought to be given a canonical trial, or, what takes its place in the United States for the present at least, a quasi judicial investigation. This is the common and general law of the Church. In civilized nations the most hardened criminal is given the benefits of a trial by a jury of his fellow-citizens—he is never condemned unheard. Need we be surprised then, that the Catholic Church, the advocate and champion of justice, the guardian of liberty and the mother of freemen, grants to her ministers a like right?

The principles underlying ecclesiastical tribunals of justice are founded on the law of nature itself, as I have already shown. Moreover, as intimated in the Constitution of Innocent III., *Qualiter et quando*, they are laid down in the very Gospel. In the eighteenth chapter of St. Matthew, we read: "If thy brother shall offend against thee, go and rebuke him, between him and thee alone. If he shall hear thee, thou shalt gain thy brother. But if he will not hear thee, take with thee one or two more; that in the mouth of two or more witnesses every word may stand. And if he will not hear them: tell the Church. And *if he will not hear the Church* [contumacy] let him be to thee as the heathen and publican." And again we read in the sixteenth chapter of St. Luke, " How is it that I hear this of thee? Give an account of thy stewardship: for now thou cánst be steward no longer."

The Catholic Church accordingly has established ecclesiastical tribunals of justice, at which every one of her ministers, even the poorest and humblest, who may be charged with any crime, has a right to seek and demand justice. Not only this, but should he feel that justice is denied him at the tribunal of his own ecclesiastical superior, he has the right of appeal from bishop, archbishop, primate, patriarch, or cardinal, to the highest ecclesiastical tribunal in the Church, the Court of Rome. Rome is eminently just, and in matters of justice has no respect of persons. The golden mitre even will not outweigh in the scales of Rome's impartial justice the poor and humble cassock. Well may we all, bishops, priests and people, rally around the Chair of St. Peter, not only the Centre of Unity and the Guardian of Faith and Morals, but also the Protector of the weak and helpless, the Defender of Right, the advocate of the wronged, the champion of the oppressed, ever holding in her hands the evenly adjusted balance of justice, to be administered to rich and poor alike, prelate and priest, prince and people. This justice, so evenly, and uprightly, and impartially administered at Rome and by Rome, the Church wishes to see administered by her ecclesiastical tribunals in every part of the world.

The United States government, or any state government, does not oblige every citizen to go to Washington, or to the capital city of the State, to have his grievance heard or redressed, or to answer for any violation of law. Their courts of justice are within reasonable reach of all their subjects. In like manner, the more perfect government of the Church wishes that her tribunals for the administration of justice be within easy access of all those who may be necessitated to have recourse to them. As the civil government has its judiciary in every State and county, and moreover a Court of Appeals and a Supreme Court, whose decisions are ultimate and conclusive, so the Church wishes her tribunals of justice to exist in every part of the Church, with the right of appeal to Rome, the supreme or ultimate tribunal for the settlement of all ecclesiastical matters. With this arrangement, every priest in the world, no matter how remote soever the corner of the globe in which he dwells, can easily obtain justice, nor is any one ever left to the mercy of one man, or to the persecutions of his enemies, of the evil-disposed and the godless, but is protected by the ecclesiastical tribunal of his diocese either from being condemned when innocent, or too rigorously punished when guilty.

Hence the "Instructio" *Quamvis* of July 20, 1878, directed to all the bishops of the United States. As soon as Rome became convinced that Decree N. 77 of the II. Plenary Council of Baltimore was either disregarded, or inadequate for the ends of justice, she immediately issued a code of laws for the observance of all our venerable prelates in criminal and disciplinary causes of clergymen, which she commanded to be rigorously observed. "S. C. de F. P.... providendum esse duxit, ut saltem illæ de admisso crimine accurate peragantur investigationes, quæ omnio necessariæ existimantur, antequam ad pœnam irrogandam, deveniatur. Itaque SSmo. Domino Nostro Divina Providentia PP. Leone XIII., approbante,. . . . Sacra Congregatio *decrevit ac districte mandavit*," etc.

Even later than this "Instructio" is other sterling evidence that the Church never wishes any of her children to be condemned without a hearing, but that a judicial process should either determine their innocence, or the extent of their guilt, as well as, in the latter case, the punishment to be undergone in expiation of it. As late as June 11, 1880, a document was issued by the S. C. Ep. et Reg. confirming all I have said on this matter of judicial investigations. It can be found in the *Acta S. Sedis*, vol. xiii., p. 324, and is entitled " Instructio pro eccclesiasticis Curiis quoad modum procedendi œconomice in causis disciplinaribus et criminalibus clericorum." This, like all the other canonical documents found in these pages, shows forth the spirit of mercy and justice which animates all the criminal and disciplinary legislation of the Church.

The wisdom of the Church's judicial legislation is apparent to every just and sensible man. What more wise, and just, and merciful even, than that a clergyman accused of crime should be canonically tried, and, if found guilty, canonically punished? Without such canonical investigation, the bishop is exposed to condemn a priest for a fault of which he is innocent—for a fault which had no existence, except in the imaginations and base hearts of malicious, suspicious, or evil-disposed persons.

If the annals of our ecclesiastical government as it has been, alas! but too often administered, were ransacked, more than one instance of such condemnation of the innocent would be found! But if only one innocent priest in a century suffered such crying injustice, would not this alone be a sufficient reason to sweep away forever the tribunal in which one man alone sits as judge and jury, in which often the prosecution alone is heard, and in which little or no opportunity of defence is given, a tribunal ever and always "odious," no matter how good, or just, or upright the judge may be—the only tribunal that has practically existed in the United States, up to the promulgation of the late "Instructio" *Quamvis* of the Sacred Congregation of the Propaganda, and, alas! that I must add with heart-felt sorrow, ever since.

Again, when no judicial or quasi judicial investigation is made of a charge brought against a clergyman, the consequence is, that the accused, if guilty, is condemned in some instances, perhaps in most cases, for an offence far greater than he committed. His fault is often made by *Madam Rumor* as unlike the actual transgression as the noonday sunshine is unlike the darkness of midnight. The story of the Three Black Crows finds its parallel in every fault, indiscretion and sin of a clergyman beyond any one else.

The Church has a dread and a horror of committing the slightest injustice against any one. By her the humblest clergyman, without friends or influence, is judged as justly and impartially as he who has both to help him in his difficulties. The love of justice and horror of injustice inherent in the Church is clearly seen from the fact, that even when the crime is notorious, she does not permit the delinquent to be condemned without a citation and a hearing, as we have seen in the chapter treating of procedure *Ex Notorio*. Even then, there may be extenuating or palliating circumstances to lessen the grievousness of his fault, and to mitigate the severity of his sentence. This clearly shows the desire of the Church that all her officials be just, and the dread and fear she has, a fear and dread in which they should participate, of punishing even the most evidently guilty beyond their deserts. The same spirit of strict and impartial justice, and horror of injustice, should animate the deliberations of every ecclesiastical tribunal, and the heart of every member thereof.

Canonical punishments canonically inflicted for cannonical offences are the *norma agendi* of the Church towards delinquent clergymen. This *norma agendi* is in accordance with the Holy and Œcumenical Council of Lateran under Innocent III., with that of Trent, with that of Baltimore, and with the decree of Gregory XVI. It is likewise in accordance with the spirit and letter of the " Instructio" recently issued by Rome, commanding that in every diocese of the United States a quasi Judicial tribunal be constituted, whose object is to examine, carefully and impartially, the causes of clergymen, to the end that, if innocent, they may be acquitted, and punished canonically if found guilty.

Those in power, therefore, who set at naught these venerable authorities in their treatment of their clergy cannot but be derelict to a just, sacred, and well defined duty of conscience, as well as disobedient to the voice of the highest authority in the Church.

Moreover, a canonical trial, or quasi judicial investigation of all important charges made against clergymen, would reconcile the rights of all concerned, of bishops, priests and people. It would shield the honor and conscience of the bishops, protect and do justice to the priest, and give satisfaction to the faithful, who do not wish either to see a priest condemned unjustly, or retained in office if he is unworthy. It would put an end also to the heart burnings and bitter feelings and just complaints of priests and people to which uncanonical proceedings have sometimes given occasion in this country, CULMINATING, SOMETIMES, IN SEEKING REDRESS IN CIVIL COURTS, to the great disedification of the people, and to the scandal and dishonor of religion.

The wisdom of the Church in insisting upon canonical trials, and now, for this country, on quasi-judicial investigations, and canonical punishments for delinquent clergymen would moreover be seen from the happy results of good order and discipline in general, and the correction of the guilty in particular, that would necessarily follow therefrom.

I know very well, that as there was one, even among the Apostles, who threw himself away, blinded and led astray by the devil of avarice, and who wilfully went to perdition, so, alas! we may possibly find, though seldom if at all, an unfortunate clergyman, whom no charity will save, no mercy soften, no law curb or restrain. But if such a case is found, he is, like Judas, the exception. The most part of clergymen who have fallen from grace might have been saved by canonical treatment. No one who has given any attention to this subject will deny, that many a priest in the United States has been actually and efficiently driven to ruin by being made a helpless outcast on the world, instead of being canonically punished for his fault. Many of them sleep to-day in silent and premature graves, but those who were instrumental in digging them, are not without accountability before God. I say this in view of the spirit and letter, and in the name of the Canon Law of the Church, which never wished, nor does wish, nor ever will wish, that even the most unworthy of her ministers, not contumacious, should be cruelly and uncanonically punished, by being abandoned by their lawful superiors, and thus exposed to imminent danger of utter ruin, spiritual, temporal, and sometimes eternal.

I am no believer in total depravity. The same God, praise and glory be ever given to his most holy and adorable Name, reigns over us, as over our brethren in other parts of the Catholic Church, and his grace is as freely given to us, and is as efficacious now, as that which converted a Peter, afterwards made head of the Church, or an Augustine, who became a shining light and glorious pillar of the same. As sure as his merciful arm is not shortened, so sure am I, that many an erring priest in these United States, would never have suffered complete shipwreck, nay, might have become, if not an ornament, at least an honor to religion, and a useful member of the Church, had they been treated with the Christian charity and the Christian justice the Church inculcates, and according to the laws of right which she has so frequently and explicitly made known for the rule and guidance of her officials—in a word, had canonical punishments been canonically inflicted upon them, when they offended against the law.

If the wise punishments prescribed and regulated by the salutary Canon Law of the Church, had been applied in the proper spirit, weight and measure, to erring clergymen in the beginning of their downward career, they probably would have been checked in time, and saved. But abandoned altogether by their bishops, punished uncanonically by being dismissed helplessly from their dioceses, they in their wanderings fell headlong over the precipice of despondency and despair, to perish in the abyss of moral ruin beneath. Condign punishment, inflicted according to the spirit and letter of the Holy Canons, and according to the gravity and frequency of the fault would have corrected them and saved them. I said according to the gravity and *frequency* of the offence. But, had these punishments been inflicted in time, and in the proper manner, the fault most probably, would not have been committed frequently.

If after a clergyman's first misstep, his bishop were to admonish him, "rebuke him between him and thee alone" as the gospel and the Canon Law of the Church direct, might it not save him? If this paternal admonition failed of having the desired effect, were he then to summon the culprit before his ecclesiastical court, or quasi judicial counsel to answer for his offence, and to receive the proper, just and canonical punishment in expiation of the same, this very fact, together with the punishment thus inflicted, would make such an impression on his mind, it seems to me, that in all probability, the offence would not be repeated. The very fact of a trial is sometimes considered by the Church a sufficient punishment. Hence we have in Canon Law the acquittal "Ex quo satis," of which I have spoken in a previous chapter. If, however, he erred a second time, the same proceedings with a punishment increased, or doubled, would, for the most part of men at least, be an infallible remedy against the recurrence of the fault. I can scarcely conceive it possible for a delinquent, punished with rigor for the third time, to ever again fall into the same fault.

But it may be here objected, that a clergyman has fallen into the same fault a dozen times or more. No one, I dare affirm, ever heard of such a case, when the delinquent was treated in the manner I have just laid down, which is the canonical way enjoined by the Church. I have heard of clergymen falling into the same fault frequently, but I again venture to say, that it was more the fault of the uncanonical manner in which they were treated by their ecclesiastical superiors than their own.

This assertion I will prove by an example or illustration taken from ordinary life. Let us take the case of a merchant, or of a student broken down in health, in consequence of over application to business or study in their respective avocations in life. That physician would be an unskilled one indeed, who would simply recommend the one, to set up business in some other locality, for the recuperating of his physical energies, and the other, merely to remove to another college for the invigorating of his mental powers. A wise and experienced physician, on the contrary, would prescribe for the one and the other, the giving up altogether for a year or longer, of the duties of their respective callings, and in quiet and retirement, by subjecting themselves to strict bodily discipline as regards eating, sleeping, exercise, etc., to thus seek the permanent cure of their bodily or mental ailments.

In like manner, the clergyman who loses the spirit of his vocation, or his spiritual health, and commits some indiscretion or fault in consequence, should be prescribed for by his bishop, or the quasi judicial Counsel of the diocese, and be retired to the quiet of some religious monastery, or ecclesiastical Home for one year or more, to recover the health of his soul. If, after having regained this, he should have a relapse, it only proves that his retirement, and the medicinal waters of prayer, recollection, holy reading, silence, study and penance, were not continued sufficiently long, to insure a permanent cure. If his infirmity is radical, or incurable, he ought to be left in the hospital altogether, or in other words, be kept permanently in holy retirement. It is much more cruel to employ a priest in active duty when he is unfit for it, than to put a poor, asthmatic invalid to breaking stones on the turnpike. Humanity revolts at the latter, well ordained charity reprobates the former.

We sometimes hear bishops complain of the incorrigibility of such, or another clergyman. And yet, perhaps, they never gave him the opportunity of retiring to some

Religious House for a year or more, to establish himself in his good resolutions by prayer and the practice of virtue. Many a bishop in the United States, on the contrary, has acted precisely like the foolish physician mentioned above. He contented himself with simply sending his subject, sick and weak in soul as he was, to another field of labor. No wonder indeed, that he succumbed after a short time to a new attack of his old malady. It would rather have been a wonder if he did not. After a few such removals and falsely so called trials, his patience is exhausted. He declares that all has been done for him that could be done. He pronounces him incorrigible, dismisses him from his diocese, and abandons him to himself and almost certain ruin.

Such ecclesiastical superiors may flatter themselves that because they gave a clergyman three or four chances to pick himself up, they acted most kindly and mercifully towards him. But in reality, they did little or nothing for him. *Their mistaken mercy was bitter cruelty.* For, like the foolish doctor, they set him to work when his malady imperatively demanded rest and retirement. Under the soothing hallucination that they did their whole duty for him, and acted most charitably and mercifully towards him, in giving him two, four, or even a half dozen chances to recover himself, their consciences are at rest, though in the end, they sent him adrift on the world, a wanderer and an outcast on the face of the earth. I think, and I say it in all the sincerity of my heart, and at the same time in all kindness, and charity, that such ecclesiastical superiors have much reason to feel great uneasiness of mind and conscience, for of a truth, and without any exaggeration, they acted cruelly towards that poor priest, in sending him, like the quack doctor, to work in another portion of the diocese, before he was even convalescent.

How much wiser and beneficial would it have been for these bishops who have treated their clergy in this manner, to have observed towards them the method of treatment laid down by the Holy Canons of the Church, or in other words, how much better for their own consciences, the good of the faithful, and the advantage of their erring subject, had they imitated the skilled and experienced practitioner, who sends his patient into the quiet and retirement of the country, to drink pure milk, and inhale fresh air, and take health-giving exercise. In like manner, the pure milk of recollection and pious meditation, the fresh air of seclusion from the world, and the life-giving exercises of mental and vocal prayer, study and holy reading, would have reinstated his infirm subject in his former health, if not have made him more robust than ever.

The canonical treatment, therefore, of clergymen, according to the prescriptions of that most skilled physician of souls, the Catholic Church, is the one which every bishop on earth should follow, the importance, necessity and utility of which have been proved by the test of centuries.

The Church, in insisting that all clergymen accused of any infraction of law, be canonically tried and canonically punished, not for the sake of punishment, but "ut emendentur" shows in this, as in all things else, her consummate and heaven inspired wisdom.

CHAPTER XXV.

APOSTOLIC DELEGATE.

In a few generations at most, the population of this immense territory which we inhabit may, and probably will be, doubled; every acre of the fertile valleys of the South and of the vast prairies of the West will be occupied. If the Catholic church in this land makes the same progress in the future as it has in the past, the religion of the Cross will be the prevailing religion in the United States. Such assuredly will be the case if the marvellous growth of the church in the last fifty years continues during the fifty years to come.

It behooves therefore, nay, it is an imperative duty incumbent on the pastors of the flocks in our day to take the means necessary to secure this glorious destiny of the church in these United States. What are those means? There are many which will suggest themselves to the minds of all, and some of which I will indicate in this chapter, but there can be no doubt, that a uniform and just discipline throughout the length and breadth of the land is of vital importance. We must have the same Catholic Church in the West as in the East, in the South as in the North, not only in matters of faith, but in matters of discipline, likewise; one homogeneous Catholic Church, united in indissoluble bonds to Rome, the centre of unity; the faithful, obedient to their pastors, these latter obedient to their bishops, and the bishops themselves obedient the voice of Peter, to the voice of Rome; all kept in unity and harmony, not only by the charity of Jesus Christ, but by wise and uniform laws, strictly and conscientiously observed by all.

The Catholic Church, it is true, cannot fail. She is founded on the everlasting and impregnable rock of Peter. She will last and perform her divine mission, notwithstanding the obstacles her enemies, either within or without, may place in the path of her success. But we know, likewise, that God in his all-wise and inscrutable providence has left His work in our hands. We know that organization directed and controlled by law and order will effect wonders, where individuals left to their own lights and to their own arbitrary methods of governing will effect little or nothing, or be instrumental in bringing confusion and sometimes positive injury on the mystic body of Christ. Those conversant with the history of the Catholic Church in this country, can readily recall sad instances demonstrating the truth of this assertion.

Therefore we need all the laws of ecclesiastical discipline already enacted, and those which Rome may yet think proper and good to impose on us, to be universally promulgated and universally observed. We do not want the interests of the Church to be jeopardized by irresponsible and arbitrary action on the part of any of those in power, whether of the first or second order of the hierarchy. We wish all, bishops, priests and laity, to be governed by wise and fixed laws, and in consequence possess that holy and inviolate liberty which that grand old faith of Jesus Christ grants to her children, and to all of them. Such, alas! is not the condition of the Catholic Church in these United States as has been abundantly proved in the preceding pages.

How, then, can this normal state of the Church, as it exists elsewhere, be secured for our favored land? How can the evils I have touched upon in these pages and others known to all, be effectively remedied? This question has been answered already. *Law* must take the place of all arbitrary power. But have we not law? Have we not the various Instructions issued by Rome from time to time? Have we not the Acta et Decreta of the II. Plenary Council of Baltimore? Aye, we have plenty of law on the statute books, but, alas! little of it observed. The Acta et Decreta of Baltimore, the various Instructions from Rome, not excepting the very latest, " have been laid on the shelf."

We want now, at length, the Instructions from Rome, the Acta et Decreta of the II. Plenary Council of Baltimore, to be taken down from the shelf, and opened and read, and their enactments put in force. " And all the people were gathered together as one man ;.... and they spoke to Esdras the scribe, to bring the book of the law of Moses, which the Lord had commanded to Israel. Then Esdras, the priest, brought the law before the multitude of men and women, and all those that could understand ;.... and he read it plainly in the street. . . . from the morning until midday. . . . and the ears of all the people were attentive to the book. And Esdras the scribe stood upon a piece of wood.... and there stood by him Mathathias, and Semeia, and Ania, and Uria, and Helcia, and Maasia on his right hand; and on the left Phadaia, Misael and Melchia, and Hasum and Hasbadana, Zacharia, and Mosollam. And Esdras opened the book before all the people, for he was above all the people.... And they read in the book of the law of God distinctly and plainly to be understood : and they understood when it was read." II. Esdras. ch. viii.

The book of the law of Moses had been hid away and almost forgotten, like the Acta et Decreta of Baltimore and the Instructions of Rome, until Esdras, animated with zeal for God's glory and the people's welfare, brought it forth once more in the midst of the people read it to them and insisted on its observance. We want in the United States another Esdras, who will "take down from the shelf," the Acta et Decreta of Baltimore and the different Instructions from Rome which have been given from time to time, read them to the clergy of the first and second order and insist upon their observance. Where will this Esdras be found? Not among our venerable prelates, for each one has jurisdiction only in his own diocese, and no authority to dictate outside of it. We must have one who is "above all the people." Plainly, then, we can look only to Rome for the Esdras that will put new life and vigor into the Church in these United States, who will bring law and order out of the chaos that now exists, who will govern the Church in these provinces with a just, yet mild and paternal hand for a few years, until ecclesiastical discipline has been firmly and securely established. We want an Apostolic Delegate, who, attended on his right hand by our most Rev. Archbishops, and on his left, by our Rt. Rev. Bishops, will "take down from the shelf" the almost forgotten Acta et Decreta of Baltimore, and the different Instructions from Rome, and like Esdras of old read them "distinctly and plainly to be understood" by the hierarchy of this land, and insist by virtue of his power and authority that all the laws of discipline contained therein be faithfully observed.

What other possible remedy for the grievances under which the Church in these United States labors? A Plenary Council, some one may answer. But what reasonable hope is there that another volume of Acta et Decreta will be observed any better than the one on our library shelves? What reason under heaven have we to believe that such will be the case? Absolutely none. Experience is our teacher, and in the light of past experience, were a Plenary Council to be convoked tomorrow, and make the most stringent laws, embodied in another volume of Acta et Decreta, it, like the volume of the Acta et Decreta of the II. Plenary Council of Baltimore, would in all probability be quietly "laid on the shelf," first by our venerable prelates themselves as they did before, and then by the clergy who could not be expected to follow laws and regulations which they ignored, or openly violated. No general Council, therefore, at the present time will or can for obvious reasons, remedy the evils resulting from our anomalous form of ecclesiastical government. In the judgment of many of the clergy and of some of our venerable prelates themselves, there is but one speedy and efficacious remedy for them. That remedy is the appointing by Rome of an Apostolic Delegate to these United States. Such an authority in our midst is at the present time absolutely necessary for the enforcement of the laws of discipline made by the II. Plenary Council of Baltimore, and contained in the various Instructions from Rome; necessary to relieve the Holy See itself which of late years, owing to uncanonical methods of action in those constituted in authority, has been literally overwhelmed with complaints from this country. I fear, alas! that without an Apostolic Delegate our generation will pass with Instructions, and Acta et Decreta, and Consiliarii, etc.,—on paper and—nothing more.

If indeed each diocese had well organized ecclesiastical courts of justice, or even its regularly appointed quasi Judicial Counsel as commanded by the recent "Instructio" *Quamvis* of our most Holy Father Leo XIII., and if, moreover, every ecclesiastical cause were canonically brought before it, and canonically treated, and in case of appeal, the appeal were accepted and acted upon by the Metropolitan, or Senior Bishop, with the right of ultimate appeal to Rome, there would be no need of an Apostolic Delegate, except as an occasional visitor. But as matters now stand, an Apostolic Delegate is absolutely necessary, not only for the reasons given above, but for the special reason that his presence and authority are needed to enforce obedience to the laws already enacted. For now even, although Rome "decrevit et stricte mandavit" that "Consiliarii" should be appointed in each diocese "quamprimum," and that all ecclesiastical causes should be brought before them, not many of our venerable prelates, as far as I can learn, have heeded this solemn injunction made by virtue of holy obedience, or if they have gone through the formality of constituting in their dioceses Quasi Judicial Counsels, I doubt much if there has been one case tried in the United States according to the spirit and letter of the "Instructio" since its promulgation. It is sad to think, as it is ominous of evil days for the Church in the United States, that any constituted in authority should be so heedless of the voice of the Head of the Church, whence they obtain their dignity and jurisdiction, yet it is, alas! but too true, showing to us and to them not only the importance, but the imperative necessity of an Apostolic Delegate to enforce obedience to the laws of the Church, and to the voice of the Supreme Pontiff, the Vicegerent of Jesus Christ in the government of His Church.

A Plenipotentiary, therefore, of the Holy See, or an Apostolic Delegate, is necessary for this country. The clergy are heartily sick and tired of the arbitrary and uncanonical manner in which, as a rule, they have been treated. They cry out for a representative of the Holy See in the United States. The universal complaint that has gone up for years from the clergy of the United States is, that Rome is so far distant that years sometimes are required to have causes decided by it. In consequence much injustice has been silently submitted to, rather than accept the weariness and heart-sickness of delay, necessarily attendant on having recourse to the Holy See.

When even recourse is had to Rome, from the evidence submitted by each side, devoid of certainty and other characteristics of credibility; evidence always open to doubt in the absence of the secure forms of a legal process, the confrontation and examination of witnesses, etc., it is often difficult, if not impossible for Rome even to give a definite decision. Hence the words of the "Instructio" *Quamvis* of July 20, 1878, "Dolendum autem est non raro evenire, ut in transmissis actis, plura, eaque necessaria desiderentur, atque, perpensis omnibus, gravia sæpe dubia oriantur, circa fidem documentis hisce, in causis allatis, habendam, vel denegandam."

Moreover the clergy, as a body, have silently resolved to demand, most respectfully, but with Christian firmness, their just rights so long denied them by the anomalous ecclesiastical form, or no form of government that has obtained, and is in danger of being established, or perpetuated in this land, and in this they act according to the spirit and letter of the laws enacted by the Holy Mother whom they serve. They demand in the name of the Apostolic See, when any difficulty arises between them and their ecclesiastical superiors, that the provisions of the late "Instructio" *Quamvis* be carried out *in toto;* that all the formalities and safeguards for their just liberties there and elsewhere laid down, be conscientiously and scrupulously observed, according to the letter of the law and the spirit of justice. They demand that the laws of the II. Plenary Council of Baltimore be enforced, especially that one which forbids any ecclesiastical superior to dismiss his subject uncanonically. They ask that the " Instructio" *de tit. ord.* be complied with and all the other Instructions from Rome be observed. They ask, in the name of the rising generation, and of millions yet unborn, that the voice of Rome on Christian education, and the prohibiting to Catholic children of the godless schools of the land, be enforced.

All these things and others of importance cannot be accomplished without the immediate and personal supervision of one higher in authority than any of our venerable prelates; of one who has plenary jurisdiction, or a Delegate of the Apostolic See. After he had lived in our midst for a few years, and seen with his own eyes the true status of ecclesiastical affairs in this country, then perhaps with great benefit to religion in the United States, might a Plenary Council be called together.

For even after an Apostolic Delegate had brought order out of confusion, and secured the observance of the laws of discipline already enacted by Rome, or laid down in the Acta et Decreta of the II. Plenary Council of Baltimore, much good would still remain to be done by our venerable prelates, in Council assembled.

There is a vast field open for the zeal, learning and pastoral solicitude of the hierarchy of this land, which could bring forth good fruits of glory to God and salvation to souls, only by the concerted action of our bishops in Plenary Council assembled, after an Apostolic Delegate, with their co-operation, had given autonomy to the Church in the United States. The harvest is indeed ripe. Look at the vast domain over which our country's banner floats. Was there ever a field from which so teeming a harvest of souls could be reaped ? Was there ever a people on the face of the earth, who loved fair play and justice so well, if we except a handful of bigots, whose hatred of the Church comes only from their ignorance of its truth, beauty and grandeur? Was there ever a people so open to conviction as are the great body of the American people? And yet have any extraordinary efforts ever been made to bring to them the true faith of Jesus Christ?

There are thousands and tens of thousands in the North as well as in the South, in country places especially, who would eagerly accept the true faith, were it presented to them in its beauty and simplicity, and the calumnies against it refuted. Doubtless that grand missionary order of St. Ignatius of Loyola who were amongst the pioneers of the faith in this new world, who travelled its primeval forests in search of souls, and watered it with their sweat and blood, would gladly undertake the less arduous task of converting the tens of thousands who are asking for the Bread of Life and find none to give it to them : and who in the absence of Apostolic preachers crowd to suffocation at so called *revivals*, the tabernacles of error, trying in vain to satiate with the husks of swine that craving after truth and happiness implanted in their souls by the hand of the Creator.

I appeal for example, to all who know anything of the Southern people, of their temper and dispositions, to say if zealous missionaries sent amongst them would not effect incalculable good. The same can be said of the Northern people remote from cities. The Jesuits, no doubt, would go to the people of the North or of the South deprived of the ordinary means of hearing the Word of God, as they went formerly, and go yet to the savage tribes of the West; "but how can they go unless they be sent?" These people of whom I speak, the great body of the American people remote from cities, never in their whole lifetime have an opportunity of hearing a Catholic priest, and they live and die in ignorance of the true faith, when a little zeal and a little preaching would bring many of them into the Ark of salvation. A Plenary Council might make some arrangement by which the light of truth and Christianity would reach these desolate and famishing souls.

Again, in the South is a multitude of our colored brethren, whose docility of character, and many innate good qualities would facilitate the spread of the true faith among them. But they have none to break to them the Bread of Life except a few missionaries from England, and the few scattered secular priests of the South, who are abundantly occupied with their several congregations.

There is a variety of discipline in the United States for which there is no need, and which a General Council could correct. In one diocese meat is allowed during Lent three times a day for laboring men, whilst in others it is allowed at the principal meal only. Incidently may I not ask, if it would not be wise to allow working men to eat meat three times a day during lent, excepting Wednesdays and Fridays, Ash Wednesday, Holy Thursday, Good Friday and Holy Saturday?

In some dioceses the Circumcision, Epiphany, Annunciation, and Corpus Christi are holy-days of obligation, in other dioceses they are simply feasts of devotion. Whilst in the same city some Catholics are devoutly hearing mass and listening to the word of God, other Catholics from a neighboring diocese are trying to sell their wheat and potatoes in the market place. What need is there of this diversity of laws? Is it not rather an abuse? Would it not be better, and more in accordance with the spirit of the Church to have the same feasts of obligation as well as the same fast days throughout the whole United States?

Then again the subject of Catholic education is of itself of sufficient importance to engage the attention of the hierarchy in Council assembled. Catholic education is the corner stone, and only solid and permanent foundation of the Church in these United States. It is the battlefield, as the venerable saintly Elder recently expressed it, on which the devil and the world on the one hand, and the church of Jesus Christ on the other, is contending for immortal souls, and the devil and the world will gain the day, if those who have been appointed the generals of God's army hide themselves from view, or regard the conflict with supine indifference. Thanks be to God, some of our venerable prelates have, beyond doubt, shown and proved themselves true and fearless champions of God and of his Holy Church. With Apostolic zeal they have raised their voices in condemnation of the system of education without God which prevails throughout the land, and informed their flocks that they are unworthy of the name of Catholics, and unworthy to participate in the Sacraments, if they neglect their most important duty of giving to their children a true, Christian, Catholic education. But it grieves me to say that a timidity and cowardice characterize others in authority, and the wolf of godless schools is ravaging their flocks, whilst they look on, like dumb dogs, with no voice raised in favor of Catholic education and Catholic schools. When their bones are rotting in their graves, and their souls are in eternity, the stately cathedrals and grand churches of their dioceses will be empty—emptied by the godless system of education which they implicitly sanctioned by not raising their voices against it, and neglecting to take the means to counteract its baleful influences.

No Catholic bishop, at the peril of his immortal soul, can be indifferent now-a-days to Catholic education. Let the cathedral wait, let the grand church wait, let all the other improvements of his diocese wait, he has need only of the school-house—the school-house or seminary to educate his priests and the school house to educate the children of his people. His cathedral, and the ample parish church, and all else for the glory of God will follow of necessity.

This matter of education is the grand and essential question of the day. No bishop, no priest, no Catholic layman, ought to be indifferent to it. We suffer, it is true, under many disadvantages and have many obstacles to overcome to give to Catholic youth an education in no way inferior to that of the public schools, or rather infinitely superior to it. But our venerable prelates must unanimously and unflinchingly direct the conflict. The zealous clergy and devoted laity will fight the battle and gain the victory. Nay more, if we Catholics were to openly and bravely demand our inalienable right, the right to have our schools receive a just share of the public moneys, we would obtain it in the end. The American people love fair play and they will yet see the justice and reasonableness of our request, and, moreover, convinced as they will be sooner or later of the importance and necessity of a religious education for youth, they will inaugurate a system which will not give offence to the consciences of any class of citizens.

A matter of supreme importance to the present and future welfare of the Church is Trusteeism or Committeeism, which could engage the wisdom and legislation of our Bishops. In some places Committeeism or Trusteeism is a veritable curse, undermining the authority of the priest and consequently of the Bishop, and accompanied with many other fruits of evil, of which every priest is cognizant, and I suppose every bishop in the dioceses where this system, foreign to the constitution of the Church, exists.

Could not a more satisfactory method of appointing bishops be inaugurated to the great benefit of the Church in the United States? The laity, even in the early ages of the church, had a voice in this matter. Why not give the clergy the right of indicating at least who would be acceptable to them? Rome has intimated that it would be pleasing to her, if the clergy had a vote in the selection of those who are placed over them, as is the case in Ireland. What earthly reason can there now be to refuse the clergy, at least rectors of missions, this privilege?

They know well the worth, and virtue and qualifications of each member of their body, and their choice would no doubt be characterized by prudence and justice. Another list sent by the clergy to Rome might be of avail to place in the episcopal chair men of learning, wisdom, prudence, charity, zeal, in a word, good and great men, and is not this precisely what each and every one of our venerable prelates desires?

Or if they are unwilling to give the clergy of the whole diocese a vote in the selection of their bishops, would it not be advisable for them to institute cathedral chapters like those which exist in England, who would help them in the government of their dioceses, administer the same *sede vacante*, and select the names of those suitable for the episcopal office? Smith, in the American Catholic Quarterly Review, vol. iii., p. 718, treating of this matter, says:

"Would it be feasible to institute chapters in this country on the model of those in Ireland or England? Throughout England, as we have shown, there are canonically established chapters, having corporate organizations and officers of their own. There are no prebends or canons' benefices. Hence the canons are pastors or professors, living, not near the cathedral, but in various parts of the diocese. They ordinarily meet but once a month, and are excused from the obligation of residing near the cathedral and of saying the "office" in choir, They select the three candidates to be proposed to the Holy See for vacant bishoprics, and upon them, or rather their vicars-capitular, devolves the administration of the diocese, *sede vacante*. From the above it is apparent that chapters, as they exist in England, could easily be introduced into nearly every diocese of the United States. The permission of the Holy See would indeed be requisite, but there could be no difficulty in obtaining it."

Therefore, to sum up all I have said in this chapter, there is an urgent, absolute necessity at the present time for an Apostolic Delegate to these United States. After a residence of a few years, when he was thoroughly conversant with the ecclesiastical status of this country, and understood well its wants, he could, with additional authority from Rome, call together our venerable prelates in council to establish on a firm basis what he had accomplished, and make such other laws as the circumstances of the times and needs of the Church might require.

CHAPTER XXVI.

ECCLESIASTICAL ASYLUMS.

The principle I have been contending for in the foregoing pages, and which I flatter myself I have abundantly proved to be in accordance with the spirit and teaching of the Catholic Church, is, that no priest who may have erred and is not contumacious, ought to be refused the opportunity of doing penance for his sin and redeeming it as far as in him lies—above all, that it is an outrage on the priesthood, and calculated to bring infamy on the Church, to dismiss such a one from his diocese and abandon him to the charity of the public.

Few, if any, I think, among the clergy, will dispute this proposition, especially if they call to mind the weighty and venerable authorities I have adduced in its support throughout these pages. I need not, therefore, waste time in proving the necessity and importance of providing for an erring clergyman a home or a refuge of some kind, where he can live a life in harmony with his sacred character.

When I established the fact by the most incontrovertible and venerable authorities, that any priest, not contumacious, has a right to an honest subsistence, I proved at the same time as a consequence, the necessity of placing him in some religious house or monastery where alone such subsistence can be furnished, without the obvious inconveniencies that would attend his maintenance in the world, or even in a seminary or a college.

Moreover, the forgiveness of sin and reconciliation of the sinner, one of the fundamental tenets of our holy faith,—the mercy and charity of Jesus Christ for sinners,—the clemency of the Church,—the example of her sainted and illustrious bishops in all ages who ever and always, like their Great Model, treated their clergy with mercy and charity, even when obliged to use towards them the rod of correction,—the tenor of the Church's wise, salutary and merciful canons of discipline,—the Decisions of Roman Pontiffs and Sacred Congregations, all plead, indirectly at least, if not explicitly, for such a wise and charitable disposition of a frail or erring clergyman. Cutting him altogether loose from his moorings, and sending him adrift on the open sea of the world, is to expose him to almost certain shipwreck. Something should be done to save him, unless it be said that the bishops, priests and faithful of the United States care naught for the dignity and honor of the sacerdotal character.

The easiest, surest and most efficacious means to benefit a clergyman who may have strayed from the path of discipline and at the same time save the honor and good name of the Catholic Priesthood and serve religion, indirectly at least, is to furnish him a home for a time in some monastery. There are monasteries of the different orders located throughout the United States, whose superiors would charitably receive delinquent clergymen, did their bishops make some provision with them for their maintenance. The Benedictines, Passionists, Trappists, Franciscans, and Capuchins have large monasteries in which they could give an asylum for a year or more to any clergyman, who, in the judgment of the bishop's Commission of Investigation, or of Rome, would need such retirement. Then all scandals would have an end, the bishop would have a light conscience in the matter, and the poor priest would be temporally and spiritually benefited.

In a religious house of this kind, he could expiate his error and recover from its evil effects. There he could undergo a term of probation, determined by his bishop after a quasi judicial investigation of his case, and when he had complied with it, or under a wise and prudent superior, when he had given ample evidence of a sincere reformation, and was deemed trustworthy, he could again be allowed to pursue his vocation.

Many a clergyman, were he thus treated prudently and canonically, would afterwards prove a more efficient and faithful laborer in our dear Lord's vineyard, than he would probably otherwise have been. His transient fall would ever after be a spur to attempt and to do great things for God's glory, as the soldier convicted of cowardice on the battle field will sometimes seek the post of danger, and court death to wash out the stain on his honor.

The members of the Community that have charge of clergymen sent to them on probation, should ever and always be profoundly impressed with the reverence due the priestly character, independently of any personal idiosyncrasies, or foibles, or short comings in its subject He certainly would not be a true religious, but a living parody on the religious profession, a disgrace and reproach to his order in particular, and a scandal to his more worthy brethren in religion, who would look down with contempt upon any of God's immortal creatures, much more if that contempt were manifested towards any of His anointed.

The religious should enforce strict, but not too rigorous discipline. They should have in view to bring about in the subject sent to them *a thorough conversion* and *reformation, the acquisition of true and solid piety, and of the habit of order, regularity, love of prayer and of their sublime calling,*—virtues that will insure perseverance in after life. THEREFORE, A FEW MONTHS ONLY IN A MONASTERY IS ALMOST USELESS. A YEAR, IN MY HUMBLE JUDGMENT, SHOULD BE THE LEAST PENANCE AS A RULE INFLICTED FOR ORDINARY FAULTS. Frequently a longer probation would be advisable and oftentimes necessary.

The matter of a *Rule* for clergymen thus retired is something so important, that it ought to be drawn up or at least approved by a committee of zealous bishops or priests who love the glory of God's house, and the honor of the Priesthood. Incalculable is the amount of good a wise and just rule would accomplish—much the amount of misery a lax or no rule would engender. Of course the hourly exercises of a seminary would be not only inconvenient, but uncalled for. There should, however, be a fixed hour for rising and retiring, for meals and recreation, and for the duties of Morning Prayer,

Meditation, Mass, the Divine Office, Particular Examen, Spiritual Reading, the Rosary, Night Prayers and Examination of Conscience. The rest of the day each one could devote to study according to his individual necessities and liking, and in accordance with the advice of a wise and prudent director. It is not for me to enter into the details of such a rule, yet from my acquaintance in general with the habits and sentiments of the clergy I may be permitted to make a few suggestions.

In the first place no one will accept the shelter of a religious House who has not more or less love for his vocation, and is not sincere in his desire to correct himself of any fault into which he may have fallen. Whilst therefore, for the good government of the House, for the sake of good order in general and for the comfort of all the inmates, the liberty of the latter must necessarily be restricted, yet it is evident that clergymen confined therein should not be treated as schoolboys or seminarians, much less like criminals. They are supposed to be men of good will and of common sense, and as priests should be treated with the kindness and consideration to which their sacred character entitles them.

Besides delinquent clergymen, another class of clergymen could be sent to these monasteries selected by the bishops, or perhaps to others of a less rigorous observance, viz: those clergymen whose ecclesiastical education has been so sadly neglected that they are really unfit for good in the ministry. They could there complete, or rather correct their education. It is a well known but sad fact, that some have been thrust into the priesthood after a most superficial course of study, and still more superficial course of ecclesiastical training. The consequences are lamentable in the extreme. Hence we meet priests who are such only in their external appearance, and often not even in that, priests who in their actions, speech and manner, evince nothing at all of the spirit of the Church of Jesus Christ. They are not so much to blame as the institution that pretended to fit them for the ecclesiastical state, or those who call them to orders. They are of little or no use to the Church, often a positive injury to it, and the only hope of turning them to some profit is in placing them in a monastery for two, three or four years, until they acquire something of the spirit of the ecclesiastical state and the learning suitable for it. Such disposition of them would be a mercy to themselves, to the Church, and to the faithful.

Such, briefly, are my humble views of the disposition that should be made of clergymen who have strayed from the path of virtue; of the rule of life they should follow in the asylum to which their bishops relegate them, and of the treatment they should receive from the religious thereof. All this, of course, should be maturely considered by our venerable prelates, and with wisdom and charity, zeal for the interest of the Church as well as those of the individual guiding their deliberations, they will select a Religious House or Houses, and form a rule for the government of their subjects therein, that will give satisfaction to all, and be productive of inestimable good to the Church. It seems to me that the most austere religious house in each diocese would be the proper place for any priest of the diocese, who may have erred, to do penance for his sin.

I certainly do not think it wise or prudent to gather into one Institution delinquent clergymen from the various dioceses of the United States. More evil than good would probably result from such a course. There might, however, be some Religious House designated for those whose moral or mental infirmities require years for their cure.

CHAPTER XXVII.

CONCLUSION.

I have finished the task I proposed to myself, very imperfectly it is true, but to the best of my humble ability. I have but a few words more to say in conclusion.

I have arrived at that age which mostly brings wisdom. With my long experience, I can look at things with a steady gaze and an impartial judgment. I have looked at the evil which I have discussed with the eyes of Faith, and have spoken of it with the Christian liberty of the Gospel, and that which Rome and my country give me. I have had in view the good of the Church, the honor of the priesthood, the welfare of the clergy, and the advantage and glory of the mitre.

Let no one, therefore, among my critics, say that it was in any spirit unworthy of an ecclesiastic that I penned the foregoing pages. I wrote them with all the rectitude of heart and purity of intention that I could bring to any good work, and with the full consciousness of my accountability to God and the Church. Having done my work for God, with an humble heart and a right purpose, what men may say of me or of it will trouble me little. My hope is, that in some way, and to some degree, it will promote His glory and the good of the Church, and for myself be meritorious to eternal life. I feel that hundreds of priests and laymen likewise, and may I hope the great body of our venerable Prelates, will bless me in their hearts and with their lips too, for my humble effort in the cause of ecclesiastical discipline. The subject of the practical observance of Canon Law in the Church in the United States, in the matters upon which I have written and the evils which result from its non-observance, need only be discussed, and brought to the attention of our zealous bishops, to have it established, and these evils abolished. They ought to be, and many of them are, I believe, as anxious as the great body of the clergy for *law and order* in the ecclesiastical discipline and regimen of this country.

Neither let any one accuse me of writing in the spirit of hostility to the venerable hierarchy of the United States. The preceding pages are a sufficient refutation of such an accusation. Whenever I have had occasion to speak of the Episcopate as a body, or any individual member thereof, it has been with the utmost respect and in the spirit, I think, of a true priest. I have spoken the truth, but I think in the right spirit, in a spirit which places the interests of the Church and the honor of her priesthood before any human consideration, and which fears not to speak the truth, when the one or the other demands it, lest some to whom it comes unpleasantly home may be offended. No upright, honest man, much less any true bishop or priest, will condemn me for employing my humble pen against an evil in the Church, of such dire and lamentable consequences as that is of which I have spoken in these pages, and if, in exposing this evil, to have it remedied, one or another bishop, who governs his diocese and clergy unwisely and not well, is hurt, he must make the sacrifice of his wounded feelings to the Church's interests and honor, and wheel into line with the rest of his venerable colleagues, who take not their own will and judgment for their rule of action, but the Church's laws of discipline, and the canonical rules laid down by her, for their guidance.

I flatter myself that in all I have written, no impartial critic can find one line, nay, one word which breathes any other than a spirit of loyalty to Church and Clergy. Thank God, I entertain nothing but sentiments of affection and devotion for the venerable bishops of the Church, my more honored brethren therein, whom I dearly love in Jesus Christ, to whom I humbly hope I am united in the bonds of charity, and by the communion of saints, and with whom I likewise hope to be ministering in eternity, "in sublime altare, in conspectu divinæ majestatis."

Nor can I be charged with disrespect in any thing that has fallen from my humble pen. No one would find fault with me, if I snatched hastily and with ungloved hands a bishop's golden mitre or jewelled crozier, to save it from falling into the mud; neither let any one accuse me of disrespect for having written the truth plainly, without varnish or veneering, for the honor of the episcopate and the good of the clergy.

Nor, in fine, let any one say, that I have championed the cause of the unworthy as such. I have indeed raised a voice in behalf of those whom the sainted Bishop Luers of Ft. Wayne denominated: "Qui sunt, vel recenter fuerunt indigni," but the remonstrance was prompted by charity, mercy and justice—it was suggested by the honor of the Catholic Church, and of her venerable priesthood. In this, I have not only echoed the voice of one who was a worthy, zealous, and holy member of the hierarchy of these United States, whose memory is even now held in benediction, and reverently and affectionately spoken of by priests and people, the lamented prelate just mentioned, but I have given utterance to the voice of the Holy Catholic Church herself, as my authorities abundantly prove. I am in sympathy with the unworthy, as was Jesus Christ and his saints, and all bishops, priests and people, who are animated by their spirit. Though unworthy, I would wish to see them become worthy, and though unworthy, I would not wish to see them made outcasts, and a thing of reproach amongst men, a reproach that necessarily falls upon Jesus Christ and His Holy Church.

No more than any bishop in the Church, would I wish to see a wolf in sheep's clothing devouring the flock. I, no more than he, would wish to see the Precious Blood of my Saviour poured through the Sacraments into the hearts of the faithful by profane and sacrilegious hands. Most sincerely do I say with every true bishop and priest, that an unworthy clergyman ought not to be employed in the care of souls. I say most unequivocally and most emphatically, without any mental reservation whatever, that such a clergyman ought not to receive "sustentatio," or support, by serving the altar which he may have polluted by his unholy touch, and for the service of which he may have rendered himself utterly unfit.

But when a priest is judicially convicted of being one who cannot be intrusted with the care of souls, what, I ask, is to be done with him? He ought not to be employed on the mission as long as he is unworthy. This is evident. He cannot be treated as the shepherd would the wolf that invades his flock. This is still clearer. Many a bishop in the United States, not wishing to be troubled with so useless or pernicious a subject, and not being able to employ him conscientiously on the mission, turns him loose on the world, thus increasing his opportunities of inflicting harm on religion, and of devouring souls. This is precisely the evil that I have tried to bring to the attention of our venerable hierarchy in the preceding pages.

But because a clergyman may be unworthy or untrustworthy, it does not necessarily follow that he must be abandoned altogether by his legitimate ecclesiastical superior. This is not the only remedy for the evil, or rather this is a remedy worse than the disease, or no remedy at all, whose fruits of death are greater than the original evil. The only proper and sensible remedy to apply to a delinquent clergyman is that which I have demonstrated to be such, viz: a canonical punishment canonically inflicted.

Our venerable prelates, therefore, should not only follow to the letter the provisions of the II. Plenary Council of Baltimore, and those of the late " Instructio." of July 20, 1878, but they should likewise make arrangements with the Superiors of Religious Houses of strict observance, so that their ecclesiastical courts could send to their monasteries a clergyman for one year, or more, or for his lifetime, according to the findings in his case. The fact of his having committed some fault several times, or of his uselessness for the ministry, ought not, for the honor at least of the priesthood, entail on him that frightful fate worse than death itself, of being made a forlorn and helpless outcast. He should be punished as the Church and her Holy Canons direct, " in emendationem" but never "in ruinam." To dismiss him uncanonically from his diocese without a home or a refuge of any kind, oftentimes friendless and penniless, is most assuredly " in ruinam." This is diametrically opposed to the spirit of the Church and the letter of her Holy Canons. The method of action towards a delinquent clergyman, therefore, laid down by the latter, viz : that of giving him a canonical investigation followed by a canonical punishment, blends justice with mercy, and reconciles the rights of all parties, bishop, priests and people.

And, if those even who are considered incorrigible, or whose perversity renders them unfitted for the ministry, should, for the sake of the reverence due the priestly character and the honor due the Church, be cared for, as I have abundantly proved, by being assigned a home in some ecclesiastical asylum, or other appropriate refuge, how much more should charity and justice stay the hand of a bishop from making of a priest of good will and honest dispositions a pariah among men! No matter what a priest's fault may have been, he is treated unjustly when he is refused a canonical investigation followed by a sentence canonically passed.

It requires in fact and in deed heroic virtue to bear up against the years of uncanonical punishment that have been so frequently inflicted on clergymen in the United States who have erred, but whose sin was far from being unpardonable. God sustained many of them, and brought them through the terrible ordeal, but how many succumbed through sheer desperation, eternity alone will tell. The delicate and beautiful flower of the garden, watered and cultivated by tender and loving hands, is often nipped by the chilly blasts or sudden frosts of autumn. It droops and dies. In like manner, it has happened more than once in the fair and beautiful garden of the Church in these United States, that a priest with bright prospects and flattering hopes, with high and noble aspirations, and goodly and generous impulses, has been blighted forever, by the rigorous, uncanonical treatment of his ecclesiastical superior. Like the fair, promising flower, he too droops, aye, and sometimes dies of a broken heart, in the spring time or prime of life. The unjust treatment he receives from him to whom he was taught to look up to as a *father* often causes him to lose all energy, all hope, all honorable ambition. He who, had he been taken in the kind spirit of Christian and sacerdotal charity and friendship, or been dealt with according to the spirit and letter of the just and merciful Canon Law of the Church, might have become a good and useful laborer in the vineyard of the Church, sinks into indifferentism, if not into something worse.

In the end, as in the beginning of my humble work, I appeal to our dearly beloved archbishops and bishops, to put an end to the evil of which I have spoken in these pages, and which has inflicted so much misery on religion and on individuals.

You love the Good Shepherd, of whom each of you, in your respective dioceses, is the chief representative. For His dear sake, remedy this evil. His Sacred Heart beats with unutterable love and compassion for even the vilest and most ungrateful sinner. Let yours at least feel pity and compassion for your poor, erring priest, and punish him as a father punishes his child, with mercy ever blended with justice, and according to the principles of the Gospel and the Canon Law of the Church. The crozier reminds you that you are his shepherd, whose duty is so plainly and beautifully marked out by Jesus Christ: "What man of you that hath a hundred sheep: and if he shall lose one of them, doth he not leave the ninety-nine in the desert, and go after that which was lost until he find it? And when he hath found it, lay it upon his shoulders rejoicing: And coming home call together his friends and neighbors saying to them: Rejoice with me, because I have found my sheep that was lost?" Luke xv. 4-6.

You love the Church, the beautiful and chaste bride to whom you are wedded, of which fact the ring on your finger constantly reminds you. For her sake, and for her dear honor, put an end to this disorder.

You love souls redeemed at the price of the precious Blood of Jesus Christ. They cry to you to remedy this evil.

You love the priestly character, of which you possess the fulness. To shield it from contempt and infamy and ignominy, let not him who bears it impressed on his soul, how unworthy soever, be made an object of reproach, and an outcast amongst the people.

You love the soul of your erring brother and child, upon whom you yourself may have imposed hands, who is at least a child of your diocese, who, in any case, is one of God's anointed, whom He once called friend, and may yet again, "vos amici Mei estis." In your zeal and solicitude for his salvation, give him the opportunity of redeeming his sin, or if he is incorrigible, which is seldom the case, give him a home, or a refuge of some kind, where he can live as becomes his sacred character.

You love, in fine, your own soul dearer than all things else on earth. For the love you bear it—in consideration of the accountability you, in common with all others, will one day be called upon to render to the Supreme Pastor of souls, with Whom "there is no respect of persons," treat your clergy as the Church and her Sacred Canons direct—give them the advantages of a fair, impartial investigation when charged with any fault, and a just punishment if found guilty—above all, do not dismiss them helplessly from their dioceses, until you have placed them under another superior, or have secured for them a refuge of some kind.

Dearly beloved archbishops and bishops of the United States, prostrate in spirit at your feet, most supplicatingly do I beseech you, "through the tender bowels of the compassion of Jesus Christ," the Great and Good Shepherd of souls, and in the name of hundreds of the clergy, to heed this cry of distress that now reaches your ears. Establish Canon Law as far as practicable and necessary, especially in all that concerns your relations with your clergy. This will remedy the evil which I have brought to your attention in these pages, as well as all other ordinary ecclesiastical grievances. In the meantime, be not offended, if I, in unison with hundreds of others, earnestly but most respectfully entreat of you, to carry out in practice, the laws of the II. Plenary Council of Baltimore for the protection of the clergy, as well as the provisions of the admirable "Instructio" *Quamvis* recently issued by the Sacred Congregation of the Propaganda, with the explicit approbation of the august Head of the Church. For the honor of our Holy Religion, for the good name of your clergy, for your own and their salvation, as well as for the welfare of the laity, do not dismiss, uncanonically, any clergyman from his diocese, and besides, use your influence with your venerable colleagues in the episcopate to have this evil forever abolished.

SOLI DEO

GLORIA SUPREMA,

BEATISSIMÆQUE MARIÆ IMMACULATÆ,

FEDERATORUM SEPTENTRIONALIS AMERICÆ STATUUM

ALMÆ PATRONÆ,

LAUS

PERPETUA.

APPENDIX.

Appendix I.

RESPONSUM.

S. CONGREGATIONIS DE PROP. FIDE.

Ad dubia circa modum servandum ab Episcopis Fœderatorum Septentrionalis Americæ Statuum in cognoscendis et definiendis causis criminalibus et disciplinaribus Clericorum.

Instructio diei 20 Julii, 1878, lata est de casibus, in quibus ecclesiastica pœna seu censura sit infligenda, aut gravi disciplinari coercitioni sit locus. Hinc Concilii Plenarii Baltimorensis II. decreta N. 125, quoad naturam Missionum, NN. 77, 108, quoad juridicos effectus remotionis Missionariorum ab officio nullatenus innovata seu infirmata fuerunt.

I. Episcopi vero curent, ne Sacerdotes sine gravi et rationabili causa de una ad aliam Missionem invitos transferant. Quod si de alicujus Rectoris definitiva remotione a munere in pœnam delicti infligenda agatur, id Episcopi executioni non mandent, nisi audito prius Consilio.

II. Electio Consiliariorum facienda est in Synodo ad instar deputationis, seu canonicæ electionis Judicum Synodalium, qui non a Clero, sed ab Episcopo eliguntur, audito quidem consilio clericorum in Synodo, *etsi ex causis sibi notis illud amplecti postea Episcopus noluerit*, ut bene observat Benedictus XIV. *De Syn. lib. V. cap V. num* 5. Hic absonum est, ut in casu de quo agit Instructio, horum Consiliariorum electio ad Clerum pertineat.

Extra Synodum electio absolute ad Episcopum pertinet, quem decet, ut votum audiat reliquorum Consiliariorum in casu subrogationis alicujus qui defecerit, prout Episcopus in casu deficientis Judicis Synodalis debet *exquirere Capituli consilium, sed illud sequi non tenetur*.

III. Votum a Consilio datum est semper consultivum, et sententia definitiva Episcopo est reservata; quando enim Canones dicunt aliquid ab Episcopo de Capituli vel Cleri consilio agendum esse, non propterea necessitatem ipsi Episcopo inducunt illud sequi, nisi expresse id cautum sit. Hinc recte dicitur in Instructione, hos Consiliarios *Episcopo in causis definiendis auxilium præbere*, minime vero ipsos decidere. Sed inquisitionis acta, et opinio pandita a Consiliariis est semper inserenda processui.

Ex quibus patet officium Consiliariorum judiciale quidem esse, cum instructio sit iisdem commissa, ac tanquam Adsessores Episcopo adsistant: sed patet etiam judicialis et definitivæ sententiæ prolationem Episcopo esse unice reservatam.

IV. Per Instructionem sublata non est Episcopis extraordinaria facultas procedendi ad suspensionem ex informata conscientia, quatenus gravissimas et canonicas causas concurrere in Domino judicaverint, aut gravi et urgente necessitate pro salute animarum, etiam non audito consilio, remedio aliquo providendum esse censuerint.

Liberum cuique Rectori est alium Sacerdotem ab Episcopo approbandum secum habere coram Consilio sive ad simplicem adsistentiam sive ad suas animadversiones aut defensionem exhibendam.

JOAN. CARD. SIMEONI Sacr. Congr. Præf.

J. B. Agnozzi Secret.

Appendix II.

INSTRUCTIO

S. C. DE PROPAGANDA FIDE.

De Scholis publicis ad Rmos. Episcopos in Fœderatis Statibus Americæ Septentrionalis.

Pluries S. Congregatio de Propaganda Fide certior facta est in Fœderatis Statibus Americæ Septentrionalis Catholicæ juventuti e sic dictis scholis publicis gravissima damna imminere. Tristis quocirca hic nuntius effecit, ut prædicta S. Congregatio amplissimis istius ditionis Episcopis nonnullas quæstiones proponendas censuerit, quæ partim ad causas cur fidelis sinant liberos suos scholas acatholicas frequentare, partim ad media quibus facilius juvenes e scholis hujusmodi arceri possint, spectabant. Porro responsiones a laudatis Episcopis exaratæ ad Supremam Congregationem Universalis Inquisitionis pro natura argumenti delatæ sunt, et negotio diligentur explorato, Feria IV. die 30 Junii, 1875, per instructionem sequentem absolvendum ab Emis. Patribus judicatum est, quam exinde SS. D. Noster, Feria IV. die 24 Novembris prædicti anni adprobare ac confirmare dignatus est.

Porro in deliberationem imprimis cadere debebat ipsa juventutis instituendæ ratio scholis hujusmodi propria atque peculiaris. Ea vero S. Congregationi visa est etiam ex se periculi plena ac perquam adversa rei Catholicæ. Alumni enim talium scholarum, cum propria earundem ratio omnem excludat doctrinam religionis, neque rudimenta Fidei addiscent neque Ecclesiæ instruentur præceptis, atque adeo carebunt cognitione homini quam maxime necessaria, sine qua Christiane non vivitur. Enimvero in ejusmodi scholis juvenes educantur jam inde a prima pueritia, ac propemodum a teneris unguiculis; qua ætate, ut constat, virtutis ac vitii semina tenaciter hærent. Ætas igitur tam flexibilis si absque religione adolescat, sane ingens malum est. .

Porro autem in prædictis scholis, utpote sejunctis ab Ecclesiæ auctoritate, indiscriminatim ex omni secta magistri adhibentur, et cæteroquin, ne perniciem afferant juventuti, nulla lege cautum est, ita ut liberum sit errores et vitiorum semina teneris mentibus infundere. Certa item corruptela insuper ex hoc impendet, quod in iisdem scholis aut saltem pluribus earum, utriusque sexus adolescentes, et audiendis lectionibus in idem conclave congregantur, et sedere in eodem scamno masculi juxta feminas jubentur; quæ omnia efficiunt, ut juventus misere exponatur damno circa Fidem, ac mores periclitentur. Hoc autem periculum perversionis nisi e proximo remotum fiat, tales scholæ tuta conscientia frequentari nequeunt. Id vel ipsa clamat lex naturalis et divina. Id porro claris verbis Summus Pontifex edixit, Friburgensi quondam Archiepiscopo die 14 Julii, 1864, ita scribens: *Certe quidem ubi in quibuscunque locis regionibusque perniciosissimum hujusmodi vel susciperetur, vel ad exitum perduceretur consilium expellendi a scholis Ecclesiæ auctoritatem, et juventus misere exponeretur damno circa Fidem, tunc Ecclesia non solum deberet instantissimo studio omnia conari, nullisque curis parcere, ut eadem juventus necessariam Christianam institutionem, et educationem habeat, verum etiam cogeretur omnes fideles monere, eisque declarare ejusmodi scholas Ecclesiæ Catholicæ adversas haud posse in conscientia frequentari.* Et hæc quidem utpote fundata jure naturali ac divino, generale quoddam enunciant principium, vimque universalem habent, et ad eas omnes pertinent regiones, ubi perniciosissima hujusmodi juventutis instituendæ ratio infeliciter invecta fuerit. Oportet igitur ut Præsules Amplissimi, quacunque possint ope atque opera, commissum sibi gregem arceant ab omni contagione scholarum publicarum. Est autem ad hoc, omnium consensu, nil tam necessarium quam ut Catholici ubique locorum proprias sibi scholas habeant, easque publicis scholis haud inferiores. Scholis ergo Catholicis, sive condendis, ubi defuerint, sive amplificandis, et perfectius instruendis parandisque, ut institutione ac disciplina scholas publicas adæquent, omni cura prospiciendum est. Ac tam sancto quidem exequendo consilio, tamque necessario haud inutiliter adhibebuntur, si Episcopis ita visum fuerit, e Congregationibus Religiosis sodales sive viri sive mulieres; sumptusque tanto operi necessarii ut eo libentius atque abundantius suppeditentur a fidelibus, opportuna oblata occasione, sive pastoralibus litteris, sive concionibus, sive privatis colloquiis, serio necesse est, ut ipsi commonefiant sese officio suo graviter defuturos, nisi omni qua possunt cura impensaque scholis Catholicis provideant. De quo potissimum monendi erunt quotquot inter Catholicos cæteris præstant divitiis ac auctoritate apud populum, quique comitiis ferendis legibus sunt adscripti. Et vero in istis regionibus nulla obstat lex civilis quominus Catholici, ut ipsis visum fuerit, propriis scholis prolem suam ad omnem scientiam ac pietatem erudiant. Est ergo in potestate positum ipsius populi Catholici ut feliciter avertatur clades, quam scholarum illic publicarum institutum rei Catholicæ minatur. Religio autem ac pietas ne a scholis vestris expellantur, id omnes persuadeant sibi plurimum interesse, non singulorum tantum civium ac familiarum verum etiam ipsius florentissimæ Americanæ nationis, quæ tantam de se spem Ecclesiæ dedit.

Cæterum S. Congregatio non ignorat talia interdum rerum esse adjuncta, ut parentes Catholici prolem suam scholis publicis committere in conscientia possint. Id autem non poterunt, nisi ad sic agendum sufficientem causam habeant; ac talis causa sufficiens in casu aliquo particulari utrum adsit necne, id conscientiæ ac judicio Episcoporum relinquendum erit; et juxta relata tunc ea plerumque aderit, quando vel nulla præsto est schola Catholica, vel quæ suppetit, parum est idonea erudiendis convenienter conditioni suæ congruenterque adolescentibus.

Quæ autem ut scholæ publicæ in conscientia adiri possint, periculum perversionis cum propria ipsarum ratione plus minusve nunquam non conjunctum, opportunis remediis cautionibusque fieri debet ex proximo remotum. Est ergo imprimis videndum utrumne in schola, de qua adeunda quæritur, perversionis periculum sit ejusmodi, quod fieri remotum plane nequat; velut quoties ibi aut docentur quædam aut aguntur, Catholicæ doctrinæ bonisve moribus contraria, quæque citra animæ detrimentum, neque audiri possunt, neque peragi. Enimvero tale periculum, ut per se patet, omnino vitandum est quocumque damno temporali etiam vitæ.

Debet porro juventus ut committi scholis publicis in conscientia possit, necessariam Christianam institutionem et educationem saltem extra scholæ tempus rite ac diligenter accipere. Quare parochi et missionarii, memores eorum, quæ providentissime hac de re Concilium Baltimorense constituit, catechesibus diligenter dent operam, iisque explicandis præcipue incumbant veritatibus Fidei ac morum, quæ magis ab incredulis et heterodoxis impetuntur; totque periculis expositam juventutem impensa cura, qua frequenti sacramentorum usu, qua pietate in Beatam Virginem studeant communire, et ad religionem firmiter tenendam etiam atque etiam excitent. Ipsi vero parentes, quive eorum loco sunt, liberis suis sollicite invigilent, ac vel ipsi per se, vel, si minus idonei ipsi sint per alios, de lectionibus auditis eos interrogent, libros iisdem traditos recognoscant, et si quid noxium ibi deprehenderint, antidota præbeant, eosque a familiaritate et consortio condiscipulorum, a quibus Fidei vel morum periculum imminere possit, seu quorum corrupti mores fuerint, omnino arceant atque prohibeant.

Hanc autem necessariam Christianam institutionem et educationem liberis suis impertire quotquot parentes negligunt; aut qui frequentare illos sinunt tales scholas, in quibus animarum ruina evitari non potest; aut tandem qui licet schola Catholica in eodem loco idonea sit, apteque instructa et parata, seu quamvis facultatem habeant in alia regione prolem Catholice educandi, nihilominus committant eam scholis publicis, sine sufficienti causa ac sine necessariis cautionibus, quibus periculum perversionis e proximo remotum fiat; eos, si contumaces fuerint, absolvi non posse in Sacramento Pœnitentiæ, ex doctrina morali Catholica manifestum est.

CONTENTS.

Dedication... 5

Address to the Most Rev. Archbishops and Rt. Rev. Bishops of the United States................................ 7

Preface.. 9

CHAPTER I.
Origin of Canon Law................................. 29

CHAPTER II.
In the Catholic Church no one possesses Absolute, much less Arbitrary Power................................ 32

CHAPTER III.
Our Anomalous Condition of Ecclesiastical Government...... 41

CHAPTER IV.
Necessity of a comprehensive and well-defined Code of Ecclesiastical Discipline for the United States........... 53

CHAPTER V.
The evil of Dismissing Uncanonically any Clergyman from his Diocese....................................... 60

CHAPTER VI.
The II. Plenary Council of Baltimore and the Spirit and Letter of the Council of Trent prohibit the Uncanonical Dismissal of a Clergyman from his Diocese....... 75

CHAPTER VII.
Charity and Justice forbid the Uncanonical Dismissal of a Clergyman from his Diocese......................... 87

CHAPTER VIII.

To dismiss Uncanonically a Clergyman from his Diocese, is to reduce him, as a rule, to Beggary, or to oblige him to engage in Secular Pursuits to gain a Livelihood, both of which are positively forbidden by the Church........ 105

CHAPTER IX.

The Church has legislated that all her Ministers in Sacred Orders receive a Becoming Support during their Lifetime... 116

CHAPTER X.

Reasons of the Title of Ordination........................ 135

CHAPTER XI.

Even an Unworthy Clergyman not Contumacious has a Right to a Becoming Support......................... 150

CHAPTER XII.

The Same Subject continued............................. 168

CHAPTER XIII.

The Same Subject concluded............................ 180

CHAPTER XIV.

Spirit of Rome towards the Clergy...................... 192

CHAPTER XV.

Recapitulation.. 209

CHAPTER XVI.

Documents pertaining to Canonical Trials............... 222

CHAPTER XVII.

Compendium of important Principles and Decisions for Sacred Congregations concerning Canonical Trials..... 231

CHAPTER XVIII.

Trial *Ex Notorio*.................................... 246

CHAPTER XIX.
The Summary Trial.................................... 252

CHAPTER XX.
Sentences *Ex Informata Conscientia*..................... 261

CHAPTER XXI.
The "Instructio" *Quamvis* of the Sacred Congregation of the Propaganda of July 20, 1878, as to the Method to be observed by the Bishops of the United States, in taking cognizance of, and adjusting the Criminal and Disciplinary Causes of Clergymen.................... 280

CHAPTER XXII.
A Brief Commentary on the preceding "Instructio."....... 287

CHAPTER XXIII.
On Canonical Punishments.............................. 316

CHAPTER XXIV.
Wisdom of the Church in her Judicial Legislation......... 328

CHAPTER XXV.
Apostolic Delegate....... 341

CHAPTER XXVI.
Ecclesiastical Homes or Asylums.................. 357

CHAPTER XXVII.
Conclusion.. 364

Appendix... 374

JURA SACERDOTUM VINDICATA.

THE RIGHTS
OF
THE CLERGY VINDICATED.
OR
A PLEA
FOR
CANON LAW IN THE UNITED STATES,
BY
A ROMAN CATHOLIC PRIEST

"Canonum Statuta custodiantur ab omnibus: et nemo, in actionibus, vel judiciis ecclesiasticis, suo sensu, sed eorum auctoritate ducatur." *Ex Con. Meldensi in Gallia*, *A. D.* 845.

Perhaps no book of late years has gone forth from the Press which will be so warmly welcomed by the Clergy of the United States as the above. It is a brave, modest, erudite, outspoken, yet withal most respectful plea for the Rights of the Clergy. The need of just such a book has been long felt. It is the right thing at the right time—most opportune indeed. It gives expression becomingly to the sentiments of nine-tenths of the clergy throughout the land, if not of the entire body.

The main subject of the work, the uncanonical dismissal of Priests from their dioceses, was a delicate and dangerous one to handle, yet it is treated well. In choice language, and with apostolic liberty, the author combats a glaring abuse, showing by a multitude of weighty authorities, viz: by Acts of Œcumenical Councils, Rulings of Popes, Decisions and Decrees of Sacred Congregations, Teachings of Theologians, etc., the impregnability of his position, whilst at the same time, there is not throughout the work from title page to end, one line or even a word at which any Catholic, bishop, priest or layman, can justly take offence. It is written in the spirit of a true priest, zealous for the honor and glory of God's Church and for the welfare and happiness of its venerable hierarchy in these United States.

Apart from the main purpose of the work, which is to abolish a long-standing abuse, deplored by all Catholics, it is valuable for other considerations. It contains the "Instructio" of July 20, 1878, a document well worthy of preservation. A chapter is devoted to a clear and lengthy explanation of this important "Instructio." This chapter alone is worth more than the price of the volume. The Chapters on Canonical Principles and Decisions of Sacred Congregations, the different kinds of Criminal Processes, all of which, as the occasion may require, could and ought to be employed in this country in criminal and disciplinary causes of clergymen, in a word, every chapter in the work will be of absorbing interest or practical utility to the clergy, as well as an invaluable book of reference.

The author wishes us to state that he hopes the bishops and priests of the United States will show an appreciation of his labors in the cause of ecclesiastical discipline, by a cordial and generous support of his work. He feels confident that the matters contained therein will amply reward them for their patronage, and for any efforts they may make to bring it to the attention of their brethren in the Holy Ministry. He is thoroughly convinced that the Canon Law of the Church which it earnestly advocates is the palladium of the liberties and happiness of bishops, priests and people, and that consequently, the sooner it is established in our land the better.

Considering the nature of the work, the valuable matter contained therein, and its size, Octavo, containing nearly 400 pages, the price is put at a very low figure. It is printed on fine heavy paper and strongly bound in cloth extra. It will be sent to any part of the world, postage prepaid, for TWO DOLLARS AND TWENTY-FIVE CENTS NET. Early orders from the clergy especially, are kindly and respectfully solicited.

Address

JAMES SHEEHY, PUBLISHER,

33 MURRAY STREET,

NEW YORK.

LIVES OF
THE CATHOLIC HEROES AND HEROINES
OF AMERICA,
By JOHN O'KANE MURRAY, B. S., M. A., M. D.,

AUTHOR OF "THE POPULAR HISTORY OF THE CATHOLIC CHURCH IN THE UNITED STATES," "PROSE AND POETRY OF IRELAND," "LITTLE LIVES OF THE GREAT SAINTS" AND "LESSONS IN ENGLISH LITERATURE."

Illustrated with 32 full-page engravings, and printed from large, clear type on fine paper, 884 pages, 8vo, cloth, elegant.

PRICE, $3.00 : GILT EDGES, $3.50.

Branch Offices. { Boston, 63 Devonshire Street. Philadelphia, 30 N. 5th St. Baltimore, 74 W. Fayette St. Washington, 615 7th Street.

JAMES SHEEHY, PUBLISHER,
33 Murray Street, New York.

It is now nearly four centuries since Columbus doubled the size of the world by his sublime achievement, the discovery of America. In the words of Dr. Murray, "he was the pioneer of a long line of Catholic Heroes and Heroines" whose deeds are told in countless volumes and many tongues. The present work, however, is the *first attempt* ever made to bring within the compass of *one volume* a truthful and interesting account of those great representative Catholics who have left bright, immortal names and enduring footprints on this Western Continent.

The "LIVES OF THE CATHOLIC HEROES AND HEROINES OF AMERICA" embrace twenty-four biographies, chronologically arranged. The following are the illustrious personages sketched, the nationality being given after each:

1. COLUMBUS.—Genoese.
2. OJEDA.—Spanish.
3. BALBOA.—Spanish.
4. CORTÉS.—Spanish.
5. ST. ROSE OF LIMA.—American.
6. CHAMPLAIN.—French.
7. FATHER JOGUES, S. J.—French.
8. FATHER DE BRÉBEUF, S. J.—French.
9. FATHER WHITE, S. J.—English.
10. VEN. MARY OF THE INCARNATION.—French.
11. VEN. MARGARET BOURGEOIS.—French.
12. MISS JANE MANCE.—French.
13. FATHER MARQUETTE, S. J.—French.
14. DE LA SALLE.—French.
15. DE MONTCALM.—French.
16. COMMODORE BARRY.—Irish.
17. ARCHBISHOP CARROLL.—American.
18. MOTHER SETON.—American.
19. CHARLES CARROLL.—American.
20. BISHOP BRUTÉ.—French.
21. FATHER GALLITZIN.—Russian.
22. BISHOP ENGLAND.—Irish.
23. ARCHBISHOP HUGHES.—Irish.
24. FATHER DE SMET, S. J.—Belgian.

The Publisher would call attention to the following points of interest:

(1). Nearly every profession and state of life has an heroic representative in this elegant volume. The great Columbus and the gallant Barry were seamen. Cortés stands, without a peer, the most splendid military genius the New World has yet seen. Montcalm was a fearless and faithful soldier. Balboa, Champlain, Marquette and La Salle are the princes of American discovery and exploration. The holiness and devotion of the nun are well represented by St. Rose of Lima, Ven. Mother Mary of the Incarnation, Ven. Margaret Bourgeois and good Mother Seton. De Brébeuf, Jogues and De Smet are among the brightest of America's illustrious missionaries. The statesman, the patriot, the ecclesiastic—all, in short, are fitly represented in this galaxy of great names.

(2). Each Life is complete in itself and is sketched in a most attractive style—a style that unites the fascination of romance to the beauty of truth.

(3). Dr. Murray's good judgment in his selection of names is evidenced by the fact that several publishers are even now issuing, at the heels of the present volume, separate biographies of a number of the famous personages whose careers are recounted in the "Lives of the Catholic Heroes and Heroines of America."

(4). The reading of this very attractive work will put any one in possession of most of the great landmarks of American History, from the discovery of the Continent to the present time.

(5). As can be seen at a glance the volume is a most handsome and substantial specimen of American Book-making.

LIVES OF THE
IRISH MARTYRS AND CONFESSORS,
By MYLES O'REILLY, B. A., LL. D.,
AND REV. RICHARD BRENNAN, A. M., LL. D.

ALSO

A HISTORY OF THE PENAL LAWS,
By PARNELL,

Illustrated with 32 Engravings, and a Colored Map of Ireland

Showing the Localities and Titles of the Principal Old Irish Families.

756 Pages, 8vo, Cloth, Elegant, $3,00. Gilt Edges, $3.75.

Branch Offices:
Boston, 68 Devonshire Street.
Philadelphia, 30 N. 5th St.
Baltimore, 74 W. Fayette St.
Washington, 615 7th Street.

JAMES SHEEHY, Publisher,
33 Murray Street, New York.

This valuable work, the first that has attempted to give the public, in a succinct and authentic form, a true account of what the Catholics of Ireland suffered for their religion during the sixteenth, seventeenth, and eighteenth centuries, from the moment of its appearance received the cordial welcome and hearty endorsement of the hierarchy, priests, and people of Ireland. Such a record of Irish suffering and fortitude had long been wanting, and its reception by the public was commensurate with its great merits.

It was a labor of love, as well as a noble and patriotic impulse, that prompted the gallant Colonel O'Reilly, commandant of the Irish Papal Zouaves, to collect, translate, and thus present to the world, the rich and precious records of Irish piety, learning, and unswerving devotion to the Church in the past, as a fitting sequel to the present efforts of that gifted gentleman to maintain the rights of the late revered Sovereign Pontiff, Pius IX., in his own dominions, and of those of the Irish Catholics in the British Parliament, in his capacity of member for the County of Louth.

Through Colonel O'Reilly's labors, nearly every prominent ecclesiastic and laic who resisted the inroads of the "Reformation" in Ireland is placed in a true light; his unassuming piety, inflexible devotion to his duties, and heroic determination to fulfil the duties of his station, receive ample justice; and thus is presented to his descendants and countrymen a record of which in these more fortunate days all ought to be proud. There are few districts in Ireland over which the polluting track of the "Priest-Hunter" has not been traced in those pages, and very few genuine Irish or Anglo-Irish names that are not in some measure associated with that desperate, heroic, and successful struggle of the children of St. Patrick to preserve pure and undefiled the Faith he bequeathed them.

This it is that has made this great book not only nationally, but personally popular wherever the Irish race exists.

The present edition, however, has marked advantages over all others. It has been greatly enlarged and enriched by the pen of Rev. Richard Brennan, A. M., New York, the well known author of "A Life of Pius IX.," who contributes nearly three hundred pages of most valuable biographical and historical matter,

Including a full history and synopsis of the Penal Laws,

beginning with a *resumé* of the condition of the Irish Catholics in the time of the infamous Cromwell, and ending with the present time.

LIVES OF THE
IRISH MARTYRS AND CONFESSORS,

We have perused with great pleasure the interesting pages of this volume. It is a needed and very valuable addition to Catholic literature, and whilst it will elevate the character of the popular author in the estimation of the public, it will also reflect credit on the publisher who presents it in so neat and attractive a form. The work richly deserves a prominent place on the shelves of every Catholic library in the country. In vivid, glowing narrative it details the sufferings of the most prominent of Irish martyrs for the Faith from the reign of Elizabeth to that of George III., inclusive. The history of the times in which those heroic champions of the Cross sealed and verified their mission by death is deftly interwoven with the admirable portraiture of life and character. We are justly proud of the valor of the Irish soldier, tested on nearly all the historic battle-fields of the world. We rejoice at many of the noble traits of our national character—generosity, love for fatherland, deep reverence and sympathy for aged and infirm relatives and friends—but our chiefest glory lies in the heroic record of the men who lived and died the devoted champions of Catholic orthodoxy. We are told by one of the most eloquent of ancient orators that Greece took all-conquering Rome captive by introducing among her people the fruits of a higher culture and a more advanced civilization. From a religious standpoint we may well predicate the same of Ireland with regard to England, her merciless persecutor in the past, even now her ungenerous, plundering taskmaster.

The descendants of the worshippers of mammon, of the iron abettors of cruelty and plunder, have read the history of our suffering and endurance, and pronounced the religion that inspired them of divine institution. We might apply the phraseology of the auctioneer to the rapid defections from the ranks of Protestantism in England—going, going, gone. No one can for a moment doubt that much of the modern triumph of Catholicity in England is due to reflection on the age of persecution in Ireland, recorded, as it is, in the blood of heroic martyrs and confessors. When the people of England learn the lessons of faith from the history of our trials and unwavering allegiance to purity of faith and morals, surely Irish men and women and their children should dwell with pride and pleasure on these memoirs, every page of which is tinted with the deepest piety and the most heroic fortitude. The inhuman cruelty and absence of all justice so graphically and grandly described in "Fabiola," when Christianity had to bury itself in the Catacombs to avoid the rage of the heathen, will be found repeated with no less brilliancy and force in the "Lives of Irish Martyrs and Confessors."

Besides the biographical sketches, accompanied by a lucid review of the history of the times, the work contains a masterly synopsis of historical events before and after Limerick's siege and broken treaty, as well as an accurate account of the Penal Laws and their baleful consequences. The whole is given in a free, flowing narrative style which swells into bold and stirring eloquence when the writers become animated in describing the grievances of their countrymen.—*N. Y. Tablet.*

Branch Offices:
Boston, 68 Devonshire Street.
Philadelphia, 30 N. 5th St.
Baltimore, 74 W. Fayette St.
Washington, 615 7th Street.

JAMES SHEEHY, PUBLISHER.
33 Murray Street, New York.

LIVES OF THE
IRISH MARTYRS AND CONFESSORS,

(From THE SUNDAY HERALD, Boston.)

"Lives of the Irish Martyrs and Confessors," by Myles O'Reilly, LL.D., with additions including the Penal Laws, by Rev. Richard Brennan, is a handsome 8vo. volume of nearly eight hundred pages, containing the biographies of those faithful and earnest souls whose sufferings and trials make up so large a portion of the Church history during the sixteenth, seventeenth, and eighteenth centuries. It cannot be doubted that these brief records of those who suffered for conscience' sake, as did the fathers of New England, will be dear to their descendants in this country, as well as to those on the other side of the ocean, and we doubt not the work will find a ready sale among those who treasure in their hearts the precious memories of the piety, faith, and fidelity of their ancestors.

(From the CATHOLIC WORLD.)

This is a new and enlarged edition of a very valuable work which has already been noticed in our columns. The period embraced by Mr. O'Reilly in his martyrology consists of the sixteenth, seventeenth, and eighteenth centuries, those darkest days in the Irish calendar. The only light illumining them shines from the lives of these holy confessors and martyrs, whose touching history is given here. Apart from its personal and Catholic interest, the work is really a valuable contribution to the history of the times in which these men lived and died. This feature of the work is still further enhanced by Father Brennan's important additions, which take in the Penal Laws of the various periods and bring the record down almost to our own day. Those who study the history of England as an imperial power cannot pass by this book. It is a page that Englishmen would wish blotted out and forgotten; but history stands, and you cannot blot out blood. These records are written in blood and tears. They are noble and ennobling, and Catholics, Irish Catholics particularly, should know them by heart. Nothing in their country or their history is so great as the lives of these Christian heroes and saints. The volume is a very handsome one, and we understand that the publisher offers every facility to those who wish to procure it.

(From the AMERICAN CATHOLIC QUARTERLY REVIEW.)

A glorious record of the Martyrs of a nation which is eminently a nation of Martyrs and sufferers for their faith—these are her true honors, of whom any people might be proud, and constitute Ireland's greatest glory. Oh, that her mock heroes and pseudo patriots would learn the lesson of true heroism from these records. The author was very competent to write about these things, for he is a hero and has the spirit of a martyr in him, as he proved by going to Rome with the intention of shedding his blood in defence of our Holy Father against the hordes of Garibaldi, and by the gallantry of his conduct at Spoleta and elsewhere. He brings his history down to the reign of George II., but Father Brennan continues it down to our time.

"The work is well presented, and is of especial value for a controversial library."—*N. Y. World.*

Branch Offices:
- Boston, 69 Devonshire Street.
- Philadelphia, 30 N. 5th St.
- Baltimore, 74 W. Fayette St.
- Washington, 615 7th Street.

JAMES SHEEHY, PUBLISHER,
33 Murray Street, New York.

LIVES OF THE
IRISH MARTYRS AND CONFESSORS.

The Catholic Church has ever met with persecution. Generally those who first preach the Gospel in a Pagan country lose their lives for the Faith. As the twelve Apostles suffered, so have their successors. The history of Ireland is singular in this respect. St. Patrick was not compelled to die for his belief ; and those who assisted and those who succeeded him were not obliged to give to Pagan tribunals the martyr's proof of the Catholic Faith. "But," as the author of this work remarks of Ireland, "the litany of her saints was to be completed, and He who was the 'Master of her Apostles,' 'Teacher of her evangelists,' and 'Purity of her virgins,' was also to be the 'Light of her confessors,' and 'Strength of her martyrs'; and the Church whose foundation had been laid in peace, was to see her persecution-shaken walls cemented and re-built with the blood of her martyrs." Ireland could not but have at some time what is one of the *marks* of the true Church of God, the glory of martyrs.

There is, however, a peculiar element in the history of the Irish martyrs. The persecutions that have been the lot of the Irish Church have come from aliens in country as well as in creed. We might be led at first to suspect on this account in the narrative of the trials of Irish Catholics a color prejudicial to truth. The historian has been careful to avoid such a blemish. The history which Father Morris has given us of the martyrs of England in the first years of the "Reformation," would have been deprived of its best qualities if he had not presented us the story in the quaint, simple, unimpassioned language of the original narratives: WE CANNOT READ WITHOUT BEING AT ONCE CONVINCED AND CHARMED. Mr. O'Reilly has pursued a similar course; he has given us as far as possible the very words of the early chroniclers. We cannot but appreciate their moderation.

The Romans may read the "Acts of the Martyrs," and feel tender sympathy for the tortured victims, but the blood of the persecutors and persecuted now mingles in peace, and no one can tell whether his ancestor was among the executioners or among the martyrs. Such is not the case in Ireland. Side by side, ever separate, the race of the Catholic and the race of his enemy ever descend, and when we think of the trials of our fathers we cannot but remember that the heirs of the blood and the hate of their enemies are still with us, and we need the example of martyrs to make us do with our foes as our more afflicted ancestors did with theirs—pray that God may forgive them. We are told frequently of the wrongs of Ireland past and present, and exhorted to remember them and *avenge* them. REDRESS IS LAWFUL, REVENGE IS NOT.

Mr. O'Reilly has shown us a page that has been seldom turned. We know the lives of the patriots—may their deeds be ever recorded—but the life of the saint is still more worthy of our study. We see in these pages the unity of the Catholic faith ; we see that we are in harmony with those whose faith received at its start the seal of blood. Ireland after the lapse of eleven centuries from the first reception of the Faith shows in her children all the glorious attestations that accompanied the establishment in first fervor of the Faith of Christ under the Pagan Cæsars. We see again the catacombs, the rack, the hunted priest ; centuries roll back, and we realize that we are the co-heirs of Him who died on Calvary.—*The Catholic Universe.*

LIVES OF THE
IRISH MARTYRS AND CONFESSORS.

(From McGee's Illustrated Weekly.)

This book should be eagerly welcomed by the Catholic public. Although none of the early teachers who spread the Faith in Ireland suffered martyrdom, yet since their time the roll of Irish martyrs has been filled with names which "angels and men call holy." The reign of Elizabeth was exceedingly prolific in martyrs, and the story of their glorious suffering and death cannot fail to move our hearts to deeper love for our religion, and admiration for their courage and fortitude. The additions made by the Rev. Father Brennan—particularly the History of the Penal Laws—make the work remarkably complete and valuable. Among the men commemorated are several who, though they did not shed their blood for their faith, yet earned their right to the title of confessor by reason of their life-long exile in foreign lands. "Let us remember," says Father Brennan, in a beautiful little preface, "that we are closely related to those elect of heaven, that they are bone of our bone, and flesh of our flesh; that we and they are members of the one great Church of God, which reaches from the recesses of purgatory to the surface of the earth, and extends aloft to the highest vaults of heaven." The publisher deserves great credit for the elaborate and careful manner in which he has issued this most excellent work.

(From the Catholic Mirror.)

Mr. James Sheehy has gotten out a new edition of Myles O'Reilly's "Lives of the Irish Martyrs and Confessors," to which Rev. Richard Brennan has made additions, including a complete collection of the Penal Laws. This book shows the sufferings for the Faith of the bishops and priests and people of Ireland, and records the history of the most infamous and bloody legislation that ever stained the statute-book of any nation. It can be procured on weekly payments of 25 cents, until the full price, $3 or $3.75, according to the style of binding, is paid.

(From the Catholic Review.)

The valuable work of Major Myles O'Reilly on the Irish Martyrs has been reprinted by Mr. Sheehy, with additions on the Penal Laws collated by Rev. Father Brennan. The book is a useful one, and ought to increase the devotion of Irishmen and their children to the Faith for which their ancestors suffered so heroically.

(From the New York Freeman's Journal.)

"It is good, in an age of softness and luxury, for Catholics to read and meditate how their predecessors made their way to heaven. It is especially good for the children of Irish Catholic parents to study the footsteps of their forefathers."

(From the Boston Pilot.)

"It is a martyrology of the Irish Church—a work of thrilling interest, great edification—a work that will make one's heart grow more and more attached to that ancient and glorious Island of Saints."

"We have read it throughout with thrilling interest."—*Irish People.*

Branch Offices:
{ Boston, 68 Devonshire Street.
Philadelphia, 30 N. 5th St.
Baltimore, 74 W. Fayette St.
Washington, 615 7th Street. }

JAMES SHEEHY, Publisher,
33 Murray Street, New York.

LIVES OF THE
IRISH MARTYRS AND CONFESSORS.

The new edition of the well known volume published several years ago by **Myles** O'Reilly, entitled *Lives of the Irish Martyrs and Confessors,* has afforded me the greatest pleasure, particularly on account of the interesting additions made to it by Rev. Mr. Richard Brennan, of New York. I cannot but express my most sincere satisfaction with regard to everything it contains.

Colonel O'Reilly has been one of the modern heroes of Ireland. As Commandant of the Irish Papal Zouaves, he gave the noblest personal proofs of his country's deepest feelings, by his bravery and religious enthusiasm. The books which such men as he was write ought to be in the hands of all their countrymen. The more so, that the subject of his work is eminently both national and Christian. As all classes of Irishmen—lay and clerical, noble and plebeian—had honored their country in shedding their blood for its religion, nothing is so well calculated to excite feelings of true patriotism in the heart of all, as the simple chronicles of THEIR LAST FIGHT AND VICTORY IN DEATH. The style of these narratives, besides, having all the simplicity and truthfulness of the primitive Acts of Christian Martyrs, produces on the reader the deep and entrancing impression well known to those who have perused the death-records of Polycarp of Smyrna, Ignatius of Antioch, and Perpetua of Carthage.

I would, therefore, very much wonder if a single Irishman's house in this country should be henceforth deprived of Colonel O'Reilly's book.

But the new matter contributed by the Rev. Richard Brennan, of St. Rose of Lima, New York, adds a great deal to the value of the work. A number of very interesting lives which the first edition did not contain would of itself induce even those who possessed it to buy this new one. There is in particular the story of a little Irish Sister born in Tipperary in 1835, and martyrized in China in 1870, whose life alone is a precious gem which all Irish people's casket must henceforth contain.

But best of all, the *History of the Penal Laws* introduced into this edition alone is worth the money. I personally know how difficult it was formerly for a student of modern Irish history to form a right conception of that atrocious policy known under that name of the "Penal Laws." Doctor Madden's *work on the subject must be now acknowledged as very imperfect. Rev. Mr. Brennan has rendered a great service to the cause of historical truth by compiling from Parnell's volumes a complete and impartial account of these heartless enactments. I wish I had a copy of it a few years ago; but better late than never.*

The remarks I have so far thought just and proper to make would be completely misunderstood if the inference was drawn from them that this work is good reading only for Irish people. I had no idea whatever of the kind. Americans of all races and creeds—as the usual expression has it—or of no creed at all, cannot but profit by looking over these pages, which will transport them into a world of which they can scarcely have an idea, but which, after all, is a great *world*, full of harmony and moral beauty, because it is blessed by the priceless virtues of faith, hope, and charity.

AUG. J. THÉBAUD, S. J.

Branch Offices {
Boston, 68 Devonshire Street.
Philadelphia, 30 N. 5th St.
Baltimore, 74 W. Fayette St.
Washington, 615 7th Street.

JAMES SHEEHY, Publisher,
33 Murray Street, New York.

AGENTS WANTED!

LIVES OF THE IRISH MARTYRS AND CONFESSORS

Including a History of the Penal Laws.

BY MYLES O'REILLY, B. A., LL. D., AND REV. RICHARD BRENNAN, A. M., LL. D.

751 Pages, 8vo., Cloth, Elegant. Price $3.00, Gilt Edges $3.75

From the New Orleans Morning Star and Catholic Messenger.

This work is all of Myles O'Reilly's, with many additions, including a history of the penal laws by Rev. Richard Brennan, A. M.; so that all who have read the beautiful work of O'Reilly, entitled "Irish Martyrs and Confessors," will find in this second volume additional records of heroism and martyrdom, with all of the valuable memoirs contained in the first.

On the top cover we find the design of a golden monument, on which are inscribed the names of those Irish heroes and martyrs who lived and died in the cause of God and their country. The idea is a beautiful one, and we hope some day a golden pillar may indeed be raised on Irish soil, all shining with the names of the great men who were "men of renown and fathers in their generation;" but we think this beautiful book of O'Reilly and Father Brennan is itself a glorious monument, standing not alone upon a few feet of Irish sod, but shedding its light wherever there is an Irish heart to prize, or an Irish home to enshrine, it.

The pagans of St. Patrick's day received the faith with love and veneration, so that no martyr's blood was shed by barbarian hand, nor martyr's heart broken by barbarian persecution, but in the civilized days of Queen Elizabeth and later of Cromwell, Irish blood was poured out like rain upon the soil, and the names of Irish martyrs gathered thick and fast upon the pages of the sixteenth and seventeenth centuries.

Their names—at least a large number of them—are recorded in this book, and their heroic lives are given us as examples worthy of perpetual remembrance.

We wish we could give the record of Very Rev. Peter O'Higgins' martyrdom during the reign of Charles I. How he was accused of sedition, treason, etc., and yet was offered a pardon and large gifts if he would but renounce his faith. How, with this document in his hand, he stood on the first step of the gallows, and nobly proved that it was only the Catholic religion that in him was condemned to death, and then, freely rejecting the proposal, and throwing the paper to a friend in the crowd, went to meet his doom.

The names upon the cover are Brady, Creagh, Lynch, Moriarty, O'Brien, O'Hurley, O'Neil, O'Reilly, Plunket, Sheehy and Walsh, but within the pages are a host of glorious names; which, dear to **every** Catholic heart, ought to be doubly so to every Irish heart.

Branch Offices:
Boston, 68 Devonshire Street.
Philadelphia, 30 N. 5th St.
Baltimore, 74 W. Fayette St.
Washington, 615 7th Street.

JAMES SHEEHY, PUBLISHER.
33 Murray Street, New York.

GERALD BARRY;
OR,
THE JOINT VENTURE,
A TALE IN TWO LANDS.

BY E. A. FITZSIMON.

Dedicated to the Sons and Daughters of Ireland, and their American Cousins.

327 pp. 12mo. Cloth, Elegant, $1.00.   Gilt Edges, $1.25.

Branch Offices,
{ Boston, 68 Devonshire Street.
Philadelphia, 30 N. 5th St.
Baltimore, 74 W. Fayette St.
Washington, 615 7th Street.

JAMES SHEEHY, PUBLISHER,
33 Murray Street, New York.

(From JOHN O'KANE MURRAY, Esq.)

BROOKLYN, Aug. 1, 1878.

During my stay amid the scenery of the Catskills, I found time to give a perusal to the elegantly bound volume which I owe to your kind courtesy—"The Joint Venture," by Miss Fitzsimon. I am much pleased with it. The style is good. The plot is skilfully worked out. A tone of lofty morality breathes through the whole book, as the gifted young author writes in the true spirit of a Catholic. Though overflowing with interest, it is flavored with no sensational nonsense. In short, it is a healthy, well-written, deeply interesting, and very beautiful story.

(From the *New Orleans Morning Star*.)

"The Joint Venture, A Tale in Two Lands," is the most prettily bound book of the season, and its emblems of the two lands—Ireland and America—are tasteful and appropriate. The style of the work is excellent—not only scholarly, but classical, and flashes with beams of faith and scintillations of wit all through its pages. It contains reflections upon the divorce laws which we would like every one to read, and its pictures of broken hearts and homes are as touching as they are truthful. The chapter which relates how Mrs. Ned O'Leary became a Catholic is one of the best in the book, and will no doubt be highly appreciated by its Irish Catholic readers.

(From the *N. Y. Evening Express*.)

In "The Joint Venture, A Tale in Two Lands," Miss E. A. Fitzsimon makes her *début* in fictional literature. The scene is laid first in Ireland, and then in America. The story is an attempt to idealize Catholic, and especially Irish Catholic life. There is nothing very remarkable about the book, but the earnestness with which the young author writes is commendable and interesting. If at times she is rather too aggressive and speaks almost too loftily, that will wear off as experience increases. In "The Joint Venture" she has produced a very readable book, which will be perused by many, if for no other reason, for the moral and useful lessons which it inculcates.

(From the *Providence Daily Journal, R. I.*)

"The Joint Venture" is a story founded on the simple lesson of life as presented from the Roman Catholic point of view, and results in the triumph of the good and the defeat of the bad through the medium of its doctrines. The Protestant law of divorce is the main object of attack, and the author shows it to be a bad thing so far as the personages of the novel are concerned.

(From the *Chicago Inter-Ocean*.)

"The Joint Venture, a Tale in Two Lands," is a story dedicated to the sons and daughters of Ireland, and their American cousins. It is a love story with many mishaps, fully illustrating the maxim that the course of true love runs not smooth ; and yet, as all love stories should, it ends with a wedding. The author of the volume is a devoted Catholic, and several chapters of the book are devoted to a glowing eulogy upon the Catholic Church and the priesthood. The story is chastely written, and the interest in the different characters is well retained until the close. It is a strong plea for the Catholic Church.

(From the *Philadelphia Catholic Standard*.)

"The Joint Venture, A Tale in Two Lands," is, what its title indicates, not a romance, but a tale. It has a number of decided merits. The style is good ; the incidents are sufficiently varied to keep up the reader's interest ; the narrative is direct, and, without unnecessary complications, leads naturally up to the *dénouement*. The personages, too, are real, living persons, not mere aggregates of certain intellectual or moral qualities. There is emotion, but it is natural and genuine. There is no mawkish sentimentalism, and none of the detestable analysis and anatomical dissection of mental conflicts and "soul struggles" which are so fashionable among writers of popular fictions. The truths of the Catholic religion are occasionally referred to, and a spirit of genuine Catholicity pervades the whole story, but religion is not lugged in by the head and shoulders. The moral, which is not preached to the reader, but left to suggest itself naturally, is the sacrifice of inclination to duty.

Love is not represented after the false and pernicious manner in which it is so fashionable to depict it, as an involuntary, uncontrollable emotion, but as a rational sentiment, held in proper subjection by the will, and regulated by regard for Christian principle.

The personages generally, are well drawn, particularly those of Alice Desmond and her mother, of Father Walsh and Ned Leary; the spirit of the work is pure and healthful; the narrative well sustained and interesting to the close.

(From the *N. Y. Daily Graphic*.)

James Sheehy, 33 Murray St., has just published a highly entertaining story, by E. A. Fitzsimon, entitled "The Joint Venture, A Tale in Two Lands." The incidents which are woven together in this story are drawn from the peculiarly amicable associations which connect the people of Ireland with the United States. The field furnishes abundant material for romantic writing, and Miss Fitzsimon has turned it to good account in the present work. Her descriptions will serve to recall recollections which are doubtless familiar to thousands to whom the work will prove instructive and entertaining.

(From *McGee's Illustrated Weekly*.)

"The Joint Venture, A Tale in Two Lands," by E. A. Fitzsimon, published by James Sheehy. The story has two purposes—to fight against divorce, and to give Catholic readers a high-class Irish novel. Its Catholicity is unimpeachable, and, consequently, its moral is excellent. Without being very powerful, it is full of charming little touches which betray the grace and skill of an educated feminine mind.

Branch Offices.
Boston, 68 Devonshire Street.
Philadelphia, 30 N. 5th St.
Baltimore, 74 W. Fayette St.
Washington, 615 7th Street.

JAMES SHEEHY, Publisher,
33 Murray Street, New York.

THE JOINT VENTURE.

CHAPTER I.

AVONMORE.—PROFESSOR DESMOND GOES ON A GEOLOGICAL EXPEDITION AND FINDS A TREASURE.

Amongst the many picturesque scenes which form a lovely setting for that isle so justly called the ocean's emerald, none can surpass the vale of Avonmore. A rich upland slope forms a background for the blue ridge of Knock-mel-down, which seems to court the light touch of the fleecy clouds floating above its summit; the banks on either side are guarded by forest veterans, through whose foliage the setting sun casts a radiance over lordly castle, old abbey, and round tower, that still speak of Ireland's past glory. The tower indeed as regards its history has been enigmatical as the Sphinx—no Œdipus has yet unraveled its meaning. The abbey once resounded with the voices of three hundred choristers, whose matin psalm and vesper hymn arose in prayer and thanksgiving at the rising of the sun and

www.ingramcontent.com/pod-product-compliance
Lightning Source LLC
Chambersburg PA
CBHW020105020526
44112CB00033B/921